THE ECONOMICS OF LAW:
Property, Contracts, and Obligations

Antony W. Dnes
Professor of Economics
University of Hull, U.K.

THOMSON
™
SOUTH-WESTERN

Australia · Canada · Mexico · Singapore · Spain · United Kingdom · United States

The Economics of Law: Property, Contracts, and Obligations

Antony W. Dnes

VP/Editorial Director:
Jack W. Calhoun

VP/Editor-in-Chief:
Dave Shaut

Publisher:
Michael B. Mercier

Acquisitions Editor:
Michael W. Worls

Sr. Developmental Editor:
Susanna C. Smart

Sr. Marketing Coordinator:
Jenny Garamy

Sr. Production Editor:
Elizabeth A. Shipp

Sr. Technology Project Editor:
Peggy Buskey

Technology Project Editor:
Pam Wallace

Sr. Manufacturing Coordinator:
Sandee Milewski

Design Project Manager:
Justin Klefeker

Internal and Cover Designer:
Justin Klefeker

Cover Images:
Digital Vision, Artville, and Brand X Pictures

Printer:
Webcom

Brief Contents

Contents

Preface

The Economics of Law: Property, Contracts, and Obligations provides an accessible survey of law and economics aimed at practitioners and students of both economics and law, based on the common law as it has developed in America. Anyone with an interest in the institutional framework—the "rules of the game"—governing economic activity will find this combined study useful in understanding how rules affect human incentives. The economics of law may be defined as the application of economic principles to legal instruments, questions, and procedures. It has many practical applications: for example, in helping with the drafting of laws, or in assessing the amount of damages required to return a person to the level of welfare enjoyed before an accident occurred.

The economic analysis of law is well established in North America and is currently spreading throughout the world. Part of the explanation for this development may lie in the nature of legal training in North America: law degrees tend to be taken by graduates who have already been exposed to other subjects in their earlier degrees, whereas law is often taken as a first degree in other countries. Therefore, the legal academic in the United States is likely open to the insights offered by other subjects. U.S. judges have a reputation for legal innovation compared with their more conservative overseas counterparts, which may stem from their different educational background.

The focus of the book is mainly on the economics of core areas of the common law: property, contract, and tort, with some attention given to criminal law. I have resisted the temptation to include regulatory topics except where regulation bears on the core areas, because there are other good existing treatments of these topics. Crime is covered in the book partly because experience shows that students enjoy this application of economics to legal issues. The chapter on procedural issues reflects some particularly interesting contemporary questions, as does the last chapter on the economics of family law.

The economic analysis and the legal principles are treated in a self-contained manner. This approach should enable lawyers and economists to use the book without any prior knowledge of the other "parent" subject. I have substituted common language for specialist jargon in places and have used economic analysis just up to the point necessary to show particular results. References to cases from related jurisdictions, such as England, Canada, and Australia, normally arise when the cases have had a wide influence. Consequently, there is a modest comparative element to parts of the book that helps make it interesting to students.

The main part of each chapter is written without any citation of literary references and without footnotes. The material is therefore summarized without pause and as simply as I know how. At the end of each chapter is a section giving notes on the literature, in which I comment on the source of arguments and also provide a more research-focused academic expansion of the material in the text. Therefore, the book can be read at two levels: first as a quick overview, and then as a more detailed guide to further work. The notes on the literature also contain modest guidance on some of the differences between American and other common-law jurisdictions. A full list of citations is provided at the end of the book.

The Economics of Law serves as a useful introduction to the economic analysis of law, and should encourage students to explore the subject further. International readers will find it useful as well, since there are few substantial differences between common-law jurisdictions over central matters.

BOOK FEATURES

- Boxed features highlight chapter material through legal case examples and real-world applications:
  - "Enron and Early Twenty-First Century Corporate Scandals" (Chapter 1)
  - "Would Contract Law Stabilize Families?" (Chapter 1)
  - "The Atlantic Oyster Fishery" (Chapter 2)
  - "Western Wars: Asymmetric Information and Asymmetric Technology" (Chapter 2)
  - *Coffin v. Left Hand Ditch Co.*, a classic water rights case (Chapter 2)
  - "Napster.com—File Sharing or Property Theft?" (Chapter 2)
  - *Stringfellow v. McCain*, the French-fry trademark infringement case (Chapter 2)
  - *Sturges v. Bridgman*, the classic nuisance case (Chapter 3)
  - "Bargaining over Externalities" (Chapter 3)
  - *Boomer v. Atlantic Cement Co.*, pollution nuisance case (Chapter 3)
  - "Conservation Servitudes" (Chapter 3)
  - *Nollan v. California Coastal Commission*, classic easement case (Chapter 3)
  - "De Beers Diamond Sales" Chapter 4)
  - *Alaska Packers v. Domenico*, classic opportunistic behavior case (Chapter 4)
  - "Hard Bargains in the World of Entertainment" (Chapter 4)
  - *Dimskal Shipping v. International Transport Workers' Federation*, union and nonunion labor (Chapter 5)
  - *Sherwood v. Walker*, classic case of mutual mistake and excuse for non-performance (Chapter 5)
  - "Westinghouse: "Who's Got Uranium to Spare?" (Chapter 5)
  - *Parker v. Twentieth Century Fox*, breach of contract (Chapter 5)
  - *Anglia Television v. Reed*, breach of contract (Chapter 5)
  - *Potter v. Firestone*, toxic waste (Chapter 6)
  - *Palsgraf v. Long Island Railroad Co*, classic damages due to injury case (Chapter 6)
  - *Ira S. Bushey & Sons v. United States*, vicarious liability case (Chapter 6)
  - "Three Strikes and You're Out!" (Chapter 7)
  - "The Deterrent Effect of Capital Punishment" (Chapter 7)

- "Louisiana Covenant Marriage" (Chapter 9)
- *Marvin v. Marvin*, palimony case (Chapter 9)
- *Roe v. Doe*, support obligation to minor (Chapter 9)
- *In Re Baby M.*, surrogacy contract (Chapter 9)

- Graphs and tables enhance the text discussion throughout.

- End-of-chapter "Questions for Review" provide critical thinking exercises that require students to use what they've learned in the chapters to answer open-ended and "what-if" type questions.

- Extensive chapter endnotes provide additional information on chapter specifics.

- An end-of-text case list includes all cases discussed throughout the text.

- A list of statutes at the end of the text highlights the major laws discussed in the chapters.

- All citations and references are also listed at the end of the text.

SUPPLEMENTAL MATERIALS

Four Web sites are available to provide additional teaching and study materials for instructors and students:

The Text Web Site

The Dnes Web site at http://dnes.swlearning.com provides the *Instructor's Manual* in electronic format. The *Instructor's Manual*, prepared by the text author, contains suggested answers to the chapter "Questions for Review." In addition, instructors and students can link to the Economic Applications features (http://econapps.swlearning.com) through the text Web site.

The Economics Web Site

- The South-Western/Thomson Learning Economics Web site (http://economics.swlearning.com) includes free access to Newsedge, which culls and organizes the most recent news and economic information.

- The Economics Web site also provides links to resources and information useful to instructors and students.

The e-con @pps Web Site

The purchase of this new textbook* includes complimentary access to South-Western's Economic Applications (e-con @pps) Web site (http://econapps.swlearning.com).

---

* Students buying a used book can purchase access to the e-con@pps site at http://econapps.swlearning.com.

The e-con @pps Web site includes a suite of regularly updated Web features for economics students and instructors: EconDebate Online, EconNews Online, EconData Online, and EconLinks Online. These resources can help students to deepen their understanding of economic concepts by analyzing current news stories, policy debates, and economic data. They are also useful for instructors in developing assignments, case studies, and examples based on real-world issues.

EconDebate Online provides current coverage of economics policy debates, including a primer on the issues, links to background information, and commentaries.

EconNews Online summarizes recent economics news stories and offers questions for further discussion.

EconData Online presents current and historical economic data with accompanying commentary, analysis, and exercises.

EconLinks Online offers a navigation partner for exploring economics on the Web, with a list of key topic links.

The West Legal Studies Web Site

The West Legal Studies in Business Web site at http://www.westbuslaw.com provides case updates and a case search feature for instructors and students wanting additional examples of cases relevant to chapter topics.

ACKNOWLEDGMENTS

During the process of the development of this text, I received many helpful reviews from the following colleagues, and am grateful for their comments and suggestions:

Allan C. DeSerpa, Arizona State University

Charles R. Knoeber, North Carolina State University

David B. Mustard, University of Georgia

Georgiy Nikitin, Boston University

Paul H. Rubin, Emory University

Jeffrey O. Sundberg, Lake Forest College

Mary Ramirez, Washburn University School of Law

David S. Ball, North Carolina State University

Greg Delemester, Marietta College

Gregory Wassall, Northeastern University

Thomas McCaleb, Florida State University

Jeffrey Milyo, Tufts University

Sarah Stafford, College of William and Mary

Thomas Borcherding, Claremont Graduate University

Roger D. Blair, University of Florida

I also thank the excellent team at Thomson Business and Professional Publishing, especially Acquisitions Editor Michael Worls, Senior Developmental Editor Susan Smart, Senior Production Editor Libby Shipp, and Senior Marketing Coordinator Jenny Garamy. Together, they kept the book on schedule, questioned and resolved issues, and expertly handled the copyediting, design, and production that resulted in this final text.

Antony W. Dnes

About the Author

Antony Dnes holds degrees in both economics and law. Currently at the University of Hull, U.K., he has taught at the Virginia Polytechnic Institute and State University, the University of St. Andrews in Scotland, and the University of Birmingham and Bournemouth University, both in England. He has also acted as a consultant to the World Bank, the Economics Education and Research Consortium, and the United Kingdom Department of Constitutional Affairs. In addition, he was a Leverhulme Fellow at the Boalt Law School, University of California, Berkeley, a Visiting Professor at the George Mason University Law School and at the Central European University, and a Visiting Fellow at the Centre for Socio-Legal Studies, University of Oxford.

DEDICATION

To my father, Michael, who taught me about the rule of law.

Chapter 1

THE ECONOMIC ANALYSIS OF LAW: AN INTRODUCTION

Interest has grown recently in the combined study often known as law and economics, for which the "economic analysis of law" is really a better description. Anyone with an interest in the institutional framework, i.e., the "rules of the game," governing economic activity, will find the combined study useful in understanding how rules affect human incentives. The economics of law may be defined as the application of economic principles to legal instruments, questions, and procedures. It has many practical applications, such as helping with the drafting of laws or assessing the amount of damages required to return a person to the level of welfare enjoyed before an accident occurred.

Legal instruments are devices—like damages for breach of contract—that feature regularly in the legal system and have implications for economic incentives. Legal questions, such as whether it would be appropriate to award damages for the interruption of normal business following an oil spill from a tanker, are also amenable to economic analysis. Legal procedures may interact with economic incentives as well, when lawyers work for contingent fees on a "no-win, no-fee" basis. The nature of a country's law and the reliability of its legal system also have direct impacts on economic performance. Countries possessing independent, reliable, and relatively corruption-free legal systems tend to show higher growth, less inflation, and higher levels of employment. The relationship between the legal system and the economy is definitely a two-way link, and there is some growing recent evidence that common-law systems promote economic efficiency and growth.

Economics of law has a respectable pedigree. In earlier times it was common for "political economists" (as economists were once known) to have had exposure to legal training and to work on institutionally focused questions. It is only in recent years that many economists have become narrowly technical and have tended to ignore institutional questions.

In the eighteenth century, Adam Smith saw institutional factors like the rules of property inheritance and the Poor Laws of his period as inhibiting industrialization. Primogeniture (land passing to an eldest son) caused land to be transferred in large parcels, which often meant some of it remained unused. The Poor Laws, much like state-based welfare support in our own time, made labor mobility difficult because the laborer was restricted from moving to another district—an unintended consequence of a policy meant to stop the poor of one district from becoming a burden on landowners in another.

Economists continued to show interest in policy-oriented questions, in a way that embodied some joint study of law and economics, into the twentieth century. Then, from the 1950s onward, many economists analyzed regulatory issues in considerable depth. Their work was an early kind of law and economics mainly concerned with antitrust and the regulation of natural monopoly. Regulatory economics certainly paved the way for the more recent extension of economics to the analysis of core areas of the law like property and contract.

Since the early 1960s, modern law and economics has focused on the common law of the United States and, to some degree, other common-law countries like England. The term *common law* reflects the emergence of a *standardized* approach to law in medieval courts in England that was carried to America by settlers. Common-law countries may be contrasted with civil-law countries of continental Europe, which limit judges to the interpretation of statutory codes. The key factor distinguishing common law is that judges in senior courts may independently make law by creating precedent as they encounter cases not fully dealt with by holdings from earlier similar cases. Such legal innovation must be consistent with existing law and may be challenged several times in courts of appeal before settling down to become new law. Judges in the United States are regarded as innovative and proactive in developing common law. This innovative history may partly explain why the economic analysis of law has been successful as a tool in understanding and developing the law.

Common law coexists with statute law that emanates from the legislature, and it is quite possible to use economic analysis on both. Although earlier work, with its emphasis on regulatory questions, concentrated on statute, modern economics of law tends to focus closely on core areas of judge-made common law such as the analysis of property rights, contracts, and tort (for example, nuisance or negligence issues). In recent years, the criminal common law has been added to the list of modern topics, along with areas as diverse as corporate law and family law. A useful milestone in the development of law and economics was the publication in 1973 of the first edition of Richard Posner's *Economic Analysis of Law*, which consolidated much of the old and the new work in the economics of law.

Different schools of thought can be identified within economics of law, and here we mention just a few of them. The University of Chicago Law School is broadly associated with the claim that the rules of common law evolve efficiently and has been very influential around the world. It is particularly associated with Nobel prizewinner Ronald Coase's work on conflict over property rights and with Richard Posner's analysis of the efficiency of legal rules. Chicago is the home of two major economics of law publications, the *Journal of Legal Studies* and the *Journal of Law and Economics*. Yale Law School is home to scholars of economics of law who are, by comparison, somewhat more interventionist in social and economic policy.

The property-rights school, which we discuss at some length in the next chapter, is associated with western universities such as University of California–Los Angeles, University of Washington, and Montana State University. It emphasizes the efficiency aspects of rules surrounding the use of property, such as those concerning water or land, and even has something to tell us about the range, cowboys, and the nineteenth-century westward expansion of America. Berkeley also stands out, as the home for many years (together with the University of Hamburg in Germany) of the *International Review of Law and Economics*, and as a law school where economics of law has been used to extend legal scholarship and to examine the incentive structures incorporated into the law. The *International Review* is now also edited from Columbia Law School in New York.

Economists have also applied game theory to the economic analysis of law. This technique carefully models strategic issues in areas like litigation or optimal law enforcement. We make some use of simple game theory in this text to examine problems of coordination, for example, in providing an explanation of the limited success of neighborhood-watch schemes in reducing crime. Game theory is neutral with regard to schools of thought and is really a technique that can be used in a variety of settings. There are economists who have emphasized the link between politics, economics, and the law, often using game-theoretic experimental approaches and focusing on "rent-seeking" behavior—which may be regarded as the pursuit of pure surpluses by sub-groups in society—a less optimistic view than the one taken by the Chicago School.

In this text, it is necessary to draw on various schools of thought simply to cover the principal contributions to the subject. The main developments in economics of law have indubitably come from the Chicago school and the property-rights school in the West, so these schools tend to receive the most coverage in this text. Within the constraint of covering the main developments, it will also be shown that the economic analysis of law can be seen as an important part of the "new institutional economics," i.e., the application of modern techniques of economic analysis to questions concerning institutions (defined as "rules of the game"). Legal rules create important institutional structures within society.

SOME APPLICATIONS

Because modern economics studies rational behavior, defined as the pursuit of consistent ends by efficient means, there is no difficulty in applying it to the law. Ends and means are clearly involved in setting and administering the law. A few simple examples of legal cases and issues will clarify what is meant by this application. They come from three classic areas of law and show that economic analysis can be fruitfully applied to some interesting legal questions.

Crime

We start with an example from criminal law because this explores some territory with which readers will have some familiarity. We examine economic issues of crime and punishment in depth in Chapter 7.

Some countries in the Far East impose death sentences on those convicted of smuggling hard drugs. Economic analysis shows why this might make sense to them. These countries are relatively poor and probably cannot afford to devote large amounts of money to detecting smugglers. If criminals are rational, they will respond to increases in the expected value of punishment by reducing their criminal activity. This response will follow even if criminals are often driven by factors such as an anti-social upbringing, as long as they react rationally at the margin of their activities.

The expected value of punishment equals the probability of conviction multiplied by the sentence for the crime. If a country cannot afford to increase the conviction rate, it can obtain the same effect in reducing smuggling by adopting severe sentences. This trade-off may explain the existence of severe punishments for noncapital crimes in earlier times in what are now more advanced societies. As those societies became richer, they were able to afford to move to more humane systems of criminal justice, while achieving deterrence through devoting more resources to detecting crime and prosecuting criminals.

Most modern societies are concerned about increasing levels of both violent and property crime. How should this be tackled? If the cost of increasing the length of prison sentences is low compared with the cost of increasing the detection and conviction of criminals, it can be cheaper to obtain a target reduction in crime by increasing the length of sentences. The economic analysis here is useful. It suggests that the

Enron and Early Twenty-First Century Corporate Scandals

Financial scandals surrounding companies like Enron and WorldCom have generated concerns leading to the legal reform of corporate governance. Enron used accounting techniques that accelerated or created revenues. Share prices were inflated, to the benefit of shareholders and managers holding options to purchase stock who managed to sell shares early on at high prices. In late 2001, questionable accounting practices became apparent, the bubble burst, and shareholders' equity fell to a tiny fraction of its previous level of $9.6 billion. Enron filed for bankruptcy protection. Other firms such as WorldCom, Xerox, Adelphia, Tyco, Lucent Technologies, Cisco, and Global Crossings were subsequently similarly embroiled in earnings restatements. Why did it take some time for the scandals to become apparent? In particular, why did company auditors not reveal to shareholders what was happening?

The legal liability of auditors who certify that financial reports comply with generally accepted principles is governed by the Securities Exchange Act of 1934. Shareholders may sue over fraudulent information, and there is a possibility for criminal prosecution by the Department of Justice, providing the auditor intended to defraud and was not merely negligent. The Public Securities Litigation Reform Act of 1995 (PSLRA) enhanced this defense by requiring the plaintiff to show particular facts leading to a *strong* inference of intent. The PSLRA also diluted deterrence by ending the use of the Racketeer Influenced and Corrupt Organizations Act of 1970 (RICO) as a means of seeking treble damages in civil securities fraud cases. Deterrence of acquiescence by auditors was reduced compared with the pre–1995 position.

The legislative response to Enron came in the shape of the Sarbanes–Oxley Act of 2002, which increases the incentive for disclosure of accurate financial information. Auditors must now issue a statement attesting to internal financial control in annual reports. Independent auditors are restricted over the nonaudit services they may provide for publicly held audit clients. The current Securities and Exchange Commission (SEC) requirement to rotate outside auditors is tightened every five years.

Senior management of all public companies must now certify the accuracy and completeness of financial reports to the SEC. The chief executive officer (CEO) and chief financial officer (CFO) must now certify that *based on their knowledge* a report does not contain any relevant untrue statement or omission. They must further state that they have evaluated the effectiveness of financial controls within 90 days prior to the report. The CEO and CFO must disclose any deficiencies in the design or operation of internal controls and *any* fraud involving management and employees. The penalty for making false statements in relation to the new disclosure requirements is a fine of up to $5 million, imprisonment for up to 20 years, or both.

To sum up, the response to Enron was a tightening of penalties, with greater reliance on criminal penalties relative to private action by shareholders. There have also been steps to increase the personal culpability of senior management. The approach is consistent with the economic analysis of deterrence in criminal law.

common response to rising crime rates by many governments around the world, which is to increase expenditure on police forces, may not be the most cost-effective. Interestingly, it seems that developed economies have not moved that far from the predicament facing less developed ones.

The principles of deterrence and the use of criminal penalties in addition to private legal action have implications for many areas of society. The boxed example (about Enron) discusses the legal response to corporate scandals.

Nuisance

Our second example comes from the legal treatment of nuisance, which is a "tort"—or private wrong—in common-law countries. Tort is covered extensively in Chapters 3 and 6. Our example is the famous case of *Sturges v. Bridgman* (1879), which concerned a candy maker who set up shop next to a physician, whom he disturbed with the vibration and noise from equipment. The doctor (Sturges, the plaintiff who brought the case and whose name appears first on the case citation—also sometimes known as the *claimant*) won the right (an injunction) to stop (enjoin) the nuisance. What are the economic implications of this?

Economists regard *Sturges* as a case of externality, i.e., there may be spillover effects caused by conflicting property rights. Externalities are inherently reciprocal in nature. The candy maker affects the doctor, but the latter has to be in the way for harm to arise. Both parties are exercising legitimate private property rights, which conflict. It does not matter from the point of view of economic efficiency whether the person causing the nuisance (Bridgman) has the right to continue or whether the victim has the right to stop him, as long as they can bargain at reasonably low cost. For illustration, assume that the candy maker's noise completely stops medical practice. If the medical business were more profitable but did not have the right to stop the noise, the doctor could afford to bribe the candy maker to stop. Conversely, if the doctor did have the right, the less profitable candy maker could not bribe the doctor to tolerate the noise. The case illustrates the Coase theorem, which we examine in detail in Chapter 3.

Courts tend to award an injunction, prohibiting the nuisance in cases like *Sturges*, rather than award compensatory damages when the number of parties is small. This would seem to be efficient because many small-numbers cases are likely to exhibit low bargaining costs. If such rules become well known to holders of property rights, they may avoid taking their disputes to court, preferring to settle at an earlier stage and avoid the costs of litigation. Observations like this have led some researchers to argue that the law evolves as if it were trying to maximize the joint wealth of the parties involved (i.e., comparing monetary gains and losses).

The Economics of Breach of Contract

Our final introductory example is drawn from the study of the law of contract. Economic efficiency is based on voluntary and informed trading, which is supported by a law of contract that enforces terms of trade and may plug gaps in agreements that would otherwise be too costly to cover. Contract law enables resources to be transferred to their most valuable uses, as people come to know what promises are enforceable and how enforcement may occur. Suppose a company does not wish to complete a service it has promised to undertake. Should it be forced to perform? Both economics and law suggest that it is unnecessary to require specific performance, except in special cases. It is not the business of the law to force people to carry out tasks for which the economic justification may have disappeared, but only to ensure they compensate the victims of breach. There can be such a thing as efficient breach of contract, when the party breaching is able to compensate the victim for nonperformance. Compensation is usually defined by the courts, although some economists argue that enforcing specific performance of the original contract ensures that the would-be breaching party is forced to pay accurate compensation to obtain the victim's consent to breach.

Would Contract Law Stabilize Families?

Older views of marriage tended to emphasize that it was a union for life, which amounted to insisting on specific performance of the implied "contract" between spouses. In the early twentieth century, many states came to allow people to obtain a divorce when the other party was at fault, for example in cases of adultery. Under older laws, property settlements for the party breached against could include most of the assets. A process of liberalizing divorce laws gained momentum across the states from the late 1960s onward, allowing no-fault divorce and establishing rules of financial settlement based either on community property or equitable distribution. In the typically western community-property states, the divorcees must share equally any property accumulated during the marriage. In equitable-distribution states like Virginia, the court will use discretion to divide the property, usually based on assessment of the parties' needs and contributions to the marriage.

Since the 1960s, there has been a considerable increase in the numbers divorcing and approximately one-half of new marriages might be expected to end in divorce. This is not surprising to many economics of law scholars. After all, divorce has become much cheaper compared with earlier periods. A spouse may be abandoned with no obligation to maintain a promised standard of living. Rather, they might receive one-half of community property, or a court-assessed award based on needs. What would happen if we allowed people to divorce but required them to obtain the consent of the other party? The prediction would be that the spouse wishing to leave would have to maintain the living standard of the one left behind, which is usually greater than a standard meeting needs or based on one-half of assets. Divorce would become more costly for "leavers" and rates of divorce might be predicted to fall.

In *Tsakiroglou v. Noblee Thorl* (1962), a company in the Sudan undertook to sell peanuts to a German firm on standard terms—in particular, at a price including insurance and freight. The Suez War erupted in 1956, and the company claimed delivery was impossible. The buyer claimed delivery was just more expensive (around South Africa's Cape of Good Hope) and won compensation from the seller for the cost of arranging a new delivery. The case also draws attention to the insurance function of contracts.

The court concentrated upon the issue of whether performance was physically possible, which is not how an economist would examine the case. The economist sees a contract as an attempt to increase efficiency by allocating future contingencies between the parties: as performing an insurance function. In *Tsakiroglou*, it seems the seller was in the best position—at the time the contract was written—to cover the contingency of blockage of the canal. It is also relevant that the price included insurance and freight, suggesting these costs were the responsibility of the seller. Efficient contracts would indeed assign risks to those able to bear them at least cost. We cover further contract issues in Chapters 4 and 5. In the meantime, the boxed example makes what may strike you as an unusual application of contract thinking to family law, which we explore in more detail in a later chapter.

ECONOMIC EFFICIENCY

Having referred to economic efficiency, for example in assessing the effects of risk sharing in contracts, we should say more about it. When we are engaged in the appraisal of policies, rules, or laws, we need a standard by which to measure efficiency. Broadly, wealth maximization is a simple and useful criterion of economic efficiency, albeit one requiring some important qualifications. Thus, a contract in which risk is borne by the person who can avoid the contingency at lowest cost is efficient, as this maximizes the joint profit (an example of wealth) of the parties. Wealth maximization ignores the *distribution* of benefits.

The main alternative to wealth maximization as a welfare criterion is utility maximization. *Utility* refers to the direct psychic benefits experienced by people as they consume money income. Although utility may often be measured by individuals' willingness to pay for a benefit (or to avoid a cost), this is not always so. The principal difficulty arises when two individuals have very different levels of wealth. If the value placed on additional units of money falls in a similar manner for different people, their preferences reflect the principle of diminishing marginal utility of money income. In this case, a unit of money is likely to be worth less to a rich man than to a poor one.

It is often suggested that we should use utility measures of the costs and benefits in comparing the costs of a nuisance to one individual with the benefits another enjoys from the same nuisance. There is simply no straightforward method to do this, and the criterion of utility maximization lacks definition. Using a test of utility maximization would require us to make assumptions about individuals' utility scales as we made interpersonal comparisons. The wealth-maximization approach avoids making difficult interpersonal comparisons of utility (at least to the extent that one accepts the distribution of income in society as given), although it will influence the distribution of wealth by conferring legal awards on some people rather than others.

Much of the time, it will not matter much to the parties concerned whether their interests are measured by money or in terms of utility (utils): Money will do fine. This is because the law often requires compensation to be paid to an injured party. If A can breach a contract with B by paying $100 to cover B's losses, it does not matter that the money is worth five utils to A but 10 utils to B, assuming (unrealistically) that we have a "black box" able to measure utility (in utils). The expected benefits to B from the contract are preserved, and A is free to pursue some alternative business deal giving a net benefit greater than $100. If compensation is paid, we have an example of a Pareto improvement (named after the economist Vilfredo Pareto), where at least one person is made better off without lowering the welfare of another.

Problems may arise when courts use market values to calculate compensation: For example, governments are often required to compensate for the compulsory taking of land by paying market value. Awarding market value ignores any special benefits (consumer surplus) enjoyed by the owner, although trying to incorporate special factors may lead to excessively costly calculations. In market-compensation cases, there is a major issue concerning the effectiveness of compensation, and we cannot be sure of a Pareto improvement

If courts do not insist upon payment of compensation, wealth maximization will not necessarily result in a Pareto improvement, but it will always give a potential Pareto improvement. This is illustrated by the courts' application of tort law, which deals mainly with accidents. If the costs of preventing an accident are high relative to the victim's losses, the person causing the injury is held not to have been negligent and is not required to pay damages. Conversely, if the victim's foreseeable losses exceed the injurer's avoidance costs, the injurer must pay. This encourages cost-effective precautions and is a form of wealth maximization. Tort law effectively says that the net benefit from the hazardous activity (for example, trucking) is maximized if the accident victim (for example, a pedestrian who may be run over) bears some of the risks, in cases where expected damages are low and avoidance costs to the injurer are high. It reflects a *potential* Pareto improvement, i.e., a Kaldor–Hicks test of whether the injurer could in principle compensate the victim and retain a profit, but with no requirement actually to hand over compensation.

What about nonefficiency-based criteria in relation to legal issues? An appealing approach is to seek fair solutions to conflict. Fairness criteria are notoriously difficult to define, as a browse through any text on the philosophy of ethics will show. It is a sad fact that many people see their own preferences for favoring the welfare of some individual or group as an expression of justice. The advantage of an economic approach is that it avoids interpersonal assessments and is more neutral in its efforts. Efficient changes, rules, or policies have the capacity to make everyone better off (although such changes might be resisted by true egalitarians if they made the distribution of wealth more unequal). An efficiency criterion can illuminate many legal issues adequately. We may not be able to agree on an ideal distribution of benefits from economic activity, but most people probably can accept that we should avoid anything likely to make everybody demonstrably worse off.

AVOIDING "NIRVANA" COMPARISONS

It is worth elaborating further on the notion of economic efficiency and the nature of normative comparisons. Many writers on economic policy ignore relevant constraints affecting a particular problem. These practitioners of "nirvana economics," as they have been called, typically commit one or more of three fallacies. Nirvana is a state of ultimate perfection.

It is easy to commit the *fallacy of the free lunch* by ignoring the costs of corrective economic policy. People seem to see a dual-cost universe, in which the cost of government intervention is ignored whereas the costs affecting the nongovernment sector are recognized. We often encounter the cry that "the government should do something about it" but rarely see an informed examination of the benefits *and* costs of policy steps.

A second fallacy, *that people could be different*, arises when commentators ignore the true tastes and preferences of the individuals who make up society. Some economists argue for increasing taxes on oil products to slow rates of depletion. They argue that oil companies heavily discount future benefits from conserving oil partly due to their sensitivity to the risk of political appropriation of their assets. This risk is purely distributional and, so it is argued, society would prefer a slower rate of depletion. However, intervention to slow depletion ignores people's preferences as they stand and substitutes the hypothesized preference derived for society as if it were a person.

The fallacy of *the grass is always greener* assumes that social situations are perfectible. This perfection may in reality be unattainable: For example, there may be no set of policies that can improve on open access to high-seas fisheries. The problem of over-fishing attached to open access may in reality be no worse than other problems, such as the encouragement of expensive lobbying by fishing groups, set up by attempts to control fishing.

Comparative Institutionalism

Courts are not required to intervene with the economy in the interests of public policy, although they do sometimes need to identify and interpret policy. In judging cases, they are nonetheless frequently engaged in welfare comparisons, albeit often on a modest scale. Consequently, it is important for the courts to be realistic and to avoid the fallacies of nirvana economics. In fact, the record may be good in this respect. The alternative to nirvana economics is *comparative institutionalism*, in which available alternative institutional arrangements are realistically examined to see which is superior. The courts may quite naturally practice comparative institutionalism, owing to procedural rules that limit case costs and a traditional emphasis on the practical demonstration of costs and benefits attached to activities. The comparison between costs and benefits is often seen as assessing the reasonableness of a case.

Comparative institutionalism is an important qualification to the use of wealth maximization as a standard. In aiming for wealth maximization, we must, in practice, recognize the possibility of irremovable institutional constraints, as in the earlier discussion of open-access fishing. Often, assessing the rationality of rules of the game is a matter of choosing the least-worst option in a highly imperfect world. Where there are irremovable constraints, we talk of seeking a second-best option and recognize that the first best may not be attainable.

Positive Law and Economics

This book is not only about rules and normative questions. We also examine work drawn from positive economics, where the aim is either predictive or explanatory. An example of a normative question was just given in the previous section: If we wish to encourage efficient contracting, how should the courts allocate risks? It is also possible to make predictive (i.e., positive scientific) arguments, for example, that the common law evolves as though judges consciously try to maximize wealth. An alternative hypothesis is that special interest groups influence the development of the law for their own benefit. Ideally, hypotheses need to be formulated in such a manner that they are testable: For example, data may be available to test whether, for each dollar spent, increases in sentence severity had a larger impact in reducing crime compared with increases in policing activity.

Much applied work testing hypotheses in the economics of law shows that the common law does show a tendency towards efficiency. Nonetheless, although efficient rules may dominate the common law, possibly because of the incentive to appeal against inefficient rulings, instances of inefficiency (including rent seeking) can be found. Legislation, on the other hand, can often be seen to favor particular groups in a checkerboard fashion, but this time efficient exceptions can sometimes be found.

Part of the reason why the common-law system tends towards wealth maximization may be that it is a simple criterion. Attempts to assess payoffs in terms of utility would involve the courts in lengthy and costly assessment procedures. Many of the costs of court actions are not borne by the parties but are spread more widely by taxation. The possible gains to the parties from refining the measurement of their gains and losses (if feasible) could easily be outweighed by increased costs of measurement, which would imply the loss of tax-funded projects to the wider community. It may be very sensible for the wider community to place limits on the measurement costs in court cases.

Work on the positive economics of law is often given an explanatory interpretation, rather than a predictive one. Frequently, we are more interested in how legal institutions have come to look as they do, rather than necessarily predicting their future. A good example of the explanatory branch of the economics of law occurs in the next chapter in connection with water rights. The difference between the systems of water rights used in east-coast and west-coast states is explained in terms of the arid conditions in the west, requiring greater ease in trading water.

PLAN OF THIS BOOK

We begin in Chapters 2 and 3 by examining the formation of and conflict over property rights, which is a well-established topic in law and economics. The idea is to see how a secure system of property rights is essential to support economic efficiency. Some less obvious property rights, such as those for intellectual property, are also considered. We move on in Chapters 4 and 5 to questions of contract, which is a classic area of legal doctrine. The effect of contract can be seen as moving resources to their highest valuing users. In Chapter 6, we examine tort, which is best regarded as covering negligence issues. Chapter 7 covers criminal law, which is our main area of public law. Chapter 8 covers procedural issues such as cost rules in court cases and contingency-fee litigation. The final substantive chapter applies economics to family law, an area of inquiry that has grown in recent years.

SUMMARY AND CONCLUSIONS

Economists have contributed much to recent legal analysis. An analysis of the incentive structures created by laws helps to explain the function of many traditional legal instruments, questions, and procedures. This has a positive-economics aspect to it, as we are interested in explaining the world and making scientific predictions. There is also a normative aspect, for economics of law is concerned with the efficiency of legal rules or procedures, which is often interpreted in terms of wealth maximization—albeit qualified in this book by a comparative-institutional focus.

Economics of law has had a considerable influence throughout North America and is spreading worldwide. Academic lawyers have been heard to comment that they need training in the economic analysis of law to understand the *law* literature, not just the law and economics literature. There is also a thriving market for the services of economists in providing litigation support in court, as in the recent Department of Justice prosecution of Microsoft for infringements of antitrust laws. Finally, there is also a growing interest in law and economics in both of the parent disciplines throughout the world.

QUESTIONS FOR REVIEW

1. A factory emits smoke that damages the paint on nearby houses. The court estimates that each of 20 households suffers damage over the foreseeable future worth $2,000 (in present value terms). Because it would cost the owners of the plant $60,000 to avoid the damage (by fitting smoke filters), the court rules in favor of the plant continuing operations as before. This is

    a. wealth maximizing.

    b. utility maximizing, assuming each household is paid $2,000.

    c. utility maximizing, assuming no compensation is paid.

2. Why is it unimportant whether the injunction was awarded to Sturges or to Bridgman? Would this conclusion be altered if there were many widely dispersed victims of a nuisance?

3. The CEO of a company that makes components for other firms asks for your advice when a customer seeks to reduce the prices paid under the terms of a sales contract. The customer claims that there have been unforeseen changes in the demand for its final output. What economic function of contracts would you highlight in giving your advice?

4. Consider whether the following studies belong to normative law and economics, positive law and economics (explanatory branch), or positive law and economics (predictive branch).

    a. An analysis of the desirability of dividing marital property equally following divorce.

    b. A statistical test of whether weakening academic tenure would lead to less research in universities.

    c. A statistical test of whether improved weaponry contributed to late nineteenth-century increases in battles between settlers and Native Americans over land tenure in the American West.

NOTES ON THE LITERATURE

- Adam Smith (1776) explores the links between economic institutions extensively in the *Wealth of Nations*, his *tour de force* on the economic underpinnings of society.

- Care is needed in distinguishing civil-law from common-law traditions. Some civilian countries have no code (for example, Scotland, which is really a mixed system), and some common-law countries have codes (for example, the U.S. Uniform Commercial Code and state-based legal codes that summarize the law as it has emerged from the common law). Care should also be taken not to overlook recent growth in interest in the economics of law in countries with civil codes (rather than a reliance on common law) such as Germany.

- The economic analysis of civil-law systems is found in Schäfer and Ott (2002).

- The links between institutions and economic efficiency are explored in a number of recent papers focusing on the redevelopment of eastern Europe, or on the causes of economic growth (see Crafts, 1998; Temple, 1999; Mayer and Sussman, 2001; La Porta et al., 1998).

- George Priest (1993) gives a masterly summary of the early law and economics work on regulated industries, in particular focusing on natural monopoly.

- The seminal work on nuisance is Nobel prizewinner Ronald Coase's (1960) *The Problem of Social Cost*. Coase analyzed the *Sturges v. Bridgman* case and several others to show that courts adopted an approach emphasizing the maximization of total net benefits by either permitting or restraining a nuisance.

- Calabresi and Melamed's (1972) work on the appropriate treatment of cases of nuisance can be regarded as fitting into a more interventionist strain (Yale). They argue in favor of compensating sufferers of dispersed nuisances but encouraging bargaining in two-party cases. Their work is updated in Ayres and Goldbart (2003).

- An example of the application of game theory to economics of law is in the area of optimal law enforcement (Garoupa, 1997; 1999).

- The main professional gatherings for scholars in the economic analysis of law are the annual conferences of The American Law and Economics Association and The European Association for Law and Economics. The societies hold conferences that discuss papers ahead of their eventual publication in journals like *Journal of Law and Economics, Journal of Legal Studies, International Review of Law and Economics, Journal of Law Economics and Organization, Journal of Institutional and Theoretical Economics, American Law and Economics Review, Research in Law and Economics,* and *European Journal of Law and Economics.* Papers in the economics of law also appear in mainstream economics journals and in law reviews.

- The New Institutional Economics refers to work in which modern techniques of economic analysis are applied to questions concerning institutions. Institutions are defined as "rules of the game" (North, 1990; Furubotn and Richter, 1997). In 1997, the International Society for New Institutional Economics was formed, and its annual conferences include much work with an economics of law content.

- Gary Becker (1968) is responsible for the conjectured trade-off between severe punishment and the probability of enforcement.

- John Coffee (2001) has argued in testimony before the Senate Committee on Commerce, Science, and Transportation that the Public Securities Litigation Reform Act is far more protective of auditors than of anyone else. His main focus in explaining the Enron debacle is on the incentives for gatekeepers like auditors to acquiesce in financial shenanigans.

- Posner (1981, p. 88) has gone further than just claiming that wealth maximization is a convenient simplification and has argued that it is a morally superior standard of justice compared with either utility maximization or other ethical standards. In particular, Posner recognizes that one of the problems of utility maximization, in addition to difficulties of measurement, is the implication that monstrous activities with net gains should be imposed on society. We might, for example, encourage theft whenever the thief obtained a higher utility value from a stolen watch compared with the owner. However, wealth maximization respects individual autonomy and encourages economic progress. Wealth maximization supports activities whenever free trade indicates that individuals are happy to see a change. No one is imposed upon but rather the watch changes hands if the seller receives a higher price than the reservation valuation for keeping the watch and the buyer values the watch at least equal to the money spent. We know from the evidence of gains from trade that there is no imposition: It is probably the imposition of change, so disrespectful to individual autonomy, that causes monstrous outcomes in the utility-maximizing approach.

- Some philosophers are quite hostile to economics of law, regarded as *positivism* or *pragmatism* in the wider literature on jurisprudence. Dworkin (1980; 1986, p. 302) is the major opponent and attempts to fashion a criteria of adjudication from a rights-based egalitarian perspective: his integrity. Dworkin called his 1986 book *Law's Empire*, clearly as an attempt at regaining ground from imperialistic economists, among others. Dworkin's integrity requires recognition of liberal democratic values (see also Dworkin, 2000) and the avoidance of checkerboard laws affecting similarly placed individuals differently. Raz (2001) has argued that Dworkin's approach is at best a possible fit for America, England, and similar societies; is not general; and should be labeled "law's province." Friedman (2000) has suggested that outside of economics of law most attempts to guide institutional change or social policy are not general in approach but rather are efforts by individuals to convert others to their preferences.

- Fischel (1995b) has argued that compensation for takings typically ignores consumer surplus.

- The Kaldor-Hicks test for a welfare improvement is so called after two famous economists, Sir John Hicks of Oxford University and Lord Nicholas Kaldor of Cambridge University. (Kaldor was Hungarian by origin but settled in England and became a member of the House of Lords.) Both proposed that a welfare improvement occurred if those gaining from the change could in principle compensate the losers and still be better off. Payment of compensation was not required, and, hence, a Kaldor-Hicks test is often referred to as a hypothetical welfare test. The test can become ambiguous if valuations of benefits change over time because it might tell you to revert to the original position.

- Demsetz (1969) is responsible for the colorful arguments about nirvana economics and coined the descriptions used in the text—i.e., the fallacies of the free lunch, the grass is always greener, and the people could be different.

- Posner (2002) argues that the common law evolves as though judges consciously try to maximize wealth. Rubin (1977) has generated a similar hypothesis by noting that there is more to be gained from litigating an inefficient legal rule. Rubin and Bailey (1994) are responsible for the alternative hypothesis that special interest groups influence the development of the law for their own benefit, which Posner accepts in the case of statute law but not for the judge-made common law.

- Mahoney (2001) focuses on the common law's association with limited government to show that common-law countries experienced faster economic growth than civil-law countries between 1960–1992. He presents statistical (instrumental variables) results that suggest that the common law produces faster growth through greater security for business dealings. Economists have also found that common-law legal institutions contribute to economic growth by supporting the operation of financial markets, which reduces the cost of credit (La Porta et al., 1998) particularly in comparison with the French civil-law tradition.

PROPERTY

Property rights are central to the operation of any economy and, not surprisingly, there is a distinct literature in economics concerned with the significance of different property-rights regimes. Indeed, work in this area was partly responsible for the emergence of modern law and economics. A major economic issue in this chapter concerns the efficiency of alternative systems of property rights. As well as looking at resources like land and wildlife stocks, we also examine intellectual property rights in inventions and works of art. Conflict over property rights and the effects of legal remedies to such conflict are dealt with in Chapter 3.

SOME DEFINITIONS

Economists and lawyers regard property in terms of a bundle of rights specifying what a person can do with resources, i.e., a bundle of entitlements. These rights are constrained by various statutes, by common law, and by the details of contracts that may have been established. However, three things in particular stand out as characterizing the bundle of rights attached to *private* property. Private property rights are saleable, the owner is free to exercise rights or neglect them, and the interference of others is forbidden once the rights have been defined.

Consider a parcel of land: The owner may be entitled to farm but may be constrained by laws prohibiting real-estate development and may be obligated by an easement to allow access over the surface for separately owned rights of mineral extraction. The same land-owning farmer may have access rights over neighboring property to reach a main highway and may have rights of use over adjacent water. The farmer therefore has a bundle of affirmative rights relating to access, farming, and the drawing of water; some separate company has the right to extract mineral wealth and the associated access rights. Both are constrained by laws, e.g., those relating to development and safe working practices. Part of the farmer's bundle, the right of access to a road, even refers to an altogether different parcel of land. The division of property rights allows particular bundles to be matched to specialist skills: A farmer might make a loss trying to mine on the land but may be able to sell the mineral rights to a more efficient specialist.

Some other categories of property rights are of interest. In particular, private property contrasts with common property, from which people may not be excluded. Examples of common property include open-access fisheries and unregulated common land. The legal rule applying to open-access wildlife stocks is that of first possession. Open access to an unregulated common property resource is generally judged to lead to its overuse, because people use the resource as long as there is any return from it and are not concerned with maximizing the total surplus.

There are also some less-obvious categories of property rights that are neither fully private nor common in nature. Among these, usufruct rights—which give the right to use privately and to exclude others but do not give the right to sell the resource—are particularly interesting. Primitive tribal societies often had usufruct rights, with much tribal regulation of their allocation. Usufruct rights have made something of a comeback with privatization programs, particularly in east European economies as they have moved away from collective ownership of property. Governments often keep a "golden share," controlling the further sale of the formerly nationalized firm.

Private property rights probably emerged as individuals protected favored pieces of land by the use of force, or took land from others through force or negotiation, when the costs of doing so were outweighed by the expected benefits. Economies of scale in protection services suggest creating some form of government to safeguard private property rights once they are established. Government then comes to have a natural monopoly of coercion and can be funded by the savings that individuals make from no longer needing private security measures. Interestingly, when modern governments become seriously weakened, as in the countries of the former Soviet Union, we find organized crime emerging as an alternative enforcement mechanism that extracts payments from business for providing some order.

The most important factors in the creation of private property rights are the bargaining and enforcement costs involved relative to the benefits of creating a new right. These transaction costs can be so high that it is not always worth creating private property rights, as has been recognized in the case of oil production from common-pool reservoirs serving several pieces of land, where oil companies often agree simply to share access. This problem of high transaction costs is also probably why open access persists for wildlife stocks such as fish and seals. If it were possible to fence areas of the sea to contain stocks, we would probably see attempts to create private rights.

ECONOMIC ANALYSIS OF PROPERTY RIGHTS

Economic analysis suggests that private property rights are more efficient than common rights. We can distinguish between a dynamic and a static view of the superiority of private rights.

The dynamic view is that private property rights give an incentive for the long-term efficient use of a resource: For example, you would not fertilize and prepare land if someone else could come along and use it to plant crops. Common property is often a feature of a nomadic lifestyle, in which a local supply of a resource becomes exhausted before the tribe moves elsewhere. An indication of the low productivity of common rights is given by the observation that a European settler typically needed about two acres of land to support a family in colonial America, whereas a family from a native tribe needed 2,000 acres.

Another dynamic view of the superiority of private rights emphasizes the role that transferability plays in encouraging efficient use of resources. Private property rights can be sold to higher valuing users, which is not possible with common rights. Therefore, private rights are necessary and *transferable* private rights are sufficient for efficiency. Transferability interacts with the separation of particularly valuable property rights, such as mineral rights, to enable specialist firms to operate alongside each other. If a farmer and a mineral company operate on the same land as owners of different bundles of property rights, the farmer does not have to find and manage employees who could extract the minerals. The mineral company can in all probability operate at a much lower cost than would a farmer trying to supervise the same work.

The static view of the inefficiency of common rights dates from the 1950s. Common property rights appear to cause overexploitation of a resource as new users ignore their impact on existing ones. We now turn to a classic examination of this proposition by looking at the economic theory of the open-access fishery. The logic of the fishery case applies to all open-access resources, including hunted animal stocks, woodlands, whales, common grazing land, and common pools of oil.

THE FISHERY

High-seas fisheries are the most significant modern examples of common property. Figure 2.1 shows a relationship between fishing effort (standard boats with crew) and total revenue, which is based on an underlying effort-yield relationship. The yield (i.e., catch) is initially measured in weight. Total revenue is found by multiplying the yield in weight by the price of fish. We assume a fixed price, which would result from a competitive market for fish and which is normalized to a unit value. Therefore, the total revenue curve in Figure 2.1 is simply a yield curve that has been given a monetary value.

The fish population will adjust to give the total revenue (yield) levels shown as fishing is varied on the horizontal axis. Increases in effort reduce the underlying population. The total revenue curve shows the usual bell-shaped relationship that is used as a starting point in models of fisheries management. At first, increasing fishing effort increases the yield as a smaller fish population puts less demand on its food sources, and breeding and growth of the fish stock show greater gains. However, past point *M*, the falling fish population implies that fish experience increasing difficulty in locating partners for

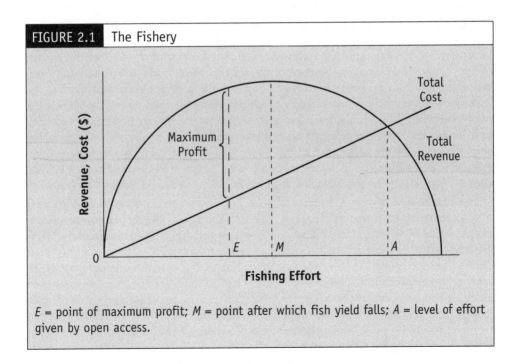

FIGURE 2.1   The Fishery

E = point of maximum profit; *M* = point after which fish yield falls; *A* = level of effort given by open access.

The Atlantic Oyster Fishery

The efficiency of private rights is indicated in cases where it is possible to compare private and common property, as in the case of oyster fishing, which is spread across 16 contiguous Atlantic and Gulf states. Research work carried out by Agnello and Donnelley has shown that private rights indeed lead to a more efficient fishing industry. The proportion of private property rights in oyster beds varies across states and years. Generally, natural oyster beds are treated as common property in the United States, but other areas may be leased and seeded for oyster farming, giving some private rights. Common property oyster beds are likely to be less efficient because harvesting removes the base on which the oysters grow, which fishermen will not replace even though states often prohibit dredging and other very harmful techniques. There is a statistically significant positive link between labor productivity and the presence of private rights in the oyster fishery. The finding supports the suggestion that private rights cause fishermen to take better account of the impact of fishing upon future yields.

breeding so that yield falls. Hence, the derived total revenue curve has a bell shape, giving a maximum at point *M*.

Assuming a constant unit cost of fishing effort gives the linear total cost function. A private owner of the fishery would fish, where profit is maximized, at point *E* in Figure 2.1. With common rights, people enter the fishery as long as there is any profit to be had in excess of the (normal) profit they could earn on their investments elsewhere in the economy. If we assume that the fishermen's costs include an element of required normal profit, open access gives a level of effort shown by point *A*. The entire surplus on the fishery is dissipated by open access. The lack of private property rights leads to overfishing. If we could reduce fishing effort from *A* to *E*, we could release inputs for use elsewhere in the economy and increase the catch in the fishery.

Unfortunately, the world's remaining examples of common property resources arise in cases where it is apparently still too costly to create the private rights. The costs would be attached to enforcing private access and to suppressing conflict over the distribution of the benefits of fishing. The analysis of the fishery model leads to a "first-best" optimum that ignores the very real costs of enforcing the ideal solution. Introducing the irremovable constraint of meeting costs of enforcement that would more than erode the maximum profit shown in Figure 2.1 would cause common property to be the "second-best" optimum. Nonetheless, many economists make the general point that introducing common property where the cost of enforcing private rights is low would lead to overexploitation of a resource. The general prediction is supported by observations of fisheries and particularly by the empirical work summarized in the boxed application.

Fisheries regulation tends to favor approaches toward controlling overfishing that rely on simple enforcement mechanisms. There is a history of the regulations not working. A simple device like a closed season is simple to enforce. If a boat is discovered fishing, the authorities just arrest the crew. However, fishermen will then intensify their efforts during the open season. The regulation does not overcome the inherent problem of the excessive use of common property but just raises fishermen's costs. An even more striking case of irrational conservation occurred some years ago in the Pacific salmon fishery, when powerboats were banned from the Bristol Bay and fishermen had to revert to sail boats. What is ideally needed in these cases is a *reduction* of costs as effort is withdrawn, not an increase of costs.

A positive recent development is the move toward individual transferable quotas (ITQs) by the eight Regional Fishery Management Councils established by the Fishery Conservation and Management Act of 1976 (as amended in 1996). A system of ITQs places an overall limit on catch and allocates transferable shares in it among recognized fishing interests. It effectively creates private (albeit group-based) property rights in fishing. Fishermen have been given ITQs based on their historical catch records, a system of grandfather rights that creates private rights through first possession of the stock. Prior to setting ITQs, there is still the issue of determining overall catch levels, which are unlikely to be set at profit-maximizing levels by the councils.

Recent evidence from the behavior of halibut fishermen in British Columbia supports the case for using ITQs. During the 1980s and 1990s, authorities first introduced technical regulation such as closed seasons and restrictions on total catch, and then relaxed technical regulations but introduced private fishing rights from 1991 onward. The private rights eventually took the form of ITQs and resulted in a reduction in the number of vessels fishing and an increase in their productivity and profitability. After privatization, the catch was reduced compared with some regulated years, or was very similar for other years. In particular, the fishers' response to closed seasons and limits on total catch seemed to have been to pile in more and more vessels and waste fuel in a "Derby" race for the briefly available fish. The empirical results are consistent with the idea that open access encourages conflict-orientated investment that tends to dissipate rents in fishing.

RENT SEEKING

Common property rights also encourage rent-seeking activity. *Rent* is defined in economics as any payment over and above the amount necessary to keep a factor of production in its current use. Rent seeking may be defined as the devotion of resources to gathering pure surpluses—for example, managers may try to influence the award of public contracts in favor of their companies by mounting a lobbying campaign aimed at persuading political decision makers of their merits in areas of competence subject to political judgment. The idea can be applied to common property resources as participants seek rents, even if overuse means they get none.

Common rights imply an increased incentive to spend resources on conflict. Taking the example of animal stocks, hunters might equip themselves with technology designed to beat rivals to the stocks. Much of this expenditure on conflict could be saved if hunting rights were owned privately because the only issue would be maximizing the surplus on the animal population. In the case of high-seas fishing, savings would also arise from avoiding the periodic episodes in which fishermen become aggressive and damage other fishermen's nets, as often arises when Spanish fishermen try to deter others from fishing for tuna in the Bay of Biscay.

From a practical point of view, independently governed, well-defined, and secure private property rights tend to make rent seeking unproductive. The security of private rights encourages people to obtain income from productive, entrepreneurial activity, i.e., to be innovative in terms of products or production processes. Furthermore, privately owned resources will only be transferred by sale if there is indeed a higher valued use in the hands of a more able owner. Rent seeking could well transfer resources to inefficient uses. A rule of first possession applies to wildlife stocks, but the fastest fisher or hunter is not necessarily the one with the lowest costs.

THE PROPERTY-RIGHTS PARADIGM

It is possible to define economic theory largely in terms of the creation, enforcement, and transfer of property rights. Property rights emerge to control externalities, which are defined as unpriced spillover effects between the activities of different individuals. An externality is internalized when property rights cause its effects to be fully recognized by the party creating it. There is a general tendency in economics texts to see externalities as minor problems in a sea of otherwise well-functioning markets. The property-rights paradigm actually inverts this view: In the beginning, there are externalities, which individuals then internalize by creating property rights whenever this is worth doing.

Private property rights develop to internalize externalities when the gains of internalization exceed the costs. This process typically results from changes in economic values that follow from changes in technology and from the opening of new markets. Early work on property rights often made use of examples drawn from the history of North American tribes. Early settlers noticed that the indigenous tribes of the Labrador Peninsula had a long-standing tradition of private property rights, whereas those of the American Southwest did not. A good case can be made that private rights emerged as the fur trade developed in scope and value.

Before the fur trade developed, tribal members hunted for meat and furs for the hunter's family. An externality was clearly present as each hunt imposed a loss of stock on subsequent hunters, just as fishing affects stocks in the model considered earlier. Accounts by Jesuit explorers in the 1650s contain evidence of common, rather than private, property rights.

The fur trade had two consequences: The value of furs rose, and the scale of hunting increased sharply. The gains from internalizing the hunting externality became much higher, and the property-rights system began to change toward private rights. Relatively immobile forest animals dominated the fur trade so that the costs of enforcing private rights were not particularly high. By 1725, travelers began to report that territorial hunting arrangements by individual families were developing. The earliest references to the emergence of these private rights indicated a temporary allotment of hunting territories. The Iroquois, for example, divided themselves into bands and appropriated pieces of land for each group to hunt exclusively. Interestingly, after private hunting was established, a starving tribal member could kill and eat another's captured animal if he left the fur.

The absence of similar rights among Southwest tribes resulted from the lack of a high-value, contained wildlife stock. On the plains of the Southwest, grazing stocks roamed large distances and could not be economically contained within boundaries. This all changed with the arrival of Europeans with cattle and, later, barbed wire. Tribes of the Northwest also developed family-based private rights to hunting grounds. Again, forest animals dominated the Northwest and fur traders visited the area.

Private property rights with few owners for any piece of property appears to be a dominant pattern, suggesting that this minimizes the cost of taking decisions over the future use of the resources involved. What then of modern examples of joint-stock enterprises, which allow many equity participants to combine their capital? Economies of scale in production and the avoidance of the transaction costs of combining many small firms suggest running a large corporation. However, it is cheaper to raise funds from many equity participants or outside lenders, who can diversify their risks. The delegation of authority to a management board overcomes the high costs of making decisions that should follow from having so many owners of the modern firm. In addition, limited liability allows investors to be liable for the company's debts only to the extent of any personal investment and helps to diversify risks. In general, it makes sense for property rights to be created over the unit of ownership that best keeps costs to a minimum.

THE "WILD" WEST

There has been much interest in testing property-rights theories using data from the history of the development of the American West. In the nineteenth century, there were many examples of property rights and associated institutions evolving in response to clearly observable changes in economic values. The "raid-or-trade" model analyzes the choice faced by European settlers between attacking native tribes and taking their land, or negotiating with them for it. Property-rights economists Terry Anderson and Fred McChesney (see the Notes on the Literature at the end of this chapter) developed the model.

Negotiation and war have different costs to each group, and each has a different valuation of the property at stake. It may be in the interests of tribes to overlook small trespasses upon their land if both negotiation and war are costly. There would also be some land of too low a value to interest settlers. Therefore, there will be some land over which disputes will not arise, and a region will exist where conflict is possible. This analysis contrasts with the view that European settlers set out to annihilate native tribes as some form of ethnic cleansing.

Figure 2.2 on page 22 shows the key features of the raid-or-trade model. Assume that there is one group of settlers and one tribe. There is a finite amount of land (L_{max}) that is initially held entirely by the tribe. The value of each unit of land to settlers is shown by the marginal benefit function MB_S and diminishes as more land is obtained. The marginal value to the tribe is measured from L_{max} and also diminishes, as shown by MB_I. Marginal benefit can be measured in terms of the price each group would be willing to pay for exclusive use of the land, assuming the use of force was ruled out. Early units of land given up by the tribe (e.g., from 0 to L_1) are of low value to them but are of high value to settlers. If neither side could use force, and if negotiation costs were zero, the settlers would negotiate to take over L_0 units of land as they could easily compensate the tribe for its loss.

However, both sides will possess credible threats of force. The cost of settlers taking additional units of land by force is shown by the marginal cost function, MC_S, in Figure 2.2, whereas the marginal cost of the tribe defending land is shown by MC_I. Marginal costs of force increase for each party, measured from their respective origins in Figure 2.2, as it is more difficult to attack or defend land that is distant from headquarters. The model demarcates a zone of controversy between L_1 and L_2 within which settlers will find it worthwhile to attempt to take land from the tribe and within which the tribe would wish to resist them. However, settlers can take up to L_1 units with impunity as the costs of defending exceed the benefits to the tribe, which cannot credibly threaten to defend their interests. Similarly, settlers will have no interest in land beyond L_2 because the costs of obtaining it are too high relative to the benefits. The model does not predict that there must be war in the zone of controversy. This will depend on factors that influence the cost of negotiation relative to that of war for the

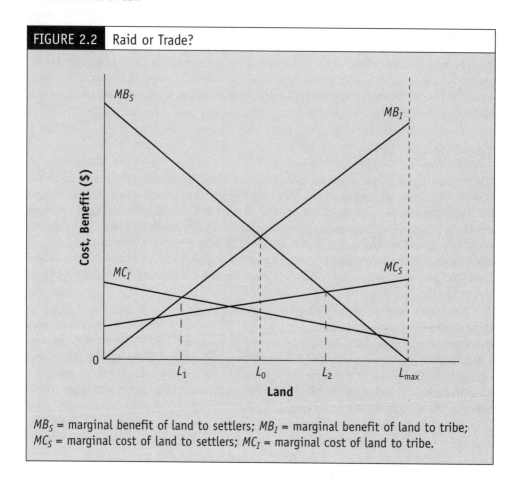

FIGURE 2.2   Raid or Trade?

MB_S = marginal benefit of land to settlers; MB_I = marginal benefit of land to tribe;
MC_S = marginal cost of land to settlers; MC_I = marginal cost of land to tribe.

parties. Figure 2.2 does imply that war to annihilation was never an issue, provided marginal benefit and cost functions intersected as shown.

Consider the influences upon negotiation as an alternative to war. To develop this aspect of the model, assume settlers have trespassed and the issue for both parties is whether to negotiate or fight. In general, negotiation could have many outcomes (e.g., settlers stay, settlers leave, or settlers compensate the tribe), but for it to be preferable to fighting for both parties we must have

$$S = S_I + S_S > 0 \qquad (2.1)$$

where S is the surplus from negotiation, made up of S_I for the tribe and S_S for settlers. For settlers we have

$$S_S = CF_S + LF_S - CN_S > 0 \qquad (2.2)$$

where CF_S is the cost of fighting, LF_S is the value of previously taken land lost in fighting, and CN_S is the cost of negotiation. The surplus from negotiation increases for settlers as the cost of fighting and the value of lost land increase.

For the tribe, a similar condition is

$$S_I = CF_I - GF_I - CN_I > 0 \tag{2.3}$$

where CF_I is their cost of fighting, GF_I is the value of land retaken by the tribe through fighting, and CN_I is the tribe's negotiating costs. The tribe's surplus from negotiation increases as the cost of fighting increases and falls as the gain from fighting increases. For both the tribe and settlers, increases in negotiation costs reduce the surplus from negotiation.

Condition (2.1) may be expanded to show a sufficient condition for fighting:

$$S = S_S + S_I < 0$$
i.e., $$[(CF_S + CF_I) - (CN_S + CN_I)] + [LF_S - GF_I] < 0 \tag{2.4}$$

If we assume that the value of land in dispute is the same (T) to settlers and to the tribe, and letting $CF = [CF_S + CF_I]$ (the joint cost of fighting) and $CN = [CN_S + CN_I]$ (the joint cost of negotiating), then

$$S = CF - CN < 0 \tag{2.5}$$

implies that fighting will occur. However, if the (joint) costs of negotiation are always less than the costs of fighting, negotiation will result.

To introduce an element of risk into the model, assume that there is uncertainty over the prospect of gaining or losing land. Condition (2.5) becomes

$$S = CF - CN - (P_I T) + (P_S T) < 0 \tag{2.6}$$

where P_I and P_S refer to the probabilities the tribe and the settlers assign to gaining and losing land valued at T. Now (2.6) holds only when

$$(CF - CN) < (P_I - P_S)T \tag{2.7}$$

or

$$(P_I - P_S) > (CF - CN)/T \tag{2.8}$$

Condition (2.8) indicates that the parties' assessment of their probability of winning land and the relative costs of negotiation versus fighting influence the likelihood that war will ensue. Assuming $CF > CN$, we obtain the simple result that the tribe must be more optimistic than settlers about their ability to win back land for fighting to occur.

The raid-or-trade model has been tested using the patterns of fighting and negotiation over tribal land that developed between 1600 and the late nineteenth century. The first testable prediction concerns the zone of controversy affecting land. This predicts that disputes will not occur at the first point of contact between settlers and tribes, which appears to have been the case; for example, the Pemaquid tribe acceded 12,000 acres of land to English colonists in 1625. Bearing in mind the low value that tribes placed on large tracts of land that they did not use efficiently, this lower level of conflict would be expected. Two key features of nineteenth-century tribal-land policy are consistent with the details of the model. These were the removal of tribes from the Southeast to

Oklahoma and the creation of reservations for western tribes. Both of these policies removed tribes to areas of land of comparatively low value and avoided costly conflict.

Even where land was contested, there was an early tendency to settle by negotiation rather than through costly conflict. Early English settlers recognized the value of trade with natives, and, in the early 1800s, U.S. governments made considerable efforts to protect tribal rights and to avoid costly war. This had changed by 1871, when Congress voted to ratify no further treaties. Table 2.1 shows the history of battles and treaties.

The increase in the relative use of violence from about 1840 onwards can be explained in terms of the raid-or-trade model. It was not the result of technical change in weaponry occurring over the period (see the boxed application). The principal explanation is the move west by both tribes and settlers. Western tribes had a nomadic lifestyle, chasing bovine herds on horseback, even if they were displaced eastern tribes that had originally farmed under some form of private property system. Property rights were not well developed, and bargaining with tribes over land was thereby made more

Western Wars: Asymmetric Information and Asymmetric Technology

Technical change cannot in itself encourage war. In the first place, many technical developments in firearms may have been outweighed by the excellent guerrilla-warfare techniques of the natives. Weapons would eventually become available to both sides. Generally, the effect of superior weapons is hard to predict. The settlers might have been more eager to fight, but the natives might have been deterred by a weapons difference. Anderson and McChesney found that one test of the effect of weapons asymmetry, the change in the ratio of settler to tribal deaths in battle, shows no significant trend over the period 1850–1891.

Tribal assessment of the chances of winning battles probably increased with the move west. The natives' nomadic existence and guerrilla-warfare tactics made it difficult for the settlers to estimate the number of Native Americans facing them. A well-documented tactic was to use small raiding parties to decoy settlers or the army into a trap where many more warriors lay hidden. George Custer's last stand at the Battle of the Little Bighorn in 1876 Wyoming—with just a few hundred bluecoats—was the result of unusually poor information about the true size of the opposing force of over 3,000 Sioux and Cheyenne.

Information asymmetry could also sometimes work in the settlers' favor. In 1867, Sioux losses were exceptionally high at the Wagon Box Fight. The soldiers were equipped with new Springfield repeater rifles, of which the Sioux had no experience. The model developed earlier suggests these costly mistakes would not have happened with better information that would have encouraged the losing side to avoid conflict. At any rate, information asymmetry may have grown from the middle of the nineteenth century onward, encouraging more conflict.

A further possible explanation of the increase in battles is found in the growth of a standing army, particularly after the Civil War of 1861–1865. The army enabled local citizenry to avoid direct personal costs when fighting with natives. Locals probably also liked an army presence because of the demand for supplies. In addition, officers and army bureaucrats increased the pressure for wars to further their careers. Broadly, the effect of military growth was to reduce the local costs of fighting relative to negotiating for settlers in the West. Anderson and McChesney discovered that growth of the army had a statistically significant effect in increasing the number of battles for the period 1790–1897. Their result allowed for other factors likely to influence incentives to fight, and they did check for possible reverse causality.

TABLE 2.1	Battles and Treaties	
YEAR	**BATTLES**	**TREATIES**
1790–99	7	19
1800–09	–	30
1810–19	33	50
1820–29	1	51
1830–39	63	84
1840–49	53	18
1850–59	190	60
1860–69	786	62
1870–79	530	2
1880–89	131	3
1890–97	13	–

SOURCE: Anderson and McChesney (1994, p. 58), based on federal U.S. data. List of treaties compiled and edited by Charles J. Kappler. Washington: Government Printing Office, 1904. Web site hosted by the Oklahoma State University Library. http://digital.library.okstate.edu/kappler/index.htm

difficult. Also, western tribes tended to have a system of government that made it harder for chiefs to commit individuals to honoring treaties. This increase in the cost of negotiation made fighting relatively more attractive for both tribes and settlers.

The raid-or-trade model is a fascinating perspective on westward expansion in nineteenth-century America. It represents a careful application of property-rights theory to institutional development.

PUBLIC AND PRIVATE ENTERPRISE

It is important to distinguish common-property problems from issues concerning the efficiency of public enterprise. Public enterprise is not an example of common property but occurs where the state nationalizes one or more firms by purchasing or, possibly, simply taking the private property rights attached to some activity. In the United States, there are few examples of nationalized industries, although there is a history of local government involvement in some utility industries—particularly electricity and gas—and in municipal transportation.

Around the world at large, the picture is different. Many industries like telecoms, electricity, gas, and steel were nationalized, particularly after World War II. Many countries became dissatisfied with the performance of nationalized industries and embarked on privatization programs in the 1980s and 1990s. The history of nationalized industries shows that there were great problems of achieving cost control, attributable to a softening of financial constraints given that the taxpayer stood by to pay off any losses that were incurred. Notable privatization programs have occurred in the United Kingdom, Latin America, and New Zealand.

As shares in formerly nationalized industries are sold to the public, efficiency gains typically result from privatization programs, usually in the order of 20 percent reductions in operating costs. These savings are driven by the establishment of incentives to achieve simple cost efficiency. Property rights do matter, and in the private sector the firms have a residual claimant with an interest in maximizing profits. Profits and general welfare go together under competitive conditions, as lowering costs compared with rival firms enables lower prices to be charged to consumers while profits on sales can also be increased. Where there are issues of limited competition, perhaps because the formerly nationalized industry runs as a natural economy to achieve economies related to the size and scope of operations, foreign governments have often introduced the sort of regulatory laws that have been used in the United States for many years.

PUBLIC GOODS

A public good is one where it is either not possible, or perhaps undesirable, to exclude individuals from sharing in the consumption of the good. National defense is often cited as an example of a public good: If it is there for one, it is there for all. The production of public goods must be carefully distinguished not only from the production of *private* goods by nationalized firms, but also from production using common-property resources, where open access yields private but *less than optimal* benefits for users. Our main interest in public goods is that some economic problems of law can have public-goods aspects.

There is a traditional argument that public goods are not suitable for provision through private markets. A pure public good arises when it is not desirable to limit access to the use of some facility. In addition, it may be difficult for a producer of a public good to practice exclusion, although this is not the key characteristic. Pure public goods are essentially ones for which consumption is not mutually exclusive for consumers, so that people can be added to the group of consumers without depriving existing members of benefits. It is then efficient to add to the group any consumer who would receive some benefit. Apart from defense, classic examples of public goods are said to be services like the police force, and the provision of a system of law and order through the courts.

In terms of price theory, the optimal level of provision of a public good occurs where the sum of consumers' marginal benefits equals the marginal cost. This is shown in Figure 2.3 where MB_1 shows the (declining) marginal benefit of consumption for one individual, MB_2 shows marginal benefit for a second, and MC shows (constant) marginal cost. The curve labeled ΣMB is the vertical sum of MB_1 and MB_2, showing the joint benefits from a marginal unit of consumption (i.e., point a plus point b gives point c). The application of the general rule that marginal benefit should equal marginal cost for efficient allocation tells us to provide X^* units of the public good in Figure 2.3.

If it is not possible to exclude them, consumers have an incentive to understate their preferences to a private firm trying to market a public good. If we imagine asking citizens how much they would pay for the military for the coming year, each citizen might well try to "free ride" by pretending to wish to buy very little. Each would hope that neighbors would buy the service anyway.

Table 2.2 shows the payoffs to two individuals, A and B, who each receive a benefit worth $4 from a public good. Collective provision costs $4 in total, divided equally among contributing individuals. Failure to cooperate would force them to provide their own service at a cost of $3 each. If A and B declare their preferences honestly and

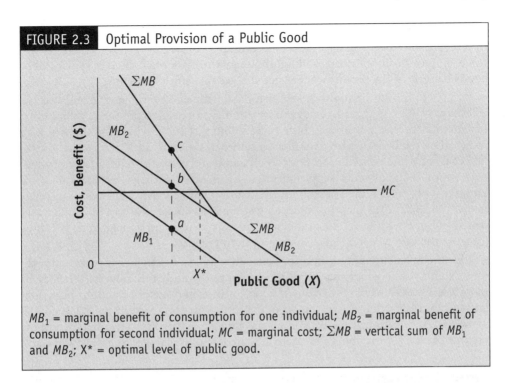

FIGURE 2.3   Optimal Provision of a Public Good

MB_1 = marginal benefit of consumption for one individual; MB_2 = marginal benefit of consumption for second individual; MC = marginal cost; ΣMB = vertical sum of MB_1 and MB_2; X* = optimal level of public good.

TABLE 2.2   Public Goods Prisoners' Dilemma

		B	
		Contributes	Does Not
A	Contributes	2,2	0,4
	Does Not	4,0	1,1

(Payoffs A,B)

share the cost of providing the service, each receives a net benefit of $2. If *A* contributes but *B* does not, *A* incurs the entire cost of providing both with the service. The net benefit to *A* would then be zero, although *B* would have a net benefit of $4. If *B* contributes but *A* does not, *B* incurs the cost and receives a zero payoff but *A* obtains $4. If neither contributes, each receives a net benefit of $1 ($4 benefit minus $3 cost).

In Table 2.2, the noncooperative strategy *does not contribute* strictly dominates for both players, which means it is always better to free ride whatever the other does. The difficulty with this is that both will evade contributing and end up at the bottom right of the table, which is the worst possible place to be (the *joint pessimum*). The table is an example of the classic problem from game theory known as the *prisoners' dilemma*.

The traditional conclusion is that public goods require the intervention of the state, which uses its coercive powers to force individuals to contribute. However, it is easy to question this conclusion, as there are many services that are often cited as examples of public goods but that have been successfully provided by private organizations. Interesting cases are toll roads and lighthouses, which are often cited as classic public goods because of the problem of levying charges on vehicles or ships.

Why were private lighthouses successful? Sometimes governments mandated the collection of dues, suggesting that government may not need to produce a public good but that its coercive power may be required. Often though, where lighthouses were provided on the basis of purely voluntary payments, suppliers could rely on a variety of nonlegal social and religious sanctions. A captain could be ostracized for failing to support a local religious order supplying the light. In small societies, a close-knit social group may succeed in the voluntary provision of public goods, as in cases of privately funded turnpike roads early in American history. The similar problem of conflict over shared use of a resource is also sometimes solved by voluntary cooperation, as can be found in the case of water rights among Western ranchers.

It is also difficult to find examples of *pure* public goods. Examples like parks and highways exhibit public-goods characteristics only until they become congested. It may be more sensible to think of a spectrum of goods, with the private good and the pure public good as extreme points. The middle of the spectrum is occupied by the "club good," where an individual's benefits depend on the amount of personal consumption and the number of people with whom the facility is shared, e.g., as with golf or swimming clubs.

SOME ASSORTED PROPERTY DOCTRINES

The legal principles affecting the creation of property rights can be linked to some of the ideas on the efficiency of private rights and the desirability of discouraging rent seeking. Several legal doctrines concerning property appear to reflect these concerns.

First Possession

Much American land was developed through the creation of private property rights following the common-law principle of *terra nullius*, which allows ownership of land to be established by first possession. The Homestead Act of 1862 enabled U.S. citizens over 21 years of age to acquire up to 160 acres of frontier land at $1.25 an acre by residing for six months and making improvements on the land. The act did not recognize aboriginal practices for this purpose and had the effect of excluding tribal claims to land.

The Homestead Act was not strictly enforced, which would have been costly, so that settlement and improvement efforts were often limited to placing the shells of houses on land claims. It is tempting to argue that the lax application of the criteria for homesteading would lead to the devotion of resources to transferring property, i.e., rent seeking, rather than to proper investment in land development. Such an argument overlooks the cost of operating the system of ownership, which is required before there can be any economic development. It is important to make a comparative-institutional analysis examining the costs and benefits of alternative approaches that might have been taken toward land rights.

The westward expansion of the United States was associated with very high costs of enforcing property rights on distant frontiers and was unsuited to a system of sales to absentee owners. The Homestead Act saved significant amounts of enforcement costs because the creation of ownership rights occurred at the local level. Disputes could be settled either through civil courts or even through claimants' associations that developed in the West. By encouraging the early settlement of land, the investment of effort in transferring land was brought to a close earlier than might otherwise have been the case. The policy of requiring settlement, although not perfectly enforced, encouraged population movement to the West, which was public policy in the mid-1800s.

In the *Mabo* (1992) case, the Australian High Court raised questions about the extent of property rights gained by settlers and mineral companies. As in the early history of the United States, the traditional legal view was that the continent of Australia represented *terra nullius*, or unoccupied land, before Europeans settled. In *Mabo*, the High Court recognized the existence of native title for Melanesian tribes living on the Murray Islands off northern Queensland. Native title gives hunting, ceremonial, and similar rights and represents a new entitlement showing an innovation in the partitioning of property rights bundles. The Murray Islanders were a settled people with a gardening culture when they were incorporated into Australia in 1879.

The extension of the *Mabo* ruling to mainland aboriginal claims of native title might be expected to produce legal conflict, particularly if native rights were to impede mineral exploration and mining. Aborigines have a highly nomadic history, and mining is an industry of great significance in modern Australia. In 2002, the Australian government announced the recognition of native rights in an area of the Gibson Dessert larger than Virginia. It now remains to be seen whether these distinct property rights, tribal and mineral, can coexist or will come into conflict. Economics suggests that conflict would be reduced and aboriginal welfare would still be recognized if native title were made a fully separable partition of property rights, so that mining companies or other interested parties could buy out the rights if they impeded more valuable conventional land use.

Tribal groups in North America have successfully claimed forms of native title in cases where they have shown that they were using and occupying land at the point when Europeans settled. These rights usually refer to some limited form of land use or an exemption from some statutory control. In the Canadian case *R. v. Sparrow* (1990), the Musqueam tribe successfully defended their right to use outsized drift nets. These partial rights reflect European movement past native tribes, with the settlers ceding rights that were not significant to them at the time. Problems may arise if native rights are *suddenly* rediscovered and adjustments are needed when trading cannot occur.

In the case of land, a rule of first possession moves society away from open access and toward enforceable private property rights. This is generally efficiency enhancing, although it may be tough on nomadic tribes who may never share in the benefits from enclosure. The result contrasts with the effect of first possession for "fugitive" property such as wildlife stocks, where the prize is the product of a renewable natural resource that cannot be privately owned. Then we have a case like the fishery, where first possession is simply a reflection of open access that never stops. With land, first possession brings open access to a halt.

Water Rights

The manner in which water is owned and used in various countries illustrates the effect of scarcity on property rights. In the eastern United States, water is plentiful and riparian owners (owners of the shore alongside a body of water) have the right to use the flow of water past their land. Traditionally, riparian rights do not allow significant diversion of water to the detriment of the flow available to downstream owners of land. The eastern states adopted riparian water rights as a part of their continued use of the English common law following American independence.

The American version of riparian water rights protects the right of the riparian owner to the natural flow of the waterway. Typically, this flow may be diminished by the reasonable use of similar riparian owners, primarily for domestic and livestock purposes, a matter that can be judged in court if necessary. The earlier English version of riparian rights was more restrictive in requiring an undiminished "natural flow" of water, which could not be reduced at all even if there was no other use for the water. The distinctive economic feature of riparian rights is that the law generally restricts the use of water for irrigating more distant, nonriparian land, because this would tend to reduce the downstream flow. In water-abundant eastern states, this poses no great problem.

As settlement spread west in the mid-nineteenth century, it rapidly became apparent that riparian water rights were ill suited to dryer conditions. Western states followed the East in adopting Anglo-American common law, not least owing to the need to recruit legal personnel in a national labor market, but gradually lost strict adherence to riparian water rights. Problems became particularly severe when mineral deposits were discovered and mined and there was a pressing need to divert water for mining operations. Mining camps began to establish their own customary law of prior appropriation under which water could be treated as private property and diverted by the first to possess it. In eight western states (Arizona, Colorado, Idaho, Montana, New Mexico, Nevada, Utah, and Wyoming), the law eventually came to reject riparian rights in favor of prior appropriation.

A landmark case was *Coffin v. Left Hand Ditch Co.* (1882), in which the Colorado Supreme Court formally adopted prior appropriation and rejected riparian rights. The *Coffin* case shows the emergence of a separable entitlement to trade water and is examined in detail in the boxed application. Prior appropriation separates rights to water from ownership of contiguous land, making it possible to divert water.

An interesting question is whether prior appropriation is strictly necessary to encourage efficient use of water where it is scarce. The argument in favor of the greater efficiency of prior appropriation is that the separation of water from land rights more clearly defines the rights and aids bargaining over the use of the water. It is certainly the case that a rule of prior appropriation will encourage efficient use of water. One way to see this is to consider a case where the water appropriator has a low-valued use compared with a downstream user. We would expect the downstream user to buy the right to an undisturbed water flow from the appropriator, who could be bribed to give up some diverted use. Prior appropriation is certainly sufficient to support efficient use.

When bargaining occurs, following the Coase theorem (discussed in Chapter 3) we would expect the initial assignment of water rights to affect the distribution of financial benefits but not the eventual location of water use. Water should end up in its most highly valued use. This observation raises the question of whether prior appropriation is necessary for efficiency in situations of water scarcity. The crucial thing may be that the law facilitates bargaining, and there may be more than one way to do that.

Bargaining could remove obstacles to efficiency under a regime of riparian rights, but possibly just in special cases. In riparian systems, the legal presumption is that downstream water rights cannot be disrupted, which is consistent with an environment in which there are no valuable distant uses of water and all riverside uses are of similar value. Water diversion is legally complex. Downstream landowners could obtain a court order (injunction) stopping (enjoining) an upstream diversion and could then sell back

Coffin v. Left Hand Ditch Co., 6 Colo. 443 (1882)

The Left Hand Ditch Co. appealed against a decision upholding the right of George Coffin to divert water to which he claimed a prior right. Coffin owned land to which water was diverted by virtue of a ditch running from the south fork of the St. Vrain creek. The ditch ran on to the Left Hand Creek, where it was again diverted and used for irrigation by the Left Hand Ditch Co. In 1879, there was an insufficient quantity of water in the St. Vrain to supply water to both parties, and Coffin dammed the ditch, preventing onward flow of the water. The Left Hand Ditch Co. tore out the dam, and Coffin sought damages and an injunction preventing further removal of his dam. Coffin won the case, clarifying his right to the water.

The reasoning of Justice Helm, which is reported in abbreviated form here, is particularly interesting.

The common-law doctrine giving the riparian owner a right to the flow of water, even though he makes no beneficial use of it, is inapplicable to Colorado. Necessity, unknown to the countries that gave birth to the doctrine, compels the recognition of another. The climate is dry, and the soil, when moistened only by the usual rainfall, is arid and unproductive. Artificial irrigation for agriculture is an absolute necessity. Water in the various streams thus acquires a value unknown in moister climates. We hold that, in the absence of express statutes to the contrary, the first appropriator of water from a natural stream for a beneficial purpose has a prior right thereto.

The territorial legislature in 1864 expressly recognizes the doctrine. It says: "Nor shall the water of any stream be diverted from its original channel to the detriment of any miner, mill men or others along the line of said stream, who may have a priority of right." (Session Laws of 1864, p. 68, s 32). The priority of right mentioned in this section is acquired by priority of appropriation, and the provision declares that appropriations of water shall be subordinate to the use thereof by prior appropriators.

The judgment of the court below will be affirmed.

Justice Helm clearly recognized the need for a different system of water rights in a more arid climate. The benefit of prior appropriation is that it creates private property rights in water. In turn, this can become the basis of water sales through which water can find its way to the highest valuing users.

the right to disrupt the water flow (condemn the injunction) if this were the more highly valued option. In principle, riparian rights could allow the bargaining that would be needed to ensure efficient use, but the process might be costly.

Where water is scarce and diversion is known typically to be the highest-valued use, it is likely to be efficient to have the rule of prior appropriation. If, for example, we knew that many miners or irrigating farmers would incur high costs from losing their water and that downstream landowners usually lost only small amounts of production from the diversion, it would be efficient to give the rights to the water appropriators. In arid conditions, prior appropriation possibly avoids costs of bargaining, as the rights go to the highest-valuing users in the first place. A rule of prior appropriation would be likely to emerge where courts were repeatedly faced with cases involving high-valued diversion of water.

Apart from the eight western states with prior-appropriation systems, nine western states have systems combining features of riparianism and prior appropriation. Texas and California are notable mixed systems. It is best to exercise a little caution over accepting the argument that first appropriation *must* be a better rule in regions facing water scarcity. It seems more reasonable to argue that water law needs to encourage bargaining between competing users whenever water is scarce and it is not obvious where the highest-valued use will be.

California gradually revised riparian rights to permit high-valued diversion of water. The courts frequently failed to prevent appropriations of water as in *Edgar v. Stevenson* (1886), where there was judged to be no damage to downstream riparian owners. The courts appear to have applied a *rule of reason*, where they attempted to balance competing interests by creative interpretation of the riparian doctrine. In *Rose v. Mesmer* (1904), the court interpreted the doctrine as giving a downstream riparian, in situations of water scarcity, the right to "so much of the water as should be reasonably necessary for use on his riparian land." There was no right to an undiminished physical flow just "for the pleasure of looking upon it," as in England. Clearly, early California law allowed irrigation of the riparian land, possibly at the cost of "less reasonable" downstream uses, and diversion to nonriparians if there was no harm.

Where downstream riparian owners had significant interests, the courts tended to uphold riparian rights and prevent diversion onto nonriparian land. In *Lux v. Haggin* (1886), the right of the riparian rancher (Miller-Lux) to an undiminished flow was upheld when water had been diverted upstream to benefit a nonriparian landowner (Haggin). Subsequently, Miller-Lux sold the right to some water to Haggin. Both *Edgar*, where there was apparently no downstream damage, and *Lux* resulted in efficient allocations of water. In the *Lux* case, Haggin paid compensation (which was used to build a dam to increase the flow of water), and we can therefore be sure the upstream appropriation was a welfare improvement.

Contractual solutions exist to allow irrigation of nonriparian land in riparian systems. In *Lux*, money was paid to overcome a downstream riparian's opposition to diversion. Another simple approach, described by the judge in *Rose v. Mesmer*, would be for a nonriparian to become riparian by joining land with that of a riparian. The new riparian could even then choose to take upstream water by negotiating access over other more convenient land (it does not matter from where the riparian takes the water). Also notice that riparian land not directly alongside the riverbank can be parceled up for sale with or without water rights. All of these alternatives to prior appropriation have organizational costs attached to them and may be too costly to be useful in many cases.

Pure riparian rights are efficient in settings where interrupting downstream water flows will almost never be beneficial. The rule of prior appropriation will be efficient where the upstream diversion is most likely to be of net benefit. Finally, a rule of reason is appropriate to regions where it is impossible to make judgements in advance about the generally beneficial rule and where it may also be desirable to define property rights to encourage low-cost bargaining. Water laws give a fascinating illustration of the range of possible responses to conflict over water resources (even if the reader had not thought so until now!).

Adverse Possession

The modern approach toward abandoned land is based around statutes of limitations affecting trespass and similar matters. If someone occupies land, they can obtain title by adverse possession if the original owner does not sue for trespass within the limitation, which differs across states but is commonly seven years. In the case of abandoned land, efficiency requires that it be returned to active use. Statutes of limitations on old land claims are efficient in this respect, as they suppress claims based on older and less reliable data, which may be very costly to pursue. The rule of adverse possession is efficient if it makes it possible to transfer unused land to a higher-valuing user, although this would not be true if the first owner has the highest valuation.

The rule of adverse possession is often associated with procedures, such as a requirement for the possessor to pay land taxes, alerting any interested first owner to the occupation of apparently abandoned land. The long period of time that must pass before adverse possession can take effect also helps, as it would be remarkable if someone with a definite interest in the land were to overlook its adverse possession over a period of seven years. In addition, adverse possession rules put landowners on notice to avoid boundary errors before improving land, which helps to avoid costly conflicts.

Lost and Found Property

Lost property is best reallocated to productive use without devoting excessive resources to questions of ownership. A suitable approach is to devote some but not too many resources to finding the original owner. The law covering lost and found property can safely follow a rule of "finders keepers," provided there is a requirement for a limited search for the original owner. Care must be taken because a danger with a simple rule of finders keepers is that people might devote too much effort to searching for lost property. A rational person would devote resources to searching if the expected return is greater than or equal to the cost of the effort. Search activity stops when the marginal benefit (*MB*) is just equal to marginal cost (*MC*), as shown by point *S** in Figure 2.4. The marginal benefit of search is shown as constant for simplicity, whereas marginal cost increases owing to the need to search more distantly.

The race to find lost property can be wasteful if people overestimate their chances of finding the property. If 10 people each have an equal probability of finding a lost

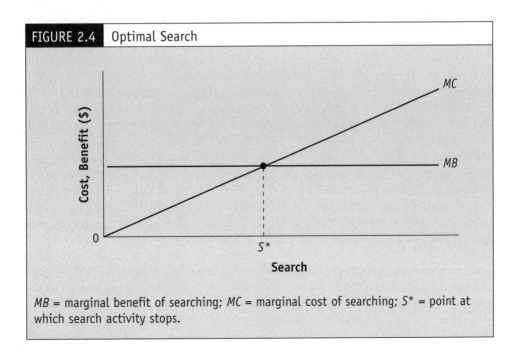

FIGURE 2.4   Optimal Search

MB = marginal benefit of searching; *MC* = marginal cost of searching; *S** = point at which search activity stops.

work of art, they should each devote 1/10 of its value to finding it. The search would be efficient because, in aggregate, no more than the value of the work of art would be spent in finding it. If they overestimate their probability of success at 1/5, they will devote in aggregate double the value of the work to its recovery.

If there were evidence of excessive devotion of resources for search activity—for example if people searching with metal detectors crowded parks—there would be a case for awarding only a portion of the value of an item to its finder. Laws covering "treasure troves" may well work in this way. Items of great historical value may have to be handed over to the state rather than sold commercially. The finder can then claim a reward that reflects a reasonable return on the search effort. Such laws may be motivated by a wish by state authorities to save money by not having to pay for valuable museum pieces. However, if people are adventurous and typically overestimate the chances of successful search, treasure-trove laws may bring search effort down to a more cost-effective level. Of course, if they were realistic in their expectations, such laws could deter efficient searching.

It is also possible to spend too much time and effort trying to locate the original owner of an item. Estray statues deliberately limit the search effort by specifying an orderly procedure, in which the finder of a valuable item declares the find to a court and attempts to locate the original owner. If the item is unclaimed after several months, the finder can claim title to the item. The point is to ensure that only cost-effective efforts are made to locate owners, where the value of this process is really the removal of uncertainty over title.

"Dead-Hand Control" and the Rule Against Perpetuities

Judges have struggled with the problem of whose preferences are to count in making decisions over land use. Economists often do not reflect sufficiently on this problem, working from given preferences and failing to recognize the context-bound nature of their analysis. The question of whose preferences are to count is a very real one in land law, as in many other areas of public policy. Consider the repercussions if, in devising land in a will, a landowner were to tie up the use of the land excessively. Suppose the landowner leaves the land to a favorite daughter on the condition that it should be kept as a cat home and must be subsequently devised by the daughter under the same conditions. There would thereby be an attempt to fix the use of the land permanently by a property rule. In particular, the will would apparently rule out later transferring the land to uses valued more highly by members of the then-current generation.

The more time that passes, the less confident we could be that the satisfaction gained by the first landowner in knowing how the land would be used outweighed any later losses from subsequent generations being unable to change the land use. In fact, the dying landowner might not give much weight to losses incurred by descendants who inherit the land. These reflections appear to explain the very strong rule against perpetuities operating in the courts. In general, and with some notable exceptions, a restriction on land use can operate only for the lifetime of persons alive at the time it is made, although the restriction can be made renewable. By forcing such restrictions out into the open for periodic reconsideration, land law ensures that the preferences of current generations dominate "dead-hand control" in determining land use.

INTELLECTUAL PROPERTY

We now consider a form of property that has grown in importance in the twentieth century. Intellectual property is the direct product of human creative activity, such as a new invention, design, or work of art. Laws covering patents and copyright allow products like these to be appropriated by their creators. The main point of these laws is to encourage valuable creative activity by defining a form of future market for the use of the intellectual property. A further type of intellectual property is the business trademark, where enforceable property rights have a useful role to play in communicating information about goods and services to consumers.

In recent years, copyright has been extended to include computer programs and even the design of integrated electronic circuits. There has also been much international activity as major industrialized countries have increasingly agreed on similar laws covering patents, copyrights, and trademarks, particularly under the Trade Related Aspects of Intellectual Property Rights (TRIPS) agreement among member countries of the World Trade Organization. Such international action gained its impetus because of worries about the trade distortions that could arise after some countries persistently permitted companies to ignore intellectual property rights, such as when music compact discs could simply be copied from their original sources and then sold. The TRIPS agreement came into effect in 1995 and sets minimum acceptable levels for patent, copyright, and trademark protection. Disputes between signatories, which include the United States, are resolved by the World Trade Organization, which can ultimately impose trade sanctions for noncompliance. The signatories are free to extend protection.

Patents

Patents exclude anyone but the patent holder from freely using an invention. The holder may choose to license use of a patented invention in exchange for a royalty payment. In the United States, a general patent lasts for a maximum of 20 years, during which time periodic (rather modest) registration fees must be paid to keep it in force. In 2000, the fees for large commercial organizations were $760 for a first registration, $940 after $3^{1}/_{2}$ years, $1,900 after $7^{1}/_{2}$ years, and $2,910 after $11^{1}/_{2}$ years.

Applications to the Patent Office must show that an invention:

1.   is a new product, process, or improvement;

2.   is capable of industrial application; and

3.   is not an obvious development.

It also must not be excluded by virtue of being a purely intellectual discovery (such as a scientific theory) or creation (like a work of art). The period of 20 years is comparable to the periods, ranging from 15 to 20 years, granted by all major industrialized countries. All such countries are signatories to the Paris Convention for the Protection of Industrial Property (incorporated into the TRIPS agreement) that allows an application to be simultaneously filed with all signatory countries after its initial registration with any one.

In the United States and Canada, patents are awarded on the basis that the inventor has a genuine claim to invention or innovation; it is a "first-to-invent" system.

Sometimes a contrast is made with the "first-to-file" systems used in many other countries of the world, including Japan and throughout the European Union. Care must be taken with this distinction as very often first-to-file systems indeed try to associate initial filing with a claim to invention, i.e., the patent goes to the first inventor to file. North America may eventually move to a first-to-file system, which encourages inventors to register as early as possible.

There is a tension in economic analysis between seeing patents as devices that restrict competition and encourage monopolistic pricing of products, and seeing them as an essential incentive for invention and innovation. Once it is in existence, the invention has the characteristics of a public good, and it would seem rational to allow others to use the information. Restricting access to the knowledge would appear to impose private costs as though they were social costs. However, this argument is not good comparative institutionalism because it ignores the cost of disturbing the long-run incentives for invention. If firms could use an invention without paying toward its costs, the price of the associated product would be driven down close to production costs in a competitive market. As a result, there would be little or no incentive to invent. Patents give a temporary monopoly to the inventor and, by raising market price, allow recovery of the costs of invention and increase the incentive to invent.

Patent law gives that temporary monopoly in exchange for full revelation of the invention. Without patent protection, firms would be more tempted than they are currently to keep their inventions secret. This would hamper further development by other innovators. Therefore, patent law can also be seen as encouraging information revelation, which may have benefits beyond the originating business. Without patent law, invention would be biased toward techniques that could be kept secret.

There is an optimal patent life based on the trade-off between the benefits and costs of extending patent life. The benefits refer to maintaining the incentive to invent (or innovate) and to avoiding investments in secrecy. The costs refer to the inconvenience to patent users, who must adhere to licensing arrangements. In principle, patent life should differ for each invention although, in practice, a uniform system is likely to prevail. Figure 2.5 illustrates the trade-off between the costs and benefits of extending patent life.

In Figure 2.5, the MC curve shows the costs of extending patent life. Marginal costs reflect costs to both firms and consumers. Firms must invent around (i.e., avoid) the patent or must pay fees to use it, and consumers face higher prices from monopoly. Constant marginal cost reflects an assumption that there is a constant additional nuisance from extending the patent. The MB curve shows the benefits from extending patent life in terms of the profit gain to the inventors, which falls over time. Over the years, more people would avoid the patent by successfully inventing around it, and the invention would become dated and of lower value. An optimum occurs at L^*, where the surplus of benefit over costs is maximized.

Fees for maintaining a patent have the useful effect of facing the inventor with some, although possibly not many, of the costs imposed. Germany has an interesting two-tier system with a full-term patent for major inventions and a 3-year patent for minor developments, and it also has patent renewal fees that rise during the life of the patent. As described earlier, the United States has also adopted an increasing periodic fee to maintain the patent.

Is it likely that patent law may encourage speculative investment in research to obtain a patent monopoly and close off a market area? One variant of such behavior, patent rac-

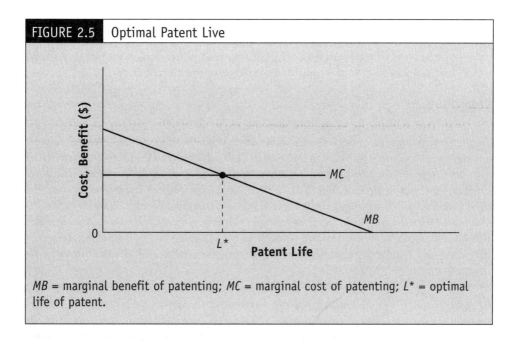

FIGURE 2.5   Optimal Patent Live

MB = marginal benefit of patenting; *MC* = marginal cost of patenting; *L** = optimal life of patent.

ing, is a bit like treasure hunting and has very clear implications of rent-seeking behavior. However, it is not obvious that rent seeking in this area is as wasteful as might be feared, and the law exhibits devices that contain the costs of rent seeking. Any wasteful expenditure on seeking patents would reflect the costs of the patenting system itself and the costs of duplicating effort over research and development. The cost of the patenting system can be regarded as an inevitable cost of administering a part of the property-rights system.

Even if research and development activity were totally protected by patents, it would not follow that duplicative research should be regarded as wasteful. It is a question of making meaningful comparisons. If there were some other means of generating the same innovation at lower cost, then it would be reasonable to regard duplicative effort as wasteful. By analogy, we do not regard competition between several gas stations as wasteful even when we know that only one will survive. We accept the cost of competition as the only way to obtain the benefits of competition. Patent races could be of this nature.

What are the alternatives to patenting? One may be for the government to use competitive bidding to allocate the monopoly right to research into a new drug to the company promising to undertake it at the lowest cost. However, competitive bidding has its own problems. For a start, it is difficult to define the right that would be exclusively allocated. Also, as defense contracting suggests, firms would devote resources to lobbying for the exclusive right. It is not obvious that there would be lower social costs with competitive bidding, or any fewer problems with any other regulatory framework that might be suggested.

Patent law itself limits rent seeking. The first-to-invent system of issuing patents in the United States communicates the knowledge that some invention has been captured. Early registration is important to avoid the risk of losing the property right to someone else. Registration leads to swift termination of other firms' efforts, an effect that is even stronger under the first-to-file rules used in other countries. Also, the patenting requirement that an invention should not be too obvious eliminates property rights in areas of innovation that might be expected to attract a lot of duplicative effort precisely because they would be the easiest in which to invest.

Copyright

Copyright law protects the property rights of authors, composers, and artists as an incentive to creative activity. It prevents unauthorized copying and gives the copyright owner a temporary monopoly on the original work. These days, the definition of creative work also encompasses the design and effective operation of computer software, and the design of integrated circuits. The TRIPS agreement incorporates the Berne Convention on copyright, which initially gave protection to an individual for the lifetime of the creator plus 50 years. In 1998, the Sonny Bono Copyright Term Extension Act extended this basic protection to the lifetime plus 70 years, following a 1993 directive issued by the European Union increasing European copyright terms to 70 years. Copyright for businesses lasts for 95 years.

Without copyright, the price of some creative work would fall to its marginal cost of reproduction. The qualification is necessary as other factors may restrict the reproducibility of some works; for example, a David Hockney painting really must be by the California-based English painter. In many cases, such as the production of novels or textbooks, consumers would be indifferent between the authorized copy and any other. An absence of copyright restrictions would benefit consumers and publishers as prices fell, as illustrated by the competition between low-cost editions of the works of long-dead authors. This benefit to consumers is based on a lack of property rights for the estates of the original authors.

The analysis of patenting in Figure 2.5 could be applied to copyright with suitable amendment of details: There is a marginal benefit to creators from copyright protection that probably diminishes the longer we look into the future, and marginal costs to consumers and publishers. An optimum could, in principle, be found from balancing marginal cost and benefit. It seems that copyright law recognizes the falling benefit to a creator from extending duration in ending copyright restrictions at a fixed number of years after death.

The blanket nature of copyright protection may be questioned. In book publishing, the original author often has a considerable first-mover advantage over possible rivals. This is particularly true in the case of popular literature, as these books must generally earn profits over their first few months on the market. An example is the book *Princess in Love*, by Anna Pasternak, which concerned the private life of Princess Diana; the book was a best-seller for just a few weeks in 1994 but is now largely forgotten. By the time a rival publisher realized the value of copying such a work, sales would have been largely completed. A contrary view is that it has become so easy to copy print, given modern electronic technology, that uniform protection is still needed unless the market is saturated very quickly. It is difficult anyway to see how property rights in textbooks and computer programs could be protected without copyright.

A stronger argument may exist against the long time period for which copyright runs. In particular, the extension to 70 years in the United States and Europe has been criticized as excessive in relation to the protection necessary to encourage creative work. In 2002, the 20-year extension under the Sonny Bono Act was challenged in the Supreme Court on the basis that it did not encourage progress, but, rather, extended

Napster.com—File Sharing or Property Theft?

Recording companies have found it particularly difficult to enforce their property rights under existing copyright law in the face of file-sharing Internet sites. The International Federation of the Phonographic Industry (IFPI) issued figures at the end of 2002 that showed world sales of recorded music had fallen by 5 percent in 2001. Consumption of music grew by an estimated 9.4 percent over the period. The difference reflects pirating of music, i.e., bootleg copying and resale of music compact discs (CDs) and downloading from free Internet sites, of which the best known is the Napster site.

The IFPI also calculated that 2.2 billion blank CDs are bought annually for recording from computer downloads. In 2002, the IFPI's antipiracy team closed down 51 bootlegging operations with a capacity to supply total music demand in a medium-sized country like France or Great Britain. Although Napster closed down after failing to "go legal" by creating a subscription, and royalty-paying, service with the German media company Bertelsmann, other file-sharing companies continued to operate for some time thereafter. The Recording Industry Association of America left it until 2002 before taking court action to close down Kazza.com and Musiccity.com, two major file-sharing sites. In all, the downloading of tracks from Internet sites grew from nothing in 1997 to 3.5 billion downloads in 2002.

Clearly, the record companies have found copyright a useful protection, but it is also clear that legal action is slow to catch up with a problem made worse for them by changing technology. The companies claim that undermining their property rights makes it much harder for them to nurture and encourage artists, whose income could in principle fall to zero as a result of bootlegging and file sharing. Interestingly, a further technical change may be coming to their rescue, as it is becoming possible to issue security-protected CDs and for the companies to set up Web search engines able to detect and stop file sharing and downloading.

the private property interests of major corporations at a time when the copyrights of some classic fictional characters, like Mickey Mouse, were about to expire.

Trademarks

Businesses invest large sums of money in developing trademarks, which are defined by Article 15 of the TRIPS agreement as "any sign or combination of signs capable of distinguishing the goods or services of one undertaking from those of others." The signs are usually words, letters, numerals, or figurative elements that form a company's logo. Trademarks associate a name or symbol with a differentiable product or service and are meant to be easily identified indicators of quality. An illustration of this is franchising, where companies like Burger King (the international fast-food chain) literally rent out trademarks in return for royalties from franchisees. The trademark indicates quality to customers who do not wish to spend much time assessing the quality of restaurants.

Under the Federal Trademark Act (1994) in the United States (and more generally around the world following the TRIPS agreement), trademarks can be registered (with the Patent Office in the United States) only if they represent a real differentiation of some product. Trademark registration is not time-governed in the manner of patents and copyright; the TRIPS agreement requires registration to be for a minimum of seven years but to be renewable indefinitely. However, if the name is a generic term for a product, it cannot be registered. Furthermore, if the trademark becomes a general description within the trade for goods of similar description, its exclusive use cannot be enforced and the trademark is broken. In the United States, broken marks

Stringfellow v. McCain (1984): A Nightclub Owner Writes . . .

Peter Stringfellow, the owner of Stringfellow's nightclub, discovered that a well-known food company had marketed oven-ready fries under the name "Stringfellows." Not being known for being too shy to come forward (check this with an Internet search of his name), Stringfellow brought suit alleging trademark infringement. The nightclub is London-based, but since United States and English laws of intellectual property are virtually identical, the case is a useful example of the traditional scope of trademark protection. The product was, in fact, an attempt to educate the British palate to the thinner (stringier) and, some would say, tastier American-style fry!

Stringfellow lost his case. The court ruled that the trademark "Stringfellows" could be enforced only in the business areas closely linked to operating a nightclub. In other areas, as the court saw it, there could be no danger of confusion of brands by consumers who would not expect a nightclub to be supplying supermarket products. The ruling is consistent with the economic interpretation given in the body of this text: Outside of the nightclub business, the name could communicate no quality signal. Therefore, there was no point in enforcing the trademark against the maker of "Stringfellows."

include "aspirin" and "super glue." One way to hold onto a trademark is to register it as a brand name: Had the company thought of it, "Aspirin-Brand Painkiller" would have been impossible to break. Furthermore, if the trademark falls into disuse, its registration can be canceled (after three years under the TRIPS agreement).

Some economists are keen to see investment in trademarks as supporting monopolies that are against the interests of consumers. However, this view ignores the information conveyed to buyers by trademarks. It is not enough for firms to produce products or services of a certain technical quality. Customers also have to receive the information. In addition to developing trademarks, firms also spend money on many other devices to indicate the quality of their service. A bank's expenditure on high-quality decor for its premises signals to customers that it is too well funded to be at risk of failure.

The information-based explanation of trademark law gains support from the observation that the law does not support trademark rights where they serve no purpose. The restriction on registering general descriptive terms may be seen in this way, as may the broken trademark. Once a name has become a general description, there can be no information advantage attached to it in relation to a particular manufacturer. Of particular interest, however, is the prohibition on stopping use of a trademarked business name by another firm in a different line of business. From an efficiency point of view, this is correct because the other line of business has no implications for the efficiency of the quality signal in the first business.

The treatment of trademarks changed in 1995 following the passage of the Federal Trademark Dilution Act, which protects famous brands, such as McDonald's, Levi's, or Ford, from unauthorized use of the brand name in any area of business. It is not necessary for a famous brand to show that consumers might be confused over *related* products. Some brands are now so famous that a possible rationale for the change in the law may be that *any* use of such a trade name carries a risk of poor-quality products damaging the brand. This argument is thin, and the traditional doctrine seems best to capture the economic logic behind branding. How can the marketing of McDonald's jeans, or Levi's hamburgers, carry a quality signal for the parent product?

SUMMARY AND CONCLUSIONS

In this chapter, we began by emphasizing the importance of seeing property rights as bundles of entitlements rather than as physical entities. We defined a number of systems of property rights and showed how these have implications for economic efficiency. In particular, private property rights encourage efficient use and transfers of resources. Common property is typically associated with overexploitation of resources, although this argument should be qualified by recognition of the costs of creating private rights. The issues surrounding ownership of resources must be carefully distinguished from those affecting the desirability of public or private provision of goods and services.

The sheer variety of property rights should be highlighted; water rights, mineral rights, intellectual property rights, and controls on land use have all evolved over time. Economic considerations are at the heart of straightforward legal rules such as those concerned with lost property or protecting intellectual property. Economic analysis can also throw light on grander institutional developments using property-rights analysis. The presumption is often that property rights, like the ones that developed as the American West was settled, tend to alter as the costs and benefits change for a particular formation. Something as simple as the invention of barbed wire may have a profound influence on enclosing common land. Encounters between European settlers and highly nomadic, weakly governed western native tribes seem to have contributed to increases in fighting relative to negotiated peace in the late nineteenth century. The analysis of property rights in economics leads to powerful insights into social arrangements.

QUESTIONS FOR REVIEW

1. Would you expect fisheries based on lakes to exhibit different patterns of property rights compared with high-seas fisheries? What factors would explain any difference?

2. In the late nineteenth century, arid areas of Australia were settled for the first time. Australia has essentially the same common-law system as the United States and also initially adopted riparian water rights. Based on your knowledge of the evolution of water rights in the western United States, what problems and legal innovations would you expect to have arisen in relation to Australian water rights?

3. Can the raid-or-trade model be applied to modern ethnic conflicts around the world?

4. Jack "The Lad" Smith is arrested walking along the street carrying a bag containing valuables. He claims that he found the items. Are there any aspects of the law of lost property that could help the police in determining whether the valuables are likely to be stolen? Comment on your answer from an economic perspective.

5. The owner of the London nightclub "Stringfellows" unsuccessfully sued a food manufacturer to prevent its calling a new potato product "Stringfellow Chips." The law in this area is virtually identical in England and the United States. What do you think would happen if a local garage owner opened a service shop and called it "Ford"? Would it make any difference if the name appeared inside a blue oval? Consider whether there is economic logic behind the legal treatment of trademarking.

NOTES ON THE LITERATURE

- Umbeck (1981) discusses the emergence of private rights in a process where the use of force gives way to settled legitimacy. Posner (1980) analyzes property rights in primitive societies. An analogy may be drawn with the emergence of mafias in settings lacking legitimate authority (Gambetta, 2000).

- The dynamic view on the efficiency of private property rights is very old and can be found in Blackstone (1766).

- Anderson and McChesney's (1994) work contains the details cited on settler and Native American land use.

- Nobel prizewinner Douglass North (1990) has developed the dynamic view of the evolution of private property rights into a theory of history. In this theory, institutional developments, such as land enclosure, occur precisely because of the efficiency gains that result.

- The static view of the inefficiency of common rights is of comparatively recent origin and is associated with property-rights theorists like Gordon (1954), Demsetz (1967; 2002), and Furubotn and Pejovich (1972; 1974). See also Furubotn (1989; 1987; 1994).

- The fisheries model used in this chapter is a development of Gordon's (1954) seminal article. The bell-shaped curve actually reflects sustainable yield, but sustainability, although important in the specialist literature on fisheries, is not important in this illustration of common property. We assume no discounting of future costs and benefits attached to the fishery. With discounting at a sufficiently high rate, it might be rational for the owner to fish out the entire stock in the current year. Libecap and Smith (2002) discuss the open-access problem in the context of common oil pools.

- Agnello and Donnelley (1975) tested the prediction that private rights lead to a more efficient fishing industry using data on the oyster fisheries of 16 contiguous Atlantic and Gulf states from Massachusetts to Texas over the period 1950–1969. They used averages of the 20 years' data for each state, finding that private rights led to greater efficiency. They regressed the average product of labor on the property-rights variable and a number of other exogenous variables (such as the capital intensity of fishing and the presence of disease) using ordinary-least-squares analysis in six different specifications of a model. The property-rights variable was always statistically significant and of the expected positive sign, indicating that it increased labor productivity.

- Crutchfield and Pontecorvo (1969) give a fascinating account of the sailing-boat regime imposed irrationally on the Pacific salmon fishery. Lueck (1995) shows that rent may not be dissipated if laws allow a race for common property to end in possession of the entire stock. Grafton, Squires, and Fox (2000) examine the privatization of the halibut fishery in British Columbia, which we discussed in the main text: Their empirical results are consistent with Dnes (1985), which examines the implications of conflict-orientated investment for the dissipation of rents in fishing.

- In case anyone should think that irrational conservation is a thing of the past, Lueck and Michael (2003) have examined the impact of the 1973 Endangered Species Act (ESA). The ESA makes it illegal to kill an endangered species or to damage its habitat. Landowners can ensure that red-cockaded woodpeckers do not inhabit their land by preventing the establishment of their habitat through harvesting timber early. They could then avoid ESA regulations that would limit or prohibit later harvesting of timber. Lueck and Michael show that increases in the proximity of a plot to the woodpeckers increases the probability that timber will be harvested early.

- Demsetz (1967) was the great innovator as far as the property-rights school is concerned. His work explains how many early and modern property-rights structures arose. His paper has an extremely interesting analysis of the development of private rights in land by American tribes, based on the research findings of two anthropologists. Frank Speck found that natives on the Labrador Peninsula had a long-standing tradition of private property rights, whereas those of the American Southwest did not. Eleanor Leacock's study of the Montagne tribe (around Quebec) showed that private property rights evolved as the fur trade developed. In the main text, we concentrate on Demsetz's analysis of Leacock's findings. More work on tribal economies is contained in Anderson (1993). Demsetz (2002) has revisited and broadened his analysis.

- Anderson and McChesney (1994) developed the raid-or-trade model of the choice faced by European settlers between attacking tribes and taking their land, or negotiating with them over it. The model is closely related to those about disputants' decisions over whether to litigate or settle a case (Cooter and Rubinfeld, 1989). Anderson and McChesney's test for the effect of army size, discussed in the text, uses ordinary-least-squares methods to regress the annual number of battles on the size of the United States Army and other variables for the period 1790–1897. In case it may be objected that causality could run the other way, the same conclusion may be obtained from an equation in which army size lagged by one year replaces army size as an independent variable.

- See E.S. Connell (1984, p. 263) for details about Little Bighorn and related matters. During the battle, there were also misunderstandings between separated parts of the Army forces. A trip to the battle site is strongly recommended.

- An earlier paper in a similar tradition to Anderson and McChesney's (1994) work is Libecap (1978), which explains the founding of the state of Nevada in terms of the need for an efficient system for creating and enforcing private property rights as the gold rush developed in the American West. Anderson and Hill (1975), which attributes the nineteenth-century move in the West from the open range to private grazing to the invention of barbed wire, is also of interest. There is more cowboy material in Anderson and Hill (2002).

- A carefully conducted research project at the World Bank (Galal, Jones, Tandon, and Vogelsant, 1992) examined the postprivatization performance of 12 companies (airlines and utilities) in the United Kingdom,

Chile, Malaysia, and Mexico. The World Bank study found net welfare gains in 11 of the cases, with an average magnitude of 26 percent. Welfare gains were measured as the sum of benefits going to taxpayers, employees, the new owners of privatized firms, and consumers. They found no cases where workers were made worse off, dismissing the allegation sometimes made that gains for shareholders in newly privatized firms are simply transfers from workers whose wages and conditions worsen.

- The classic prisoners' dilemma refers to two criminals placed in separate cells by the police. Payoffs looks like this:

		B	
		Confesses	**Does Not**
A	**Confesses**	2,2	0,4
	Does Not	4,0	1,1

(Payoffs A,B)

The criminals cannot communicate. Each is told that if she confesses and helps to obtain the conviction of the other, the police will charge her with a trivial offense carrying no prison sentence. If she does not confess but a more serious charge can be proved, the court will show no mercy and she will go to jail for four years. If they both confess, the police do not need to be so generous, but the court will make an allowance for cooperation and halve the sentence. If neither confesses, the police can only prove a lesser offense carrying a 1-year sentence for each. "Confess" dominates "does not confess" for each player and they end up going to jail for two years each, which is as bad as things could be.

Holm (1995) argues that the original interpretation of the prisoners' dilemma is illogical. The confessions of the prisoners are worthless if a judge or jury would realize, as they surely must, that even an innocent party would confess under the circumstances. This critical insight does not undermine the account given in the text of coordination problems in public goods. In practice, prisoners' dilemmas seem to resolve more frequently in favor of cooperation than might be predicted (Axelrod, 1984).

- On the private provision of public goods, see Benson (1994) and, particularly for toll roads, Klein (1990). The private provision of lighthouses is discussed in detail in Coase (1974) and Van Zandt (1993). Coase (1974) stylishly quotes Gilbert and Sullivan's *Mikado* to suggest that the lighthouse is used by economists to provide "corroborative detail, intended to give artistic verisimilitude to an otherwise bald and unconvincing narrative." The private provision of a public good could be optimal if the supplier could practice perfect price discrimination by excluding consumers unless each paid his or her marginal valuation (Demsetz, 1970).

- The coercive power of the state may not overcome the problem of obtaining a true revelation of preferences for public goods. If we knew each individual's preferences, the state could provide the service and levy taxes to pay for it equal to each person's marginal valuation of the service (Lindahl, 1919). But this information is not easily available, and special schemes, probably quite costly to implement, would be required (Tideman and Tullock, 1976). Also, it is not certain that the implied ("Lindahl") taxes would always provide sufficient revenue to cover the total cost of the service.

- The argument that a close-knit social group may succeed in the voluntary provision of public goods is found in De Jasay (1989). Anderson and Simmons (1993) examine the case of water rights among ranchers in the western United States.

- The theory of club goods is explored by Buchanan (1965), who received a Nobel Prize for work on the interface between economics and politics. It may be that the club good is the best representation of typical consumption.

- First possession and the Homestead Act, along with estray statutes, are well covered in Lueck (1998). The Homestead Act did not recognize aboriginal practices as creating occupation and had the effect of excluding native claims to land (Allen, 1991). Hulme (1993) discusses the *Mabo* case.

- Lueck (1998) also examines riparian water rights and the rule of prior appropriation. Kanazawa (1998) thoroughly examines Californian water law and extends his analysis to groundwater in Kanazawa (2003). Current water law in California permits appropriation in cases where there are no active rights over water. Thus riparians could lose water flow to appropriation. The modern developments in California strengthen the argument that appropriability is needed in arid climates. See also Johnson, Werner, and Gisser (1981) for earlier work.

- Miceli and Sirmans (1995) discuss the rule of adverse possession and other issues connected with land law.

- In *Keppel v. Bailey* (1834) the court was concerned with suppressing novel and hazardous restrictions on land use. From that case onward, Anglo-American courts have been restrictive toward allowing negative limitations on use, outside of allowing easements to preserve such things as light, air, and the physical support of land. *Keppel v. Bailey* is an English case concerning London's Leicester Square, which at that time still contained private gardens.

- A good survey of the law and economics of intellectual property matters is given in Besen and Raskind (1991). Ordover (1991) discusses the first-to-invent patent system used in the United States and Canada in relation to the first-to-file systems used in Japan and throughout the European Union. Patents started with the medieval royal prerogative to grant "letters patent" and typically applied to foreign inventors who were required to train the native population. The privilege was widely abused by monarchs and was brought under control (in England) by the Statute of Monopolies (1623).

- The tension between seeing patents as restricting competition and seeing them as an essential incentive is illustrated by an example adapted from Posner (2002). If it costs $10 million to invent a better food mixer and the marginal cost of production is $50 per machine with anticipated sales of 1 million, a market price of $60 is needed. If other companies can freely use the invention, the price of the food mixer will be driven down to $50 in a competitive market. As a result, there will be little or no incentive to invent. Demsetz (1982) makes a strong efficiency argument in favor of patents.

- One variant of patent blitzing, patent racing, is a bit like treasure hunting and has very clear implications of rent-seeking behavior (Grossman and Schapiro, 1987). The argument used in the text to suggest that there are natural and legal limits on the rent-seeking possibilities of patent racing was put forward by Dam (1994).

- The blanket nature of copyright restrictions was questioned by Breyer (1970). Some law professors must sympathize with the view as I have sometimes encountered their use of this book in photocopied form. You've been warned!

- Peter Stringfellow's (1997) autobiography, *King of Clubs*, is a very humorous account of his 30-plus years spent running nightclubs. The steelworker's son survived many adventures—including a brush with the New York Mafia—to succeed in both the United States and England.

- A modern variant on the common property problem arises when too many regulatory agencies control access to some resource. If each agency tries to extract access fees, the result can be underuse of the resource, a result known as the *anticommons* (Schulz, Parisi, and Depoorter, 2002). The result is often regarded as reflecting excessive propertization but in reality reflects open access, albeit by access authorities.

CONFLICTS OVER PROPERTY RIGHTS

Conflict over property rights, for example when a concrete plant releases dust onto nearby residential property, reflects the presence of externalities, defined earlier as unintended spillovers between separate activities. Many externalities can be dealt with by private action to stop nuisance, using the part of law dealing with the obligations of owners to make only reasonable use of property. The theory of externalities examines the question of how to settle such conflict efficiently. Although nuisance is technically a topic in tort law (the part of the law of obligations dealing with civil wrongs, which we consider more generally later), it is most sensibly examined alongside property-rights issues.

Faced with a case of nuisance, courts may give legal relief and order the defendant (the *tortfeasor*) to pay compensation (damages). Alternatively, they can grant equitable relief and issue an injunction that enjoins (stops) the defendant from generating the nuisance. The traditional approach is for courts to grant an injunction, although they may also order compensation to be paid for existing damages. In much of this chapter, we examine the economic properties of injunctions and legal relief. Courts have recently moved more toward using legal relief where the damage is spread over many victims. Later in the chapter, we look at private devices like servitudes and statutory controls such as zoning, which are further methods of controlling conflict over property rights.

We start by examining the work of Ronald Coase, a Nobel-prizewinning economist who developed the economic theory of externality by focusing on individuals and drawing in details of the law on nuisance. He concluded that the legal maxim asserting that no one may make *unreasonable* use of property reflects a balancing of costs and benefits. The courts tend to resolve conflicts efficiently by permitting activities for which there is a net gain after allowing for externalities.

THE COASE THEOREM, EFFICIENCY, AND DISTRIBUTION

Efficient resolution of conflict requires that individuals take into account the externalities generated by their activities. If an externality is made to affect the costs of its perpetrator, we say that it is internalized. Bargaining between individuals internalizes many externalities when the cost of bargaining is sufficiently low. Bargaining costs are defined as the costs of negotiating and enforcing agreements, and are a form of transaction costs. Transaction costs can often be lowered if the law is used to define property rights, for example, by issuing an injunction against a nuisance, so that someone has the clear entitlement to carry out activities without interference. When bargaining costs are very high, perhaps when many parties are involved, the law may be used to assess and award damages to victims of the nuisance. Coase examined the economics of a range of legal

Sturges v. Bridgman (1879) 11 Ch. 852

Dr. Sturges occupied premises neighboring a candy-making workshop, where noisy equipment had operated for more than 60 years. He claimed that the noise was so bad that he could not listen to patients' chests or carry out routine medical examinations. Sturges requested an injunction to stop the noise and allow his uninterrupted working. The court noted that Sturges had moved into the property after the candy business was well established, but granted the injunction anyway on the grounds that the doctor had a right to enjoy quiet because this was required for the reasonable use of his property as a consulting office. The candy maker, Bridgman, could not claim that the doctor should not have the injunction owing to his having "come to the nuisance."

The court balanced the advantages of having a quiet office for the doctor's work against the value of lost candy making. It concluded that it was "reasonable" for the doctor to prevail. The case shows a judicial willingness to assess the relative advantages of leaving the nuisance unabated or of controlling it, and is often cited in later cases. Many more cases follow *Sturges* in showing the same judicial balancing of costs and benefits, which is incorporated in the legal doctrine of controlling the unreasonable use of property.

responses to nuisance. His point of departure was a classic nuisance case, *Sturges v. Bridgman*, for which details are given in the boxed example.

The Coase Theorem and Transaction Costs

The costs and benefits of using the machinery in *Sturges* might have looked like Figure 3.1, where the noise nuisance is measured as hours (per day, within working hours) on the horizontal axis. The upward-sloping function measures the marginal external cost (*MEC*) of the noise, reflecting an assumption that each extra hour of noise creates a greater cost than the preceding one. This cost is simply lost fee income for the doctor. The downward-sloping function showing marginal net benefit (*MNB*) shows the profits (i.e., revenue minus production cost) to the candy maker from extending the use of the machinery.

Left alone, the candy maker would generate 8 hours of noise. This is where marginal net private benefit falls to zero, maximizing profits (the area under *MNB*). However, the jointly optimal level of noise is 4 hours in Figure 3.1. Up to that level, marginal net benefit exceeds marginal external cost, whereas beyond it the opposite is true. If an hour's noise adds more to the benefit from the noise than to its cost, it is worth bearing the nuisance. One way to look at this is to recognize that the candy maker could compensate the doctor for bearing the external cost up to the fourth unit (just) but not beyond. Note that a classic public-policy recommendation for controlling externality is for the state to impose a charge equal to marginal external cost on the noise polluter (*polluter pays*). This causes *MNB* to fall to *MNSB* (marginal net social—i.e., joint—benefit), giving maximum post-tax profits at 4 hours.

Bargaining can make it irrelevant whether the court had found for or against the doctor in *Sturges*, as long as a right had been defined one way or the other. This result follows easily in the case where bargaining is assumed to be costless (zero transaction costs) and is usually referred to as the *Coase theorem*. The court's granting of an injunction gave Sturges the entitlement to stop the noise. The court could have assigned the

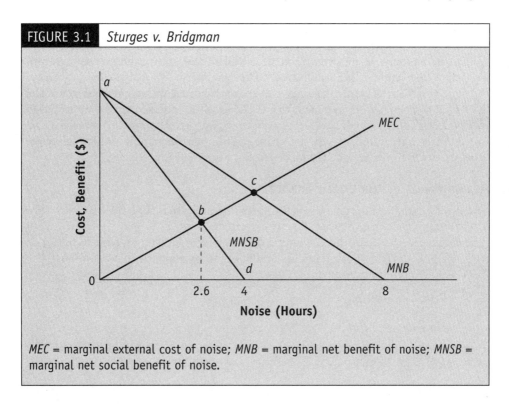

FIGURE 3.1 *Sturges v. Bridgman*

MEC = marginal external cost of noise; *MNB* = marginal net benefit of noise; *MNSB* = marginal net social benefit of noise.

entitlement to continue with the noisy work to Bridgman by not issuing the injunction. The Coase theorem states that, on the assumption of costless bargaining, the court's assignment of the entitlement is irrelevant for determining the equilibrium (and optimal) amount of the nuisance. The parties can bargain around the injunction or the lack of one. The important step is to give the entitlement to one of the parties so that bargaining can commence. Assigning the entitlement does of course create an additional dimension to an existing property right and will have distributional consequences, effectively making one of the parties richer.

In Figure 3.1, if Sturges has the injunction, he would initially like to stop all noise (moving below point *a* in Figure 3.1). However, the marginal profits (*MNB*) for Bridgman from making candy exceed the marginal external costs (*MEC*) to Sturges until they reach 4 hours of the nuisance (below the intersection of *MEC* and *MNB* at point *c*). Therefore, by paying an amount just greater than the losses, the candy maker can compensate the doctor for putting up with 4 hours of noise per day. Both parties are then better off than if there were no noise (or compared with any other period of noise). Bargaining to "condemn the injunction" automatically leads to the jointly optimal level of 4 hours of noise.

Now suppose that no injunction is granted. Bridgman would initially create 8 hours of noise, which is where marginal profits fall to zero. However, the losses to Sturges exceed the gains to Bridgman over 4 to 8 hours of the nuisance (*MEC* > *MNB*), which means that Sturges would find it advantageous to bribe the confectioner to reduce the level to 4 hours per day. Sturges would offer just more than Bridgman's lost profit on each unit of noise (*MNB*). Both parties would be better off by agreeing to the reduction.

Notice that if is cheaper to insulate rather than bear the noise or bribe the candy maker to stop, the doctor will insulate if he lacks the injunction. Similarly, if the doctor has the entitlement and it is cheaper to insulate than induce him to condemn the injunction, the candy maker will insulate. The example shows that the level of noise is the same whether the candy maker or the doctor has the entitlement. Our example of the Coase theorem shows that allocative efficiency is not affected by the initial assignment of entitlement, which has only distributional impact. All mutually beneficial trade over an externality is undertaken; the final equilibrium is the same whether the polluter is free to pollute or is enjoined; and value of production is maximized.

Assumptions of the Coase Theorem

There are a number of criticisms of the Coase theorem that students may encounter. These tend to focus on the case of zero bargaining costs. They may therefore be misplaced criticisms, as Coase did not intend the case of low bargaining costs to be a guide to public policy. The following is a list of significant assumptions that are necessary for the Coase theorem to hold.

1. Perfect knowledge

2. No strategic behavior

3. The courts operate without cost

4. No wealth effects

5. No economic rent on marginal activities

Assumption 3 is a proper statement of the requirement for costless bargaining in the context of a court system and warrants little discussion. Requirements 1 and 2 ensure in a more general way that bargaining costs are zero. It is often alleged that assumption 4 is necessary to ensure that assigning entitlement cannot affect the allocation of resources, even if bargaining costs are zero. Assumption 5 refers to special conditions that might result in small changes in entitlements, causing businesses to fail. We now examine the assumptions in more detail.

Imperfect Information and Strategic Behavior. Imperfect information, which usually implies information asymmetry, leads to great difficulties in bargaining even when parties are not attempting to mislead each other. If some individuals have information when others do not, mutually beneficial trades will not occur. As a simple example, if a seller values a house less than the would-be buyer but erroneously believes there are higher-valuing potential buyers, the house will not be sold and gains from trade will not be realized. Similarly, if the victim of a nuisance is unsure of the cost of its impact, it may be hard to reach agreement.

Strictly speaking, information asymmetry cannot affect the Coase theorem because it could not arise in a world of zero transaction costs. The cost of gathering information about a proposed trade is a part of the costs of transacting. Information asymmetry suggests there is information a trader would like to have but which is too costly to gather.

Moving on to consider the problems caused by strategic behavior, we continue to assume the mechanics of bargaining to be costless. There is a huge range within which bargaining can take place. Assuming Sturges has the injunction and again referring to

Figure 3.1, the candy maker would pay up to an amount equal to area *oacd* (the profit) and the doctor would require at least area *ocd* (the cost to him) to move to 4 hours of noise. Even with perfect information so that the candy maker knows the scale of external costs, by holding out, the doctor can increase his share of the surplus from reaching agreement. He has to be convincing about his stubbornness to extract as much money as possible, which implies he would devote resources to developing threats.

Threat strategies are a form of rent seeking that disturbs the results of the Coase theorem. With zero transaction costs, making threats would be costless, but so would a counter strategy, and a process of threat followed by counterthreat could go on endlessly and destabilize bargaining. It is also possible that information asymmetries give an incentive for the devotion of resources to influencing the beliefs of the other party, although this point moves us away from a world of zero transaction costs.

A further type of strategic problem arises when a party uses the threat of irrationally moving to a position that is bad for both parties in order to extract most of the gains from bargaining. If the opponent does not give in, the individual may be forced to carry out the threat if at all interested in preserving a reputation as a tough bargainer for subsequent "games." This implies that mutually beneficial trade over an externality may not always occur, even when promises are enforceable. However, the problem may be solved naturally if the bargaining game is repeated. If the number of repetitions is known with certainty, there exists an endgame in which the threat is not credible. Therefore, the threat is not credible in the immediately preceding game, or the one before that, and so on, to affect all bargaining games in which the threat might be used. Also, threats may be deterred if each party is unsure whether the other might irrationally adopt a strategy of tit-for-tat. The fear of retaliation may encourage cooperative behavior.

The problems of strategic interaction would be a powerful criticism of Coase's analysis if the argument really were that costless bargaining could be relied upon to internalize externalities. However, this is not the correct interpretation because Coase was really interested in cases where bargaining costs were significant. Concentrating on the case of costless bargaining takes an expository device far too literally. More recent work outside of the case of costless bargaining focuses on the design of legal rules to minimize bargaining costs, including those connected with strategic interaction.

Taxes on Pollution. In the spirit of comparative institutionalism, we should look at an alternative to bargaining (or court-governed) solutions to externality. An often-quoted alternative is for a government agency to impose a tax on nuisance equal to its marginal external cost (*MEC*) in Figure 3.1. A tax equal to *MEC* shifts *MNB* downwards to *MNSB* for the candy maker, who will then wish to create just 4 hours of noise at point *d*. The idea here is to internalize the externality by using the tax impact on the candy maker. Taxes aimed at pollution are sometimes called *Pigouvian taxes* after Arthur Pigou, whose work suggested them. The Pigouvian tax is one of several possible ways of dealing with pollution problems. Such a tax might be useful if a government agency were well informed and could operate at a sufficiently low cost so as not to erode the benefits of controlling the pollution.

However, taxing the externality leads to suboptimally low pollution levels whenever bargaining is possible. The tax ignores the strategic ramifications of changing a party's costs. In Figure 3.1, if a tax equal to *MEC* really shifts *MNB* to *MNSB* as far as the candy maker is concerned, and bargaining *is* possible, the parties will move to approximately 2.6 hours of noise (below point *b*). The moral here is that it could be reasonable to use a tax when bargaining cannot arise, but it is dangerous to do so when bargaining is possible. In reality, of course, there is no such thing as a free lunch. The costs of government intervention may be too high to justify use of pollution taxes quite apart from problems of strategic interaction.

Wealth Effects. The assumption that there are no wealth effects has a simplifying effect for Coase's analysis. Beneficiaries of changes in entitlements will feel better off after the change, which has much the same impact as an increase in income or wealth for them and may change the marginal value they place on particular items. If this happens, the award of an entitlement by the court is unlikely to be neutral with respect to allocation. For example, giving the entitlement to the victim of a noise nuisance might make him feel better off and increase his demand for noise reduction.

In Figure 3.2, the noise problem characterizing *Sturges v. Bridgman* is shown somewhat differently. On the horizontal axis, we measure noise reduction as decibel loss. For simplicity, we assume that it is always cheaper for the candy maker to pay for the doctor's cost of insulation than to cut back the noisy activity. It is also necessary to assume that there is some range of noise reduction, falling short of total silence, for which the benefits to the doctor outweigh the cost of insulating. The relevant comparison is then between the benefits to the doctor and the costs of insulation.

The curves labeled I_0, I_1, and I_2 are examples of indifference curves for the doctor. Indifference curves allow us to study changes in the doctor's level of welfare without making an unrealistic assumption that we can measure utility directly. For example, curve I_0 shows combinations of levels of noise reduction and wealth measured in money that the doctor regards as equivalent, and I_1 shows combinations giving a higher level of utility. Indifference curves merely rank different levels of utility. The

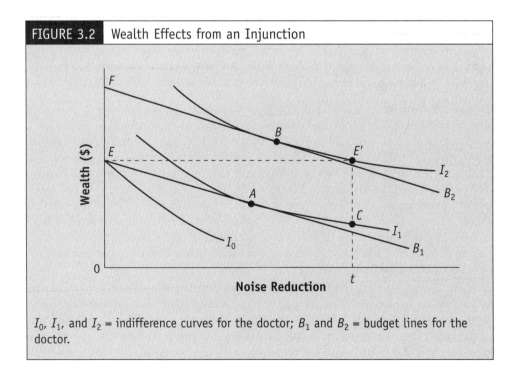

FIGURE 3.2 Wealth Effects from an Injunction

I_0, I_1, and I_2 = indifference curves for the doctor; B_1 and B_2 = budget lines for the doctor.

convex shape of the curves (they bend towards the origin) indicates a diminishing marginal rate of substitution between wealth and noise reduction: The quieter it gets, the less money the doctor will give up for further unit reductions in the noise level. A line is drawn vertically from point t, reflecting total silence. Similarly, the origin shows the maximum amount of noise.

The line from point E on the vertical axis to B_1, in Figure 3.2, is the doctor's budget line. Point E shows his situation when he has no injunction so that the candy maker is entitled to make the noise. By moving along budget line B_1, the doctor could buy insulation, with the slope of the line reflecting the assumed constant unit cost of noise reduction. The budget line is therefore also an implied price line. Remember, it is always cheaper to buy insulation than to bribe the candy operation to reduce the noise. Point E is on the lowest indifference curve shown, I_0, but by moving along the budget line B_1 the doctor can just reach the higher curve I_1 at the point of tangency, A.

Now suppose that the entitlement changes because the doctor obtains an injunction. Point E moves to E' directly above t, as the doctor can now insist on total quiet. However, we know from our earlier analysis that the candy maker will want to induce the doctor to tolerate some noise. As a simple (but not unique) solution to the bargaining problem between them, assume that the candy maker agrees to pay the doctor a sum of money sufficient to maintain the doctor's welfare at I_2 after the noisy activity is resumed. The doctor's budget line therefore moves to position B_2, showing the compensation payment as distance EF. The doctor moves from point F to a new optimum at B by purchasing insulation.

The indifference curves in Figure 3.2 are not vertically parallel, and their slopes differ at points drawn vertically above one another, reflecting the doctor's changing marginal valuation of noise reduction as his entitlement (wealth) increases. This means that point B is to the northeast of point A in Figure 3.2: There is a wealth effect, which implies that the court's assignment of entitlement does affect the level of noise reduction even with zero bargaining costs. This result contrasts with the one in Figure 3.1, where the assignment of rights has a neutral effect on allocation.

However, the non-neutrality result in Figure 3.2 emerges precisely because we allow the doctor's taste for noise reduction to change as he becomes richer. We treat noise reduction as a normal good for which the demand increases as income or wealth increases. This need not be the case if the doctor's demand for noise reduction were determined entirely by the financial impact that noise has upon his practice. He would then buy the same amount of noise reduction whatever the level of wealth. In that case, the indifference curves would be parallel, B would be vertically above A, and the assignment of rights would have a neutral effect upon allocation.

Changes in legal entitlements are likely to have small impacts on peoples' wealth levels, relative to their entire lifetime earnings. Therefore, although the changes to which they could lead remain a theoretical concern, they are unlikely to be a practical worry. Coase was probably correct to ignore wealth effects.

Economic Rent and Marginal Activities. There is a link between the Coase theorem and levels of economic rent, which refers to the difference between the earnings of a factor of production in its current use and its next best use. In Figure 3.1, the profit the candy maker earns on every hour up to the eighth hour of noise is economic rent, assuming cost functions embody a normal profit that can be earned elsewhere in the economy. Normal profit is treated as an opportunity cost, or the lost benefit from a

Bargaining over Externalities

Professors Hoffman and Spitzer presented a schedule of payoffs to subjects in an experiment aimed at testing their ability to bargain over an externality. They allowed one or more of the subjects to act as controller (analogous to having the entitlement) in distributing the payoffs among the others. The payoffs were chosen so that there were gains from bargaining over an externality. Some experimental conditions were varied to produce repeated games to see if the long-term relationship between players influenced results. In 90 percent of the trials, the gains from bargaining were in fact realized. Deviations from optimality occurred, in some early trials only, when there were three parties and joint controllers, and parties knew only their own payoffs. Hoffman and Spitzer conclude that their results are broadly consistent with Coase's proposition that agents will bargain to reach an optimum under full information and when one party has the entitlement.

A later study by Hoffman and Spitzer supports robustness in their results for groups of up to 19 individuals. Deviations from optimality turned out to be less likely in both studies if an individual earned property rights in some way, as though subjects do not take outcomes seriously if they are obtained by chance.

forgone opportunity, in standard economic analysis. The marginal external cost suffered by the doctor in Figure 3.1 can similarly be seen as a loss of economic rent caused by the noise. One way to look at the bargaining result reached in Figure 3.1 is to see it as maximizing the sum of economic rent across the doctor's and candy maker's activities. In *Sturges*, bargaining is used to adjust the margin of the competing activities.

Sometimes the activities themselves may be marginal. In another of Coase's examples, cattle damage the crops of a neighboring farmer. If there is no economic rent on either of the conflicting activities, assignment of the entitlement will have allocative consequences. Suppose that the rancher just covers costs, and the farmer would just cover costs if it were not for the losses resulting from the rancher's damage to crops. If the rancher is not liable for the damage, the farmer goes out of business. If the rancher is liable, then he goes out of business. Assignment of the entitlement would appear to affect the level of the nuisance. To be fair, this would seem to be something of a special case illustrating a need to be careful in distinguishing marginal activities from marginal adjustments in activities.

Experimental Tests of the Coase Theorem

Several experiments have directly tested whether bargaining is successful in solving externality problems. The results suggest the Coase theorem is robust in its predictions. Coase predicted that, in a world of insignificant transaction costs, the parties bargain until they agree on a jointly optimal level for some externality. Experiments generally use student subjects in an environment created to have very low transaction costs. The subjects may sometimes have private information, as shown in the boxed example.

Coasian bargaining solutions to externality problems emerge in developed experimental settings. Nonetheless, care must be taken not to overstate the conclusions that can be drawn from experiments that support the predictions of the Coase theorem in situations characterized by relatively low bargaining costs. Much more work is needed aimed at testing the suitability of bargaining solutions in environments containing significant negotiating costs. Where such studies have been constructed, they tend to support the prediction that bargaining costs are an impediment to internalizing an externality. In particular, information asymmetries create bargaining costs and make it much harder for individuals to negotiate solutions to externality problems.

The Significance of Transaction Costs

Coase did not argue that costless bargaining would correct all externalities and render government intervention unnecessary, which is a common misunderstanding of his work. The conclusions of most of his articles are somewhat anti-interventionist, but are also firmly grounded in a world of positive transaction costs. If this were not so, his 1937 work on the nature of the firm, which regards firms as internalizing some transactions to save costs attached to using markets, would have no subject. The assumption of zero bargaining costs in part of *The Problem of Social Cost* is purely an expository device and should not be taken too literally.

In 1988 Coase wrote the following notes:

> *The world of zero transaction costs has often been described as a Coasian world. Nothing could be further from the truth. It is the world . . . I was hoping to persuade economists to leave. . . . The same approach, which with zero transaction costs demonstrates that the allocation of resources remains the same whatever the legal position, also shows that, with positive transaction costs, the law plays a crucial role in determining how resources are used.*

In this sense, the experimental work discussed earlier misses the point, as do criticisms of the assumptions of the Coase theorem. Unfortunately, the literature on the Coase theorem has developed a life of its own, which is why it was necessary to examine it carefully. Coase's emphasis on the case of positive transaction costs should be more widely respected.

Government intervention in externality problems is likely to be problematic because it relies too heavily on information that governments would be unlikely to have. As discussed, Pigou's solution for pollution imposes a tax on the creator of the nuisance. Coase pointed out that this ignores alternative solutions; for example, it might be cheapest for the victim of nuisance to relocate, although a tax-imposing government agency would be most unlikely to realize this. Coase approved of the way common-law judges approach nuisance cases like *Sturges v. Bridgman* and noted their ability to compare alternative possible solutions.

Courts typically recognize the reciprocal nature of externalities. The nuisance is, in a sense, as much caused by the victim being there as by its perpetrator. They are less interested in questions of causality but concentrate on deciding which party should be induced to modify behavior to solve the problem. In *Sturges*, the doctor had come to the nuisance, but this did not stop the court from finding for him, which is correct from an economic point of view because what matters is finding the course of action that maximizes the value of joint production.

In the presence of positive transaction costs, there is no theoretical solution to the problem of externality. It may, for example, still be worthwhile for the affected parties to bargain their way to a solution, and it may even remain true that the assignment of rights does not influence the final level of the nuisance. If bargaining is prohibitively costly, the courts may be able to find the solution that would have resulted from bargaining, and at a lower cost. In some cases, the court may be able to do nothing more than decide who will benefit the most from the entitlement, knowing that bargaining cannot occur. Sometimes the optimal solution might well be for government to tax the externality—if it somehow had lower costs than the courts or the affected parties in finding the solution. Which is the best approach is a matter of empirical assessment in any particular case. Sometimes it might even be best to do nothing, if all options are very costly relative to the benefits of internalizing the externality, as appears to be the case with the high-seas fisheries discussed in the previous chapter: The grass is not always greener. What is needed is a proper comparison of all feasible alternatives, fully taking into account the cost of each. In particular, Coase makes the point that the real characteristics and possible failures of government need to be taken into account if investigating the possibility of basing policy on government intervention.

Table 3.1 illustrates one possible solution of an externality problem in a world of significant transaction costs. The table gives details of *Sturges* in the form used in Figure 3.1, where a constant noise level could be varied over the working day. Marginal net benefit again refers to the profits of the candy maker. Social benefit is found by subtracting external cost from profits. We assume that bargaining, or imposing a pollution tax, is prohibitively expensive. Also, we further assume that it is too costly for the court to enforce the optimal solution of 4 hours of noise. The court is left with the option of assigning the entitlement strictly to one or other party. Its assignment will have an allocative effect, because bargaining is not possible, and should be guided by the total net benefit from each possible choice.

Faced with a stark choice over rights in Table 3.1, it is better to assign the entitlement to the victim and award the injunction. The first-best solution is at 4 hours of noise, where the marginal net social benefits sum to 24. However, the court believes that it cannot enforce this solution, which would involve the operation of both activities. The second-best solution is to give the injunction and have no noise, which gives a total social net benefit of zero. The alternative of allowing the confectioner to create the 8 hours of noise that would maximize his profits gives a negative sum of –16 for the marginal net social benefit column, which is clearly worse. Obviously, differ-

TABLE 3.1	The Costs and Benefits from Noise ($000)		
NOISE (HOURS)	**MARGINAL NET BENEFIT**	**MARGINAL EXTERNAL COST**	**MARGINAL NET SOCIAL BENEFIT**
–	–	–	–
1	14	–2	12
2	12	–4	8
3	10	–6	4
4	8	–8	–
5	6	–10	–4
6	4	–12	–8
7	2	–14	–12
8	–	–16	–16

ent figures could give a different result, and there is no general rule. However, the approach in which discrete comparisons are made between the total net benefits of assigning the entitlement one way or the other is, generally, very much the kind of thing a court may do.

ALTERNATIVE LEGAL RULES AND THE INCENTIVE TO BARGAIN

The choice for courts is not simply between issuing an injunction and refusing it. They may award compensation for damages to victims of nuisance as an alternative to issuing an injunction. Indeed, in more complex formulations they may issue an injunction against future nuisance and order compensation for existing damage, or may even require a payment by the victim as part of the settlement. The precise nature of the entitlement that is assigned alters the incentive for bargaining, as the following example demonstrates.

Suppose that a ready-mix concrete plant (the tortfeasor) discharges dust onto an auto-sales business, which creates additional costs of $40,000 in preparing vehicles for sale. The concrete plant could fit a filter costing $100,000, or the auto business could fit a cover costing $20,000. Either option would cure the problem, for which details are given in Table 3.2. If the plant fits the filter, the auto business makes $60,000 profit. If the concrete business is left free to pollute, it makes $200,000 profit. The optimal solution is for the concrete plant to be free to pollute and for the auto business to fit a cover, as this gives a joint profit of $240,000 ($200,000 to the concrete plant and $40,000 to the cars). The court might grant an injunction to the auto business, or it might order damages to be paid by the concrete plant.

Assume that transaction costs are sufficiently low to permit bargaining, and let the gains from bargaining be equally divided. Table 3.3 shows the impact of bargaining

TABLE 3.2	Alternative Remedies for Concrete Pollution ($000s)					
ACTION	**FILTER (PLANT)**	**COVER (CARS)**	**POLLUTION (COST)**	**PROFIT (CARS)**	**PROFIT (PLANT)**	**PROFIT (TOTAL)**
Plant Filters	100	0	0	60	100	160
Cover Cars	0	20	0	40	200	240
No Action	0	0	40	20	200	220

TABLE 3.3	Payoffs to Bargaining ($000s)		
RULE	**INITIAL PAYOFF**	**GAIN**	**NEW PAYOFF**
Compensation	160, 60	20	170, 70
Injunction	100, 60	80	140, 100

on the profits of each party under the compensation rule and the award of an injunction. Using the compensation rule, but without bargaining, the plant retains $160,000 profit after paying $40,000 damages to maintain the car lot's profits at $60,000. Bargaining enables the parties to move to the optimum and gives a gain of $20,000 (the difference between $40,000 damage and the $20,000 cost of a cover, shared equally). Granting an injunction, in the absence of bargaining, would cause the concrete business to spend $100,000 on a filter. Bargaining can save $80,000 (the difference between the filter and the cover).

Table 3.3 shows that the assignment of entitlement affects the gains from bargaining. The two rules differ in their distance from the optimum. A corollary is that the assignment influences the incentive of each party to bargain. The concrete plant has a much bigger incentive to bargain under the injunction. This observation suggests that bargaining is more likely to occur when a legal assignment is seriously inefficient, given modest transaction costs.

LEAST-COST AVOIDANCE (PROPERTY AND LIABILITY RULES)

The modern view of nuisance suggests choosing between remedies on the basis of the adjustment costs affecting the parties. The costs of adjustment are another form of transaction cost. We can distinguish two principal routes that courts can take in assigning entitlements. When a court issues an injunction (or declines to do so, favoring the property rights of the tortfeasor) it follows a property rule. When it assesses and awards compensation for damages, it adopts a liability rule. When there are obstacles to bargaining, the liability rule may provide the safest approach. However, when bargaining can occur, it is safe to adhere to a property rule and issue an injunction.

Obstacles to bargaining normally arise when damages are dispersed widely in a population. It may then be very costly to get the victims together to pursue an injunction or damages, or it may just be costly to assess all the damages. This type of case is referred to in the economics of law literature (see the notes at the end of the chapter) as a public nuisance. With such dispersed nuisance, it is costly for victims to bargain with the tortfeasor. There is likely to be a free-rider problem, as the individual benefits from negotiation are probably highest if a victim sits back and lets others solve the problem. If all victims feel this way then, analogous to the prisoners' dilemma discussed in Chapter 2 in the case of public goods, the worst outcome occurs as no action is taken. In this case, the cost of keeping the victims' team together would be prohibitively high. Dispersion of damages may also simply make it difficult to gather the necessary information for bargaining. In the case of dispersed nuisance, it is more likely to be worthwhile incurring court costs to assess the level of damages.

Obstacles to bargaining are few in disputes involving a small number of people who can easily communicate. This is the case of the private nuisance. In fact, *Sturges v. Bridgman* was a classic case of private nuisance. There may even just be two people involved, the victim and the generator of the nuisance, and we would not expect them to incur high costs in negotiating with each other. An injunction is the appropriate judicial response to private nuisance, at least on efficiency grounds. By issuing the injunction, the court defines property rights and provides a basis for bargaining to discover the optimal level of the nuisance, or even to induce another party to take low-cost avoidance measures. This observation raises questions about the efficiency of the traditional judicial response to nuisance, which has been to grant an injunction regardless of the nature of the nuisance.

Another way to consider the distinction between injunctions and awards of damages is to examine ways of inducing the least-cost avoider (abater) of the nuisance to take action, which may be illustrated by adapting our earlier example of a polluting concrete plant. Suppose the concrete plant emits so much dust that it impairs the air-conditioning systems of many local factories. Each of 200 factories suffers a $700 loss but can be protected by putting filters on their air intakes at a cost of $400 per factory. The plant makes profits of $200,000 and can stop the damage by fitting a powerful exhaust filter costing $150,000. The relevant options are shown in Table 3.4.

Option 2 is the most desirable, but with high transaction costs, bargaining cannot occur. The court should not issue an injunction: With high costs of bargaining, the plant would fit exhaust filters and there would be a move to option 3 rather than option 2. Without an injunction, the victims protect themselves by fitting intake filters and move to option 2, which is the best result because they have the lowest cost of avoiding the nuisance. Notice that the court is able to use a property rule here, even though the damage is somewhat dispersed, because full information is available. This special case enables us to identify easily the principle for the property rule. We should award the entitlement to the highest-cost avoider so that the lowest-cost one does the avoiding.

Using the liability rule and awarding compensatory damages could work regardless of who is the least-cost avoider and even without the court's knowing who has the lowest costs. We could give each of the 200 factories $700 damages. The concrete plant would still make $60,000 profit and would stay in business (and would not wish to fit the exhaust filter, which is more costly than paying damages). The victims would then protect themselves by fitting intake filters at a cost of $400 each. There would be a distributional consequence: Profits would accrue as $60,000 to the concrete plant and $60,000 to the victims of the nuisance ($140,000 compensation minus $80,000 spent on filters).

Notice that if the cost of the exhaust filter fell to $60,000, the concrete plant would become the least-cost avoider (beating the $80,000 total cost for intake filters for the factories). The liability rule will still work well because the owners of the plant will prefer to pay $60,000 abatement cost rather than incur a $140,000 liability for damages. Certainly, for a wide range of problems characterized by dispersed damage, the ability of the liability rule to encourage least-cost avoidance suggests it is a safe option compared with using a property rule. It can even harness the private information of the least-cost avoider.

Care must be taken however because it is possible to find cases of dispersed damage where the liability rule will not work well. If, as before, the concrete plant is liable to pay $140,000 damages and the fitting of intake filters to the factories still costs only

TABLE 3.4	Least-Cost Avoidance ($000s)		
	CONCRETE PLANT PROFITS	**FACTORIES' LOST PROFITS**	**NET EFFECT**
1. Uncontrolled Pollution	200	−140	60
2. Intake Filters	200	−80	120
3. Exhaust Filter	50	0	50

$80,000 but the exhaust filter now costs the concrete plant $130,000, there is a problem. The factories have the lowest cost of avoidance but the plant will fit the exhaust filter, costing $130,000, rather than pay the higher damages. Remember we are assuming that bargaining is too costly. If it were possible to bargain, the concrete plant would be better off paying for the factories to fit the filters. A court could impose an effective liability rule by qualifying the strict liability approach toward nuisance and making the plant liable for the cost of fitting the intake filters to the *factories*, which implies a degree of knowledge of the ordering of costs for the parties that may sometimes be present. Airport and road developments are often made to pay for screening and double-glazing for nearby residents.

A variant on the liability rule is to award an injunction to the victim of nuisance but require the victim to compensate the tortfeasor for the costs of closing down (at a court-determined price so as to reduce transaction costs). This approach effectively permits factories to buy out the concrete plant's entitlement to pollute if they value it at more than $200,000. The efficient outcome would then follow: In Table 3.4, the victims would not seek the injunction, knowing they must buy out the concrete plant, but would instead purchase intake filters because they are cheaper.

DOES CASE LAW REFLECT ECONOMIC CONSIDERATIONS?

Until the 1970s, courts in the United States tended take much the same approach as the court in Sturges, emphasizing a property rule and the use of injunctions. In *Bove v. Donna Hanna Coke Corp.* (1932), a New York case, the court decided that no cost-effective steps could be taken to control the noise and dirt coming from a factory in an industrial part of Buffalo. Its continued existence was of net benefit relative to all other uses for the land in the area. *Bove* is essentially a case decided on similar grounds to *Sturges*, even though the injunction was withheld. The refusal was on the same basis of comparison, although this time the court decided the balance of advantage came out in favor of the activity generating the nuisance. This traditional approach still dominates in other common-law jurisdictions like England and Australia.

More recent cases show that U.S. law has moved away from a property rule and toward the use of compensatory damages (a liability rule). The move is consistent with the economic analysis of the previous section in relation to the more dispersed nuisances produced by modern industry. Perhaps, too, the courts have become more experienced in valuing nuisance so it is less costly for them to carry out a judicial cost-benefit analysis. *Boomer v. Atlantic Cement Co.* is credited with moving the courts in the direction of using compensatory damages. We describe its details in the boxed example.

In the years following *Boomer*, a tendency may be discerned to award damages for a "permanent" nuisance for which the tortfeasor is judged unable to take cost-effective avoidance steps and where it would be unreasonable, relative to the nuisance, to close down the offending activity. The payment of damages should cause the victims to adopt any cost-effective avoidance available to *them*. An injunction tends to be awarded against temporary nuisance, where the tortfeasor is thought to be able to adopt a cost-effective avoidance strategy and will do so to be back in business. The distinction broadly recognizes the conditions in which a liability rule or property rule might be expected to work, as discussed earlier.

A case from Arizona, *Spur Industries v. Del Webb* (1972) shows that the courts have been prepared to take the reciprocal nature of externality very seriously. Spur raised

To enjoin - tell them to stop (handwritten)

Boomer v. Atlantic Cement Co. (1970)

Adjacent landowners brought an action against a large cement plant and associated quarry in the Hudson River valley, asking for an injunction and damages. They complained of smoke, dust, noise, and vibration. The court weighed the loss of the plaintiffs against the cost of removing the nuisance. It was not feasible to move the existing plant, which employed 400 people. Removing the plant would cause the defendant to lose the benefits from a $45 million investment, and the locality to lose substantial tax receipts. The damage to landowners was small in comparison, and the court cited this reason in denying the award of a traditional absolute injunction. Instead, the court granted an injunction "conditioned upon the defendant paying the plaintiffs such permanent damages as may be fixed by the court" to compensate fully the neighboring landowners for tolerating the nuisance. The case went to appeal and one judge dissented, pointing out that paying permanent damages removed all incentive to reduce the harm, but the court thought there was no prospect of alleviation anyway. Actually, a long-run incentive remained for the adjacent landowners to take steps such as installing double-glazing to minimize the nuisance.

The court recognized it was setting a precedent, as the rule in New York state had been to enjoin nuisance, notwithstanding any marked disparity in the economic consequences of the injunction and the nuisance. The change was broadly consistent with the literature on the economics of law; bargaining costs in *Boomer* probably were high given the dispersed nature of the damage. However, it is a little odd that the court did not award temporary damages, which would have encouraged Boomer to adopt a cleaner technology to avoid future damage assessments. The court may have wished to avoid the cost of repetitive legal action. Also, the precedent in *Boomer* does encourage other cement companies to avoid pollution, knowing they will be liable for permanent damages.

cattle in Maricopa County, west of Pheonix, Arizona, dating back to 1956. By 1967, Spur's stock had grown to 25,000 cattle, which were producing approximately one million pounds wet weight of manure daily. Del Webb was a real-estate business that built Sun City, a residential development, in 1960 several miles north of Spur. By 1967, Sun City had expanded to within 500 yards of Spur. Del Webb complained that 1,300 plots were not salable because of the noxious smell from the cattle operation, and obtained an injunction at a lower court.

The higher court concluded that Spur created a nuisance to which Del Webb had come. At times, some courts have recognized the defense of "coming to the nuisance," although this is by no means a general recognition. The court nonetheless gave Del Webb an injunction on the grounds that many people had been encouraged to purchase houses in Sun City—which implied a high level of damage—but ingeniously made it conditional on Del Webb paying Spur the "reasonable" costs of shutting down or moving. If Del Webb had a lower-cost method of avoiding the nuisance (perhaps moving its construction sites or building environmental buffer zones), economics would predict that Del Webb would use them after the ruling.

From an economic point of view, and concentrating on the value of the location in different uses, the defense that Del Webb came to the nuisance does not make sense. If Del Webb valued the local amenity level more highly than Spur, then—without an injunction—it would compensate Spur to move. With an injunction, Spur would fail to compensate Del Webb to tolerate the nuisance. The allocative outcome is the same, although the distributional consequences are different. One problem could be that

Del Webb would be better off by coming to the nuisance, buying land cheaply, and then obtaining an injunction to raise land values. By ignoring the defense of coming to the nuisance, the court risked being an agent of Del Webb's rent-seeking strategy, incurring court costs when otherwise there would be low-cost bargaining. In the long run, following the rule in *Spur Industries* and imposing the tortfeasor's removal costs on the victim removes the incentive for rent seeking through the courts.

In summary, from two principal approaches, it is possible to identify four possible detailed approaches to nuisance. The first two of these are property solutions, and the remaining two are liability solutions. First, an injunction may be granted, which is a possible solution in small-numbers cases where bargaining costs are low, or where courts have a full picture of the costs and benefits affecting more numerous parties. Second, the injunction may be denied, reinforcing the status quo, which can also work well with small numbers or a well-informed court. Third, damages may be awarded, which can work well when there is a clear least-cost avoider and no strategy allowing the tortfeasor to avoid liability at relatively high cost. Finally, an injunction may be granted subject to its holder paying compensation to the enjoined activity as in *Spur*.

A recent development that could undermine the ability of courts to follow *Boomer* or *Spur* is the emergence of "right-to-farm" laws in several states. In Georgia, for example, agricultural activities that have continued for a year or more are protected by a section of the Georgia Code from becoming nuisances even if there are changes in surrounding land use. Such right-to-farm laws are highly controversial exceptions to the general movement toward judicial cost-benefit analysis. They reinforce the status quo entitlement but need not be inefficient providing bargaining can occur. The effect could be distributional, forcing new businesses to pay farmers to stop using problematic techniques. However, the laws could be inefficient if bargaining costs are high.

There are obstacles to the spread of right-to-farm laws. In 1998 in *Borman v. Board of Supervisors*, the Iowa Supreme Court held a right-to-farm statute to be an unconstitutional taking of land. *Taking* refers to the government's confiscating land without compensation, contrary to the Fifth Amendment of the Constitution. A law that prevents a higher-valued use of land to prevail could be said to amount to a taking because the law removes value from a property right. In *Borman*, the Constitution was pressed into service to hold onto the economic logic of comparing the benefits and costs of conflicting economic activities.

In other common-law jurisdictions, the courts behave more conservatively and tend to enjoin nuisance rather than apply liability rules. The courts in England behave more traditionally toward nuisance than do U.S. courts. Even so, some change may be occurring. In *Miller v. Jackson* (1977), the plaintiffs sought an injunction against a cricket club when balls kept damaging their neighboring property. Lord Denning (an innovative English judge) did not award one, arguing that in the days of *Sturges* the rights of property owners were more important, but that in modern times there should be an attempt to balance conflicting interests. Anyway, the club was offering to fit unbreakable glass to residents' windows. Although subsequent English cases may have returned to general use of a property rule, *Miller v. Jackson* reinforces American developments in showing that modern conditions reveal a need for judicial cost-benefit analysis. We note in passing that cricket is now a growing sport in America.

Finally, an Australian case shows that the legal definition of nuisance, in terms of interference with the reasonable enjoyment of land, tends to be narrower than the economist's idea of an externality, which refers to any nonpriced spillover. In *Victoria*

Park Racing Ground Co. Ltd. v. Taylor (1937), the defendant erected a viewing tower on property overlooking the racing ground, from which he relayed a racing commentary service for radio. The judge refused to grant an injunction on the basis that, in Australia, the natural rights of an occupier do not include freedom from the view of neighboring occupiers. Note that Victoria Park was free to bribe Taylor to stop his activity, so the judgment had a distributional rather than efficiency impact. The freedom to view enjoyed by one's neighbors is an example of the law defining "reasonable enjoyment" of land, which allows the court to follow simple rules and avoid incurring very high costs in reaching decisions.

Courts look at nuisance in terms of what is reasonable behavior and, in turn, are guided in their judgment by the benefits and costs of conflicting activities. The location of the activity makes a great difference. In *Bove v. Donna Hanna Coke Corp.*, the court was very clear in its view that what would constitute a nuisance in some locations would not necessarily be so elsewhere. Local conditions should also be expected to change over time. This view of nuisance implies that a nuisance is to be valued following the expectations and tastes of a "reasonable" person, who might or might not expect to find it in a particular situation. What is considered reasonable is to some degree governed by social convention, which reveals that the idea of externality in economics and nuisance in the law are not exact equivalents.

SERVITUDES

Owners of land can take steps to minimize potential conflicts. Historically, they have been able to use easements and covenants to define property rights in a way that anticipates and attempts to control possible external effects. Easements and covenants are examples of _servitudes_, that is, interests over land belonging to someone else. They internalize an externality by turning a spillover into a property right.

An easement is defined in the *Restatement (Third) of Property, Servitudes*, §1.2 (the American Law Institute's influential guide to the law of servitudes), as a nonpossessory right to enter and use land. It typically requires "dominant" and "servient" pieces of land in reasonable closeness to each other, in which case the benefit and burden of an easement is said to be "appurtenant"—that is, attached to land as in the case of a right of way. In the United States, easements need not necessarily be appurtenant, in which case they are held in "gross," as in the modern practice of creating conservation easements to preserve scenic amenity. Enforcement of an easement is treated as a matter of property law, with the beneficiary being entitled to require specific performance. It is difficult to abolish an easement.

An example of a positive easement would be where the owner of one piece of (dominant) land has a right of access over neighboring (servient) land. In *Brown v. Voss* (1986), land was broken off of a larger estate and sold with an easement that preserved access to the seller's land. The dominant land would otherwise have been landlocked and possibly only of value if jointly owned with the servient land. Use of the easement implies that the separate ownership increases the joint value of both pieces of land (or why would an owner incur the transaction costs in dividing land and creating necessary easements). Sometimes an easement is bought from a neighboring landowner, as in *Hayes v. Aquia Marina Inc.* (1992), where the only land access to a marina in Virginia was over neighboring land bordering a highway.

Conservation Servitudes

An interesting modern development is the *conservation easement*, or *conservation servitude,* as it is now beginning to be called, which is normally a form of negative gross easement. An organization having charitable status, such as a conservation trust, either buys the development rights to scenic land or receives the rights as a donation. The servient land value is then decreased by the loss of the development rights. Because property taxes are assessed on current land values, the reduction in value will have tax advantages for a donating landowner. The trust then manages the environmental benefits attached to the land. The owner of the servient land may continue to live there and carry out compatible land uses such as farming. However, activities ruled out by the conservation easement, such as building condominiums, are not allowed. Conservation easements are typically of permanent duration.

Traditional views of the scope of easements would cause problems for conservation easements, which have therefore been developed under state statutes following the model provided by the Uniform Conservation Easement Act of 1988. First, in traditional common law, easements over views may not be created. Second, there is no right to wander at will over land; neither are there any easements for purely recreational purposes. Third, easements cannot impose direct costs, such as those of maintaining access, on the servient land but must be acts of sufferance. Typically, conservation easements do require acts of conservation. The use of conservation statutes, based broadly on the idea of an easement, forces the courts to recognize conservation easements without invoking common-law principles against negative easements in gross.

A negative easement gives the holder the right to prevent the servient owner from carrying out defined actions on the servient land. A good example is an easement of light and air, in which a neighbor is prevented from construction of anything that would block light and air from the dominant land. Traditionally, courts have discouraged negative easements as liable to "clog title," with possibly idiosyncratic restrictions likely to be of doubtful value to future generations. There was a general tendency to encourage the use of covenants for restrictions, based on the view that covenants are less final and less likely to result in imposing restrictions that would seem irrelevant to later generations. Recently, the use of negative easements for conservation purposes has renewed interest in such burdens on land, as examined in the boxed example.

An easement runs with the land and binds all future owners, contrasting with contract law, under which benefits but not burdens can be transferred to third parties. The history of land law shows a general tendency to force renegotiations over burdens on land as generations change. This reflects the rule against perpetuities, which inspires courts generally to deny endless dead-hand control of the future by a person transferring land.

Easements typically reflect encumbrances such as rights of way where we might suppose that future generations would contract in the same wealth-maximizing way (access across land is likely to be of net value in the future). This observation is supported by the implications of features of easements such as the requirement that there be no direct costs imposed on the servient land, as these costs could change over time, undermining the net value of the easement. Also, the practice of creating easements by necessity reinforces the idea that easements can be efficient where conditions are not likely to change. This stability was shown in *Morrell v. Rice* (1993), where the alternative to a low-cost route over a neighbor's land was $300,000 of dredging work. The *Restatement (Third) of Property, Servitudes* does allow the owner of servient land to reroute a third party's right of way as long as doing so preserves the essential value of the easement, which reflects efficient land use, as the move could increase the value of the servient land.

The requirement that easements must touch and concern the land acts as short-hand in describing cases where the costs are more readily assessed objectively and without much reference to the personal characteristics of the parties. One basis for condemning an easement is if the beneficiary has developed the dominant land to increase the burden on the servient land. Another basis is failure to use the easement. Such developments would undermine the predictability of use that is necessary to be sure that a standardized, rigid restriction like an easement makes economic sense. In principle, a landowner likely to create an externality could buy an easement, such as allowing the emission of smoke over a neighbor's property. This could be bought back if the value of the servient land increased at a later date. An easement defines a property right, but it requires foresight at some point early on and may be most relevant when a parcel of land belonging entirely to one owner is transferred.

A *covenant* is a contractual agreement in which the covenantor promises to engage in or refrain from specified activities affecting a defined area of land. It is enforceable as a contract, with a standard remedy for breach being money damages, rather than specific performance. Covenants emerged in the late nineteenth century as landowners used contract law to circumvent the unwillingness of judges to apply restrictions to land use via easements. They are more specific in terms of the methods of conferring a benefit (maintain a demountable wall) compared with easements (leave access), and are said to resolve conflicts over land use, rather than to permit compatible uses like easements.

Covenants, which might be positive (maintain a neighbor's fence) or negative (do not erect a fence) for a particular piece of land, allow owners of land to be bound by personal promises, that is, to force conflict resolution into the marketplace at regular intervals. A good example is found in *Nahrstedt v. Lakeside Village Condominium Association* (1994), where a condominium association required new purchasers to accept a covenant barring the keeping of indoor cats. By analogy with contract law, the common law has resisted passing the burden of a covenant to a subsequent purchaser or transferee (assignee) although if there are similar features to easements, the courts often will let a covenant run with the land. The traditional remedy for breach of a covenant is to award damages, in line with the approach of contract law (discussed in later chapters).

U.S. courts have blurred the distinction between covenants and easements, having followed *Hills v. Miller* (1832) in enthusiastically enforcing some covenants as equitable servitudes. These arose where an assignee had notice of a covenant on purchasing land, and it was held unconscionable for that person then to benefit from increased land values. The value of land could increase if the covenant disappeared just because land was transferred. An equitable servitude, like an easement, could be enforced through the granting of an injunction requiring specific performance. The American Law Institute has recommended in the *Restatement (Third) of Property, Servitudes* that the distinction between easements and covenants be abolished. The *Restatement*, which clarifies the law and has advisory status, favors the combination of easements and covenants into a single form of servitude.

REGULATION OF LAND USE

So far, we have concentrated on the economics of the private law on conflicts over property rights. We now consider the impact of government and examine a number of regulatory, or statutory, approaches. The most important area of statutory control arises through zoning laws that regulate the location of conflicting and complementary uses of land.

Zoning

Beginning in 1916 in New York City, a comprehensive system of land-use controls has emerged across the United States. Some of the potential nuisances that are controlled through systems of planning consent and building regulation may have serious safety implications; others may simply regulate conflicting and compatible land uses. The primary control is through zoning, in which local authorities have powers to specify the type of activities permitted in different areas. Authorities usually also control the technical details of any particular development. Anybody wishing to develop land must obtain planning permission from the local authority, which may approve the plans, refuse permission, or impose conditions on the developer. The Standard State Zoning Enabling Act, dating from 1924, gave a model act that could be followed by states wishing to control development through zoning. Similar systems operate in other countries, such as Australia, Canada, England, and New Zealand.

In *Village of Euclid v. Ambler* (1926), there is a good illustration of typical zoning. Euclid is a suburb of Cleveland, Ohio. In 1926, its local authority zoned the suburb into six classes of use. Classes included single-family dwellings, 2-family dwellings, apartment houses, retail and office buildings, warehouses and works, and refuse facilities. Area districts were also established, covering space requirements for dwellings, and height limitations were also imposed. The local authority's building inspector enforced the zoning ordinance. The U.S. Supreme Court upheld the local authority's right to impose zoning conditions as an exercise of normal local government procedures. Ambler had unsuccessfully claimed an infringement of his constitutional rights to due process in finding his land bound by zoning requirements. "Euclidean" zoning developed rapidly elsewhere following the ruling.

Is development control necessary? There are examples like Houston, Texas, which for many years existed without zoning, and during which time relatively few developers tended to dominate local development, relying on covenants to control uses. Applying the distinction between property and liability rules, we might argue that compensation for damages would control conflicting use when the victims of a nuisance were dispersed, and that bargaining would control conflict when there were few affected individuals. There are two possible efficiency reasons why local authorities would become involved in development control. First, traditional remedies for nuisance are available to those with neighboring land interests but would not be available to the wider population of a locality. However, the wider population might well suffer a negative externality if, for example, a development were out of keeping with the rest of a town. Second, immediate neighbors may have little incentive to pursue a nuisance that has a wider impact.

Land Development Conditions

Local authorities also impose technical planning requirements on developers. Even if a specific type of builiding is permitted in a development zone, buildings typically

Nollan v. California Coastal Commission (1987)

Mr. and Mrs. Nollan successfully appealed against a decision of the California Court of Appeal that the California Coastal Commission could condition its grant of permission for rebuilding their house on the creation of an easement across their property. They owned a private beach positioned above the high-tide mark in Ventura County, California, a quarter-mile south of Faria County Park and its public beach. South of them was another public beach known as "the Cove." The easement would have made it easier for the public to get to Faria County Park and the Cove. Other property owners along the coastline had also found the commission seeking access easements as a part of development conditions, as it was in fact engaged in creating a continuous coastal path.

In the county court, the Nollans argued that the condition could not be imposed without evidence that there would be a direct adverse impact on public access to the beach (below the high-tide mark, or farther along). The court required the commission to hold a public hearing, after which the commission claimed that the new house would interfere with the public's ability to see the beach and would create a psychological barrier to using the public beaches. In the context of development along the coastline, the building would "burden the public's ability to traverse to and along the shorefront." The court concluded that the California Coastal Act authorized the commission to impose public access conditions only where the proposed development would have an adverse impact on public access to the sea. It ruled that there was not an adequate factual basis for concluding that replacement of the Nollan's house would create a burden on public access. The commission successfully appealed to the California Court of Appeal, which disagreed with the county court's interpretation of the Coastal Act.

Finally, the Nollans successfully appealed to the U.S. Supreme Court, raising the constitutional question of whether the requirement to grant the easement amounted to an uncompensated taking of land for government purposes. The Supreme Court accepted the commission's argument that it would be in order to allow development subject to a condition, if to do so overcame an objection raised through the exercise of legitimate powers to control development. The Supreme Court did not accept that the argument applied in the case, because allowing access across the Nollans' property would not compensate for any impediment to viewing that section of beach, nor lower any psychological barrier to using the public beaches. Prohibiting construction, or imposing height restrictions, would have been acceptable planning responses. The commission's requirement for the easement was not justified and amounted to taking a property right in land without compensation to the owner. If the commission wished to create a coastal path, it could do so by using powers it had to buy land.

must meet minimum standards for building methods, appearance, and positioning on a lot. Failure to comply with regulations may be penalized by a requirement that an offending development be removed—a costly penalty of specific performance. An inspection-based system is justified if it would be difficult for ordinary citizens to detect problems that could turn into serious nuisances. If detection were easy and temporary nuisance not too severe, it would be easier to rely on a system of fines imposed after nuisances were created as a means of deterrence.

It does not follow that local authorities intervene purely from a wish to maximize the total value of land use. Controls also could reflect attempts by the local authority to extract some of the benefits of any development, as shown in the boxed example.

The *Nollan* case shows that constitutional protection exists against local authorities trying to extract planning gain. This protection may not be as strong as it seems, in particular because courts have disagreed over where to draw the line in balancing the interests of private rights and public policy. There may be cases where local authorities could legitimately turn down development plans, such as having the power to decide that a new shopping mall is not in the local interest, unless a developer shared some of the benefits that are likely to be forthcoming. Once a developer accepted these conditions, and in the interest of future harmony with the local authority, it would not be possible retroactively to attempt to recover the development conditions. Such rent seeking may have been reflected in the inclusion on Arizona ballot papers during the 2000 presidential election of a proposition covering infrastructure development. Arizona has experienced much inward migration. The proposition required larger local authorities to adopt 10-year growth plans forcing developers to pay for roads, schools, and other facilities in return for consent to develop new residential subdivisions.

Suppose development may be permitted if the builder agrees to put in new access roads that are of wider benefit in the area. Figure 3.3 illustrates planning gain in relation to rent extraction by the local authority. The horizontal axis measures increases in the specification of a development, which is measured by the amount of road building by the developer. The vertical axis measures the marginal (external) benefit to the local authority, and the marginal cost to the developer, of the roads.

In Figure 3.3, the origin is labeled R_p, as this is the profit-maximizing amount of road building that would be undertaken by the developer in the absence of controls. The maximum amount that the developer could build before going bankrupt is assumed to be R. Costless bargaining between the authority and the developer would give a jointly optimal amount R^*. The bargaining could proceed as follows. The local authority might insist on a specification level providing R miles of new roads. The developer would then find it worthwhile to encourage the local authority to move back toward the optimum R^*. The developer will have to pay the local authority at least its forgone total benefits, measured by the area R^*BDR, for the move back. If the local

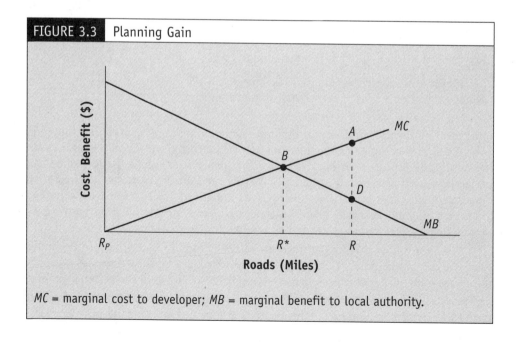

FIGURE 3.3   Planning Gain

MC = marginal cost to developer; MB = marginal benefit to local authority.

authority is a particularly good bargainer, it might extract a higher amount, worth up to area R^*BAR, representing the gain in profit to the developer from the move. Assuming local authorities do not accept cash bribes, the developer can pay in kind—perhaps offering to undertake particularly attractive landscaping in exchange for a relaxation of the road-building requirement.

An alternative strategy for the developer is to appeal against the local authority's specification of R miles of road. This was essentially what happened in *Nollan*, where the planning gain was sought as a coastal easement and the constitutional ruling protected the plaintiff. The court required the Californian Coastal Commission to buy a move from R_p to R^*. In general, the attractiveness of an appeal strategy relative to negotiating with the local authority will depend upon costs of negotiation relative to litigation. The possibility of successful appeal may be ruled out if the local authority succeeds in defining planning gain as a definite cost imposed on the locality.

Eminent Domain

Government agencies can undertake compulsory purchase (condemnation) of private property for public purposes. Compulsory purchase is referred to as the exercise of *eminent domain*, which is potentially a minefield of conflict between private and public interests. One common argument suggests a need for eminent domain because the owner of a vital piece of land in a particular position, such as land needed for a public road, could hold up the process. In particular, the owner could demand at least the entire projected net benefit from the scheme as a selling price and might extract more if there are disruption costs from not going ahead. The price of land would be raised artificially, and this would encourage the inefficient substitution of other factors of production; for example, major thoroughfares might be built in locations where they would not otherwise be cost-effective.

This argument does not lead to the conclusion that public authorities should be permitted to take land without paying compensation. Apart from the distributional consequences, governments would be encouraged to take land when it was of little public value compared with its value to its private owner. However, it is also true that a rule of full compensation fails to encourage a private owner to recognize that some private uses may conflict with public developments; the owner may have no incentive to locate a structure away from a road likely to need widening. No zero-sum compensation rule can give all parties incentives to take care. Existing compensation schemes fall short of full compensation for owners and impose process costs on local authorities, which implies that incentives for care will exist.

The Fifth Amendment governs the exercise of eminent domain and limits takings to those for legitimate public use subject to the payment of just compensation. Legitimacy and the amount of payment can be defined in the courts. Commonwealth countries like Australia, Canada, England, and New Zealand are in a similar position. Compensation is normally for the market value of the property and not for any special valuation placed on it by the owner. The payment of market price for takings corresponds to taking a liability approach over the damage to the owner. Using market value simplifies the calculation of damages.

The market-price approach ignores consumer surplus, which is the difference between an individual's private valuation of a thing and the market price for it. If someone has not sold a property, it may be valued more highly than the market price.

If we wish to be sure that the public taking is for a purpose that is more highly valued than that of the owner, we should require the authority to buy at the owner's valuation.

It is difficult to see how to get beyond some rule of thumb to help compensate at above the market price. Attempts to calculate accurate measures of ask–offer discrepancies would increase the transaction costs of public development schemes. In some countries, it used to be normal to add 10 percent to market value to compensate for the fact that compulsory purchase did not reflect a voluntary sale. This contributed something to consumer surplus, without creating great problems of valuation. Such a rule of thumb may well be as far as it is possible to go to make a contribution toward consumer surplus without severely increasing costs.

Nonetheless, it is puzzling from an economic point of view why a power of eminent domain is necessary away from situations where holdup is likely to be a problem. It could be a reserve power available when almost all landowners affected by some public development have sold out and a small proportion of them choose to hold out for prices way above the market rate. The more general use of eminent domain suggests it may be more a way of getting land cheaply.

It is important to recognize that public authorities do sometimes attempt to use their powers in ways that have some of the implications of taking land for private purposes. Apart from cases like *Nollan*, where the California Coastal Commission appeared to be building a coastal path without purchasing land, there are cases that seem to redistribute land. In *Poletown Neighborhood Council v. City of Detroit* (1981), the city compulsorily purchased 465 acres of land, at a cost of over $200 million, to convey it for approximately $8 million to General Motors for construction of an automobile plant. The public purpose behind this was said to be the preservation of 6,000 jobs and associated local revenues. Against opposition from the 3,500 residents whose homes were destroyed in the process, the Michigan Supreme Court accepted the taking as for a legitimate public purpose.

In *Hawaii Housing Authority v. Midkiff* (1984), the U.S. Supreme Court upheld the Hawaiian legislature's policy of compulsorily purchasing land from owners of large areas to resell it as smaller parcels. The perceived public benefit was reducing the concentration of land ownership in Hawaii, which had a history of highly concentrated ownership. The concentration was held to injure social stability, and the legislature also worried about upward pressure on land prices. In both *Midkiff* and *Poletown*, it is difficult to escape the conclusion that largely private purposes were pursued by using the coercive power of local authorities.

Regulatory Takings

The passage of a government regulation may blight a property and depress its value. Since *Pennsylvania Coal Co. v. Mahon*, a 1922 Supreme Court case, the position has been that regulations can go too far in reducing the value of affected property. It is as if the property had been compulsorily taken. In *Mahon*, surface rights but not mining rights had been compulsorily purchased. Subsequently, the local authority had passed an act taking away the mining rights. Later the company wished to mine, but the residents of housing built on the land objected. Justice Holmes asserted that the local act amounted to taking property (mining rights) without just compensation and was contrary to the Fifth Amendment. No compensation was paid to the company, which simply retained the right to mine.

In a more recent case, *Lucas v. South Carolina Coastal Council* (1992), a local act creating coastal zones removed the development rights for two island plots. In this case, the Supreme Court ruled that compensation was appropriate as the local act rendered the plots completely valueless, an example of categorical taking. The public purpose could not simply take private land for public purposes, unless the private use of the land was harmful (under the doctrine of reasonable use, no-one has a right to compensation for harmful use). Cases of regulatory taking do not necessarily need to be categorical, as it may be enough if significant loss of value occurs following the regulatory change. The courts have experienced much difficulty in determining when a regulation sufficiently diminishes value to be a taking.

From an economic perspective, it is rational to regard regulatory taking as equivalent to any other form of taking. Property rights are altered by regulatory change. American constitutional protection emphasizes compensation to individuals for loss of the status quo. Other countries often allow governments more freedom to impose policy without such compensation, effectively emphasizing the welfare of the beneficiaries of the change. Although it may be tempting to consider the implications of taking as largely distributional, this conclusion is false because uncertainty over future development values may distort private investment away from areas likely to be at risk from regulatory change. Also, unless there is a perceived benefit from the regulatory change after meeting an obligation to pay compensation, it is not clear that the change is desirable. The Fifth Amendment imposes a Pareto test of welfare improvement, testing whether the gainers can compensate the losers and still be better off.

Environmental Protection

Most countries have some statutory control of general environmental nuisance and do not rely solely on the private law to regulate conflict over property rights. The United States is no exception in having a range of laws that control environmental emissions. The Environmental Protection Agency (EPA) administers these controls. Environmental protection largely proceeds by enforcing technical standards for airborne and waterborne emissions, and by specifying fines that may be imposed for creating pollution.

A justification may be given for environmental protection legislation that is similar to the one that was given for the existence of development laws. The effect of a nuisance may range more widely than just over neighboring properties, and immediate neighbors may have too little incentive to take action. The choice between legislation that simply imposes a fine and legislation establishing an active inspectorate then depends on whether the nuisance is easy to detect. If it is not, then fines may not be effective and an inspectorate may be needed. Thus, a nuisance like noise is easy to detect early on, and its temporary existence would not be too harmful. Noise is typically controlled through fines. The situation is different with factory emissions, and we tend to find these to be subject to an inspectorate system.

Many countries have experienced growing environmental problems and have also enacted pollution-control statutes. Noise pollution in urban settings has grown considerably in recent years. Changing technology has made the imposition of a noise nuisance on a neighborhood an easy matter: There was a case where a fan of the singer Whitney Houston was prosecuted for playing her hit single "I Will Always Love You" almost nonstop for six weeks. In another case, a would-be disc jockey was jailed for three months after playing pop music and his own commentary at full volume from his bedroom over a powerful sound system for up to 14 hours a day: Earlier fines and even the seizure of the equipment failed to end this bizarre behavior. Even so, complaints about noisy neighbors seem to be rising every year. Note that enforcement is often based on fines, which is consistent with noise being an easily detected nuisance that neighbors can be expected to report.

An approach favored by many economists is to create markets in nuisances wherever possible. The Clean Air Act (1990) allows for the trading of pollution permits. The authorities set limits for particular airborne pollutants and allow bidders to bid for transferable licenses to pollute up to set amounts. This type of procedure allows a permit to go to the user that most highly values the units of air pollution, which is usually an industrial firm wishing to pollute. Firms will choose to control their pollution if that is cheaper than bidding for a permit.

There is also a worrying trend for statutes to undermine possible common-law solutions to cases of nuisance. Statutory dominance is embodied in the Clean Air Act, which forbids interstate lawsuits. Federal courts have repeatedly ruled that interstate suits are superseded by federal regulation of pollution. Although it is possible to justify statutory control of nuisance in terms of cost savings when damages are diffuse, there can be no support for the suppression of common-law solutions when these are possible.

SUMMARY AND CONCLUSIONS

In this chapter, we have looked at the principal methods by which conflicts over property rights are resolved. The economic analysis we have used takes the Coase theorem as its departure point. We have been careful to show that the comparative-institutions analysis of problems characterized by positive transaction costs is the important part of Coase's work. Therefore, criticisms of the assumptions of the Coase theorem are largely beside the point. The work of Calabresi and Melamed (see References) is particularly relevant in stressing the importance of encouraging the least-cost avoider of a nuisance to take evasive steps in the context of particular legal rules. In this respect, it is important to distinguish whether nuisances have public or private characteristics.

There is a considerable range to the law on nuisance. The common law traditionally favors a property rule based on awarding injunctions. A liability approach based on paying damages, which has increasingly come to be used in the United States, may be safer if damage is dispersed and the court does not know who is the least-cost avoider, although it can lead to unnecessary court costs outside of those circumstances. Statutory efforts to control externalities with a wide impact can be understood partly as unwillingness to rely on immediate neighbors to prosecute nuisance and, in the case of development control, partly as rent seeking by local authorities.

QUESTIONS FOR REVIEW

1. Would a property or a liability rule have been the best outcome had the *Boomer v. Atlantic* case involved just one or two pollution victims?

2. Some U.S. states have community-property laws affecting the division of marital assets following divorce, under which property is divided equally. If a state without community property were to adopt it, replacing a rule under which nonworking ex-wives typically received one-third of

marital property upon divorce, what would happen to the divorce rate? Is your answer different if the preexisting rule was to award two-thirds to the divorced wife?

3. Under what circumstances is it appropriate to control nuisance using
    a.   servitudes?
    b.   an environmental protection agency?

4. What is a house really worth? Is it feasible to compensate fully for takings by the government?

5. To what extent is the Coase theorem a guide to public policy rather than a textbook example?

NOTES ON THE LITERATURE

- In *The Problem of Social Cost*, Ronald Coase (1960) argued that bargaining between individuals internalizes many externalities when the cost of bargaining is sufficiently low. Bargaining costs, a form of transaction costs, are defined as the costs of negotiating and enforcing agreements. Coase took a more legally realistic view of nuisance than Pigou (1938), whose public-policy recommendation for controlling externality was for the state to impose a charge equal to marginal external cost on the noise polluter. The approach to Coase's work taken here is based partly on discussions with him. The term *Coase theorem* was actually coined by Stigler (1966, p. 113). In *Sturges v. Bridgman*, the court's granting of an injunction gave Sturges the entitlement (Calabresi and Melamed, 1972) to stop the noise. The argument that Pigou's solution of taxing the externality leads to suboptimally low pollution levels when bargaining is possible comes from Buchanan and Stubblebine (1962).

- Do people bargain after court decisions? Farnsworth (1999) examined 20 nuisance cases and found no bargaining after judgment in any of them. The lawyers in the cases thought that the possibility of bargaining was closed off by animosity between the parties, rather than by standard issues of transactions cost. Farnsworth does not consider *Sturges v. Bridgman*, but although we have no information on whether they bargained, we do know that the premises, in Wimpole Street, London, eventually became law offices!

- The list of significant assumptions used in the text, which are necessary for the Coase theorem to hold, are adapted from Veljanovski (1982). Farrell (1987) shows that if some individuals have information when others do not, mutually beneficial trades will not occur. He also argues that information asymmetries give an incentive for the devotion of resources to influencing the beliefs of the other party. Roth and Murnighan (1982) report the results of experiments showing that when people do not know one another's tastes or opportunities, negotiations can be protracted and unsuccessful. As Mumey (1971) points out, information problems imply that parties would devote resources to developing threat strategies—a form of rent seeking with associated waste of resources.

- It is possible to draw on a game-theoretic argument of Schelling (1960) to suggest that bargaining advantages may come from irrationality (one tends to be respectful toward the requests of a seemingly deranged, axe-wielding person who arrives at the house). A party may use the threat of irrationally moving to a position that is suboptimal for both parties in order to extract most of the gains from bargaining. If the opponent does not give in, it may be necessary to carry out the threat for future credibility. However, Selten (1978) showed that if the number of repetitions of the game is known with certainty, there exists an endgame in which the threat is not credible. Therefore, the threat is not credible in the immediately preceding game, or the one before that, and so on—affecting all bargaining games. Also, if each party is unsure whether the other might irrationally adopt something like a tit-for-tat strategy (Axelrod, 1984) threats may be deterred. Work outside of the case of costless bargaining focuses on the design of legal rules to minimize bargaining costs, including those connected with strategic interaction (Epstein, 1993).

- There has been some recent interest in endowment effects and the ask–offer problem in relation to the Coase theorem. The impact of changing initial endowments (of income, goods, or rights) on the valuation of goods and services has been observed to differ depending on whether the endowment is given or taken away. Individuals may offer to pay a different amount to be free of an externality compared with the compensation they ask if required to bear it. The ask–offer problem could arise as a simple result of a wealth effect. However, endowment effects have also been observed in situations where the associated change in wealth is too small to give rise to the observed effect. The ask–offer problem, referring to the impact of changing entitlements in the presence of wealth effects, is developed in Kennedy (1981), Veljanovski (1982), and Fischel (1995b). It is as if the very ownership of an item affects its value (Thaler, 1980). Knetsch and Sinden (1984) ran experiments distributing lottery tickets to groups of students and then presented the individuals with offers to buy back the tickets or demands for payment to keep them. The ask-offer difference may have picked up a move from risk aversion, when asked to pay, to risk taking when asked to sell. Therefore, Knetsch (1989) conducted riskless experiments using market goods and money that support the existence of an endowment effect. Supporting results were obtained by Kahneman, Knetsch, and Thaler (1990). Tversky and Kahneman (1991) see the endowment effect as a manifestation of loss aversion: the generalization that losses are weighed substantially more heavily in the evaluation of prospects and trades. It appears most likely to arise where items are not easily replaceable. Recent experimental work (Shogren, Shin, Hayes, and Kliebenstein, 1994) questions the existence of the endowment effect and instead relies on movement between indifference curves to explain ask–offer differences (but see Morrison, 1997).

- Wellisz (1964), Nutter (1968), and Regan (1972) have asked whether the operation of the Coase theorem depends on levels of economic rent. In the example in the text, if the rancher is not liable, the farmer cannot induce him to stop because we assume the value of the damage is less than ranching rents. Nutter (1968) has interpreted this type of case as one where bargaining makes no impact on the nuisance but just transfers economic rent (from rancher to farmer). Wellisz (1964) argues that even if there is no economic rent on either of the conflicting activities, assignment of the entitlement will have allocative consequences.

- Following Regan (1972), the predictions of the Coase theorem can be summarized as claiming that, in a world of insignificant transaction costs, the parties will agree on a jointly optimal level for some externality, and the agreement will be attained by bargaining. Experimental tests generally use student subjects in an environment created to have very low transaction costs (Roth, 1988; Smith, 1989). The subjects may sometimes have private information.

- Harrison and McKee (1985) reported experimental results suggesting that deviations from Coasian outcomes in Hoffman and Spitzer (1982) were consequences of the relative insignificance of the sums involved. Harrison and McKee (1985) had the bargainers experience an initial environment in which property rights were not defined. Harrison, Hoffman, Rutström, and Spitzer (1987) also found that Coasian solutions to an externality problem were realized, following an initial learning period, in a more complex experimental setting. One aspect of their study was that subjects traded using information that was initially private to them. Nevertheless, Harrison et al. (1987) are careful not to overstate the conclusions that can be drawn from their experiments, accepting that they only support the predictions of the Coase theorem in situations characterized by relatively low bargaining costs. They urge the construction of experiments aimed at testing the suitability of bargaining solutions in environments containing significant negotiating costs. A recent study attempting to do this is Shogrun (1993). The work of Roth and Murnighan (1982) suggests that information asymmetries create bargaining costs and make it much harder for individuals to negotiate solutions to externality problems.

- Posner (1993) accepts that Coase believes that we live in a world of transaction costs. Indeed, if this were not so, Coase's (1937) work on the nature of the firm, in which he regards firms as internalizing some transactions to save costs attached to using markets, would have no subject. Coase's notes, quoted in text, are from Coase (1988, p. 174–178).

- Calabresi and Melamed (1972) and Calabresi (1970) suggest choosing between remedies for nuisance on the basis of the transaction costs affecting the parties. Care must be taken to avoid confusion with the specialized legal use of the term public *nuisance*, as a statutorily controlled nuisance like spreading contagious disease. The specialized legal use is actually consistent with Calabresi and Melamed's analysis because nuisances with highly dispersed damage imply the need for a public body to act as plaintiff or too little action will be taken. Unfortunately, the law's technical definition of a private nuisance includes nuisances with dispersed consequences. Given the economics focus of this book, we follow Calabresi and Melamed, whose work was recently updated in Ayres and Goldbart (2003).

- Farber (1988) gives a wonderfully detailed analysis of *Boomer*. The fame of the case may have much to do with the growing environmental concerns of the 1960s and 1970s. Widespread airborne pollution was probably a low-priority concern in the case, and much was not as legend would suggest. Boomer actually ran a junkyard on an 8-acre site. There was a strike at the cement works at the time of the case. The works had state-of-the-art dust filtration. Finally, most complaints were about vibration from relatively few local neighbors.

- A retrospective assessment of Calabresi and Melamed's work is Levmore (1997), who strongly picks up on the idea of an injunction with associated compensation for the tortfeasor. Ellickson (1993) is critical of the argument that liability rules tend to be the best approach to public nuisance, noting many overlooked costs applying to injunctive remedies for private nuisance. Swanson and Kantoleon (2000) give an excellent survey of the literature on nuisance.

- Wittman (1981; 1998) criticizes the doctrine of "coming to the nuisance" as being arbitrary in allowing priority in time to determine the development of land. An interesting lawyer's view, recognizing the control of holdup by applying compensation for an injunction when the recipient has come to the nuisance, is Reynolds (1992).

- Reichman (1978) appears to have given the first economic analysis of easements and covenants, but also see Reichman (1982) and Stake (1998). Dana and Ramsey (1989) cover conservation easements. The view of covenants as contracts is from *Black's Law Dictionary*, 1891.

- Following *Tulk v. Moxhay* (1848) and *Hills v. Miller* (1832), equity principles were applied to enforce covenants against an assignee who had notice of it and where it was held unconscionable for the seller to benefit from increased land values if the covenant were to disappear.

- Fischel (1985) examines development without a system of zoning—that is, relying instead on developers' covenants to control conflicting use.

- The court in *Euclid* noted the judge's comments in *Sturges* that whether a particular thing is a nuisance is not an abstract question but is to be considered in connection with circumstances and locality.

- Knetsch (1983) argues that the market-price approach to compensating compulsory purchase ignores consumer surplus, which is the difference between an individual's private valuation of a thing and the market price for it. In the standard introductory analysis of demand, used in the introduction to this book, consumer surplus is taken to be the area above a price line and below the demand curve. Note that both the equivalent and compensating variations for a price change are alternative measures of consumer surplus. More recent analysis has emphasized the ask–offer problem in arguing for compensation at above-market value (Marshall, Knetsch, and Sinden, 1986). Fischel (1995b) concludes that compensation at market value balances the future benefits from eminent domain against the extra taxes

- Fischel (1995a) examines regulatory takings, as does Eagle (2001). Meiners and Yandle (1993) have examined the growing dominance of regulators over the common law.

Chapter 4

CONTRACT FORMATION AND EVOLUTION

Contracts have an important impact on human welfare and, not surprisingly, economists pay a great deal of attention to them. Over time, the view of contracts found in economic analysis is becoming richer and more detailed. There is particularly strong interest in the formation, modification, and enforcement of contracts. From a societal perspective, contracts allow people to negotiate fixed or predictable prices for goods and services so that they can plan for the future. There is an important insurance aspect to any contract: The enforceability of the promise it embodies shifts risks to one party and protects the other.

In this chapter, we apply economic analysis to traditional legal questions concerning contract law. In particular, we ask what makes a contract, as opposed to an unenforceable promise, and what are the economic implications of the more important rules for contract formation? We also consider several aspects of long-term contracts, including contract modifications, which have aroused much interest in economics and in law. We move on to examine the economics of breach of contract in the next chapter.

THE NATURE OF CONTRACTS

Contract law tells people when promises are enforceable and what the consequences are of breaching contracts. This is essential to business and to most forms of planning, and enables people to move resources to the uses in which they are valued most highly. Contracts are the practical means by which people bargain with one another and realize expected gains from trade. Predictable contract law implies that people can confidently pursue all transactions that yield gains from trade even when performance occurs over time, and not just limit themselves to those embodying an instant exchange. Efficient contracts are enforceable agreements that create gains from trade for all parties.

The time dimension of contracts is also important from the point of view of providing insurance. Agreements often contain express terms specifying who is to benefit or lose from increases or decreases in the prices or costs related to the transaction. Even if there are gaps in agreements, when courts fill these in a predictable manner, people can rely on precedent to specify implicitly the insurance aspects of a contract. Gaps might be left if it is too costly to specify what the parties must do in every contingency, or if the parties are happy with the typical default rulings of the courts. Such gaps need not mean that people will end up in conflict with each other. The contingencies may not materialize, or the judgment may be so predictable that the parties settle any conflict out of court.

Figure 4.1 on page 78 shows a simple contract for the supply of wheat, viewed from the purchaser's perspective. We measure the purchaser's money income on the vertical axis at point *A*, and the amount of wheat purchased on the horizontal axis. The price line (*AB*) shows the amount of income that must be sacrificed to buy wheat (i.e., the slope reflects the price of wheat). The purchaser can reach point *x* tangent to indifference curve *I*. This indifference curve is the highest attainable and shows all the combinations of money income capable of producing a given level of welfare (*I*). If a new supplier with a lower price is found, the price line pivots out to *AC*, and point *y* can be reached on the higher indifference curve (*II*). If the new supplier suddenly withdrew from the contract, we would need to increase the purchaser's income by the amount *AD* to compensate for the loss at the old price (the consumer would move to a point like *z*). The amount *AD* therefore measures the purchaser's expectation from the new contract.

Expectation refers to the net benefit associated with the contract. For the purchaser in Figure 4.1, it is the opportunity to buy at a lower price. Although the supplier's expectation is not shown, we might surmise that it would be the profit on the sale. The common law has always had a strong tradition of trying to support the contracting parties in realizing the monetary value expected from a contract.

FORMATION OF CONTRACTS

To understand the economic implications of contract formation, we must examine principles from case law that largely developed in the nineteenth and early twentieth centuries. These principles are embedded in modern case law and have also influenced efforts to codify contract law. Two efforts at codification are worth mentioning. Article 2 (Sales) of the Uniform Commercial Code (UCC) is a joint project of the American Law Institute and the National Conference of Commissioners on Uniform State Laws. The American Law Institute has also published the *Restatement (Second) of Contracts*, which is an influential guide to the general principles of contract case law

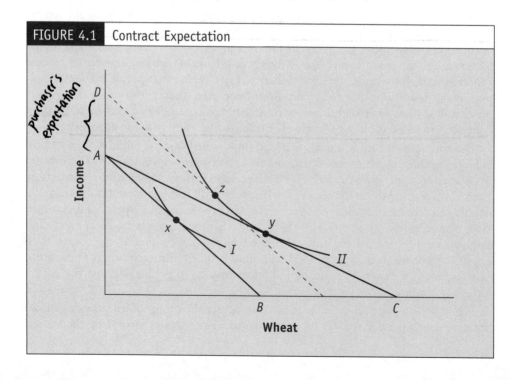

FIGURE 4.1   Contract Expectation

incorporating details of the Uniform Sales Act. Foreign common-law countries have very similar commercial laws that have also often been codified.

Traditionally, a promise is enforceable and forms a contract if it is given as part of a bargain and the parties intend to create a legal relationship. This principle excludes most gratuitous promises (unless made under seal), such as an individual's promise to donate a new library to a local university in the event of winning the state lottery. In the traditional doctrine, three basic conditions must hold for a bargain to exist and for a contract to be formed: There must be offer, acceptance, and consideration. Some economic support can be given for each of these requirements, which are mainly concerned with indicating gains from trade and an intention to form a legally binding commercial relationship.

Offer and Acceptance

The buyer or seller must have clearly offered to buy or sell the good or service. This need not be in the form of a written document: For example, a buyer at an open auction conventionally signals an offer by raising a hand. What constitutes an offer very much depends upon conventional practices in an industry.

Unwritten formal offers are often used in transactions in stocks and shares, where people routinely offer to buy and sell shares by telephoning their stockbroker. A note is taken of calls and contract notes are issued, which would be taken as compelling evidence of an offer if a dispute arose. Courts have indeed ruled that telephone and other electronic messages are permitted means of communicating offers. An economic interpretation of special trading routines like this can be given. It is important to be able to act quickly on movements in share prices, so the system really needs to operate on the principle of "my word is my bond." The gains from this to everyone outweigh the possible increase in costs from having a less certified basis for contract.

The requirement for an unambiguous offer is important from an economic perspective. Contracts normally move resources to more highly valued uses. If a clear offer was not made, then we cannot be sure that a promise to sell implies that a seller prefers the monetary price to keeping the good or service, or that a buyer really prefers to buy rather than keep the money. There is a mirror-image requirement for unambiguous acceptance of an offer before a contract can be formed. Again, the requirement for acceptance is also interpreted in relation to standard practice in an industry and may differ from case to case. (See the boxed example on De Beers.)

De Beers Diamond Sales

An interesting example of industry practice over offer and acceptance is in the standard terms used by the De Beers cartel that accounts for 80 percent of world sales of uncut diamonds. De Beers always sells mixed boxes of diamonds, which include both better and poorer stones, and refusal to accept these would probably cause De Beers not to deal with a buyer again. Clear acceptance of an invitation to purchase from De Beers carries the implication that the buyer will receive mixed stones. These are well-known standard terms, and a buyer could not turn around and demand a refund of the purchase price because of the mix received. Standard terms imply that transaction costs will be saved, because there can be less discussion at the time of forming the contract.

Courts encourage business efficiency by recognizing standard terms as a basis for acceptance. In *Allied Van Lines v. Bratton*, an interstate carrier enforced a limitation of insurance liability as a standard practice in the industry and within its company. It was not relevant that the shipper of household effects, Bratton, had not read the limitations on her bill of lading. The judge held that the court (in Florida) had long ago put to rest the issue of carrier liability in relation to industry practice. Had Bratton been deliberately misled over the availability of alternative insurance, or forcibly prevented from checking the small print, the contract would not have been enforced. Equally, companies cannot avoid well-understood standard practices. In *Agricultural Insurance Co. v. Constantine*, a parking lot was prevented from limiting its liability for the theft of a car. It could not claim that small print on its parking tickets exonerated liability, because the ticket was, by standard practice, a "mere token for identification" with no indication that the owner of the automobile consented to restriction of normal legal liability.

Standardization should help to produce efficient decisions. Shippers are on notice to insure particularly valuable items separately because of known limitations of carrier liability. Parking lots are on notice to watch for thieves due to liability if cars are stolen. A caution is in order as the courts have a difficult job in distinguishing between standardization that enhances efficiency and contracts of adhesion, where firms with few or no competitors present customers with "take it or leave it" standard contracts that are aimed at extracting the maximum benefit for the monopolist. The courts need to examine industry practices very carefully for evidence of cost savings compared with restrictive practices.

Courts determine objectively whether offer and acceptance has occurred based on the factual evidence. It is not relevant whether a seller misunderstood the buyer's acceptance or did not wish to make the offer. It is necessary that the buyer genuinely believe that the offer represents the seller's intentions and accepts the seller's terms, which was held to be the case in *Allied Van Lines*. The courts have moved away from what was in theory an older subjective approach of trying to decide whether there was a meeting of minds, which is a much harder thing to assess. This move reflects an intention to keep assessment costs within reasonable bounds. Traders are put on notice to incur the lower costs of ensuring clarity in their dealings.

Consideration

A traditional doctrine of common law is that the promisor must receive something valuable in exchange from the promisee for a contract to be formed. This consideration is typically money, but could equally well be a service, goods, or another promise. Promises lacking consideration are traditionally treated as unenforceable, and consideration has been treated quite narrowly. On this doctrine, the generous promise to donate a new library to your local university on winning the state lottery is unenforceable, as no consideration is present.

There are some persuasive economic arguments in favor of the doctrine of consideration. It reduces the number of inadvertent contracts that might be caused by careless language. Court costs are saved because trivial promises are not enforced and because courts do not have to fill in missing details for vague ones. Finally, opportunistic behavior may be prevented as a result of the requirement. The way in which consideration affects opportunistic behavior is examined in the boxed example of a contract for sailing a ship.

Alaska Packers v. Domenico (1902)

Consideration may be investigated in relation to opportunistic behavior with reference to *Alaska Packers v. Domenico*. The defendant hired a group of seamen in San Francisco to fish in Alaska. When they arrived, the men demanded more money before continuing with the voyage. The defendant had incurred unrecoverable costs in setting up the voyage (known as *sunk costs* in economics and as *detrimental reliance* in law) and was unwilling to see the voyage end unproductively. Therefore, he agreed to the demands, but—upon return to San Francisco—refused to make the extra payments. The court excused him from his promise on the grounds that the modification to the original contract was not supported by fresh consideration.

Any protection from opportunism may, in fact, be slight in *Alaska Packers*. If the seamen had chosen to add fresh consideration, they would have succeeded in enforcing the change. They could have contracted to sail for an extra day (or even for an extra hour), for example. It may be that consideration protects from postcontract opportunistic renegotiation only to the extent that individuals practicing such hold-up tactics are ignorant of the law.

Such possible opportunism was in fact a major issue in maritime matters and is often analyzed in terms of duress in legal studies, that is, one of the parties exerting coercive physical or economic pressure so as to obtain better terms. Some older maritime cases show the court's worries about coercion rather well, such as *Harris v. Watson* (1791), where the judge concluded that to enforce such modified contracts would cause sailors to threaten to sink a ship unless the captain acceded to demands. In later cases the emphasis shifted to the doctrine of *preexisting duty*, which states that it is not possible to make an additional payment for an existing contractual duty. The requirement for fresh consideration effectively rules out simple contract modifications once a contract is entered into, however much the parties wish to make them, which is of great interest from an economic point of view in relation to problems of opportunistic behavior.

Recent Developments Concerning Consideration. There has been a recent trend for courts to move away from the preexisting duty rule and toward enforcing mutually agreed contract modifications. The requirement for fresh consideration is much eroded, not least because UCC §2-209 does not require fresh consideration for a binding modification to a sales contract. There have also been moves in case law toward enforcing mutually desired contract modifications. In *Brian Construction & Development v. Brighenti* (1978), a contractor in Connecticut was allowed to enforce a contract modification entered into upon encountering unforeseen excavation work. The court used the doctrine of unforeseen circumstances to make an exception to the preexisting duty rule. There have been moves in this direction in other common-law jurisdictions, such as the very similar construction case of *Williams v. Roffey* (1991) in England. In this section, we consider whether the move to enforceable contract modifications is efficient.

Allowing contract modifications when they reflect genuinely changed circumstances is an intuitively appealing argument. According to such a view, courts should not enforce modifications if they reflect opportunistic renegotiation by one party. By implication, we should regard modern developments away from the doctrine of preexisting duty as an efficient change in the law. This type of argument can be formulated as a proposal to enforce contract modifications that are not unconscionable and that do not arise from duress.

Opportunism can arise because of a difference between (*ex-ante*) incentives when the parties enter a contract and (*ex-post*) incentives once the contract begins to roll. Ex-ante, the contract must show a normal return on all costs, as no investment is sunk and irrecoverable at that time. However, ex-post, it is only necessary that a normal return be earned on avoidable costs as earlier expenditures may have become sunk costs, or bygones no longer relevant to decision making. By playing on the distinction between ex-ante and ex-post incentives, a contracting partner might be able to practice "post-contract opportunism" and obtain a favorable revision of the contract.

Opportunistic renegotiation is aimed at extracting all or part of the value of contract-specific assets that reflect a sunk cost. Specific investment cannot be moved to another use. Therefore, ex-post an investor is entirely dependent on the honesty of a trading partner or on court enforcement of the original contract to recoup the value of the contract-specific investment. Such detrimental reliance in expectation of contract returns is a normal part of many business contracts.

An example helps to distinguish between opportunistic renegotiation by the promisor and renegotiation aimed at correcting a genuine mistake. A firm supplies components to a manufacturer of toys over a period of one year for $50,000, which is an avoidable cost for the manufacturer. There is no alternative supplier. At the start of the contract, the toy manufacturer must also spend $50,000 on specialized machinery, which has no alternative use, to assemble the parts. The manufacturer expects to sell the toys for $105,000 at the end of the year, which gives a return on the contract of 5 percent. Therefore:

$$(\text{Sunk Investment} + \text{Avoidable Investment}) \times (1 + \text{Rate of Return}) = \text{Contract Value}$$

$$(50,000 + 50,000)1.05 = 105,000$$

We assume that 5 percent is the normal profit required before anyone in business would be willing to invest.

The component supplier could adopt the following hold-up strategy: "Let the manufacturer make the $50,000 specific investment (the specialized machinery) and then immediately renegotiate to increase the cost of components to $100,000." This gives the manufacturer the normal 5 percent return, but only on the (now more expensive) avoidable investment. The supplier might claim that costs are higher than expected and that the price must rise or he must abandon the contract. Providing this threat is credible and given that the components cannot be purchased elsewhere, the manufacturer is better off accepting the revision, as shown in Table 4.1

TABLE 4.1	Contractual Revision			
	INVESTMENT		REVENUE	LOSS
	Sunk	Avoidable		
Accepts Revision	$50,000	$100,000	$105,000	−$45,000
Refuses Revision	$50,000	$0	$0	−$50,000

If the toy manufacturer knew for certain, in advance, that the supplier would behave opportunistically, it would not enter the contract. We know that the contract is of economic value because it yields the normal return to the manufacturer (and generates profits for the supplier). Opportunism discourages otherwise efficient contracts and is a serious matter going beyond distributional issues. If courts routinely resist postcontract opportunism by enforcing the original contract, the manufacturer will be reassured and would be more likely to enter into the contract. If they did not so enforce the original contract, ex-ante, businesses would be much more cautious in entering into trading relationships and economic activity could be destabilized.

The logic is different if the supplier made a genuine mistake in initially pricing the contract. Suppose $100,000 is really needed for the components and that the supplier will fail if this is not forthcoming. It might then be argued that the only relevant question is how to minimize the costs of breaching the original contract. This could be achieved in the example by permitting the revision, which gives losses of $45,000 to the manufacturer and no losses to the supplier. Abandoning the contract is worse because losses are $50,000 for the manufacturer. On this line of reasoning, the courts need methods to help them distinguish genuinely required revision from the opportunistic kind. If they are capable of making the distinction, then they should apparently enforce modifications correcting genuine mistakes.

However, the difficulties in distinguishing between genuine and opportunistic revisions of contracts are likely to be severe. First, we require a clear guide for courts as to what constitutes opportunistic behavior, which is difficult to provide. Second, enforcing apparently genuinely required modifications ignores the insurance aspect of contracts. A fixed-price contract is usually precisely intended to insure the buyer against increases in costs. There is a danger that a contractor might win a contract by pricing too low, believing that it will be possible to pass risks back to the buyer later through an enforceable contract modification (a problem known as *underbidding*).

A rule of enforceable modifications, as implied by Article 2 of the UCC (sales contracts), may encourage opportunistic underbidding by promisors, or at least gives the courts a difficult task in distinguishing opportunistic from genuine requests for revision. The transacting costs of promisees are then increased as they must devise means of protecting themselves. For example, the toy maker in Table 4.1 might insist on renting the specialized equipment from the component supplier. Opportunistic underbidding is a problem in specialized markets. The component manufacturer would be unable to raise the price of components to the toy maker, if the toy maker could simply turn to another component supplier in a competitive market. Unfortunately, specialized markets are a key feature of modern industrial life.

Efficient Contract Modifications.   Generally, it is not possible to find economic arguments to support enforceable modifications. However, three special cases are exceptions. The first occurs if the superior risk bearer cannot be identified at the start of the contract. In that case, the parties did not include insurance as part of the contract. Second, the risk may have been too small to worry about. In both of these cases, enforcing contract modifications cannot encourage opportunistic risk shifting on the part of promisors, and courts can safely allow the parties to adapt to unforeseen or trivial risks.

There is a third case in which it is safe to enforce contract modifications. This is where it was not feasible for the promisor to bear the risks. One indicator of this inability would be if the promisor obviously lacked the financial resources to cover the risks of cost increases, including the possibility of purchasing separate insurance, which is often true in cases that come before the courts. Recall that in *Brian Construction & Development v. Brighenti* (1978) the contractor was allowed to enforce a contract modification entered into upon encountering unforeseen excavation work. The court used the doctrine of unforeseen circumstances to make an exception to the preexisting duty rule. The exception appears to have been a way of recognizing that the promisee could not possibly have been buying insurance. Providing the contractor in *Brian Construction* was incapable of providing the insurance, it did no harm to enforce an agreed contract modification.

A lack of financial resources often characterizes cases in which small businesses cannot carry out tasks for which they are subcontracted in the construction industry. It is noticeable that cases coming before the courts often relate to construction work. The enforcement of modifications does not amount to discharge of the original contract if it clearly was the case that no insurance was provided. Rather, the contractor negotiated additional consideration for dealing with an unforeseen problem once it materialized. It must be emphasized that an *obvious* inability to provide insurance it is a very special case. Generally, it will be difficult for courts to distinguish opportunistic motivated from genuinely required contract revision.

GIFTS AND OTHER GRATUITOUS PROMISES

Modern courts will often enforce promises of gifts by taking a creative view of what may comprise consideration. Judges will look for signs that a promisee relied on the promise and incurred costs, and may assert that the promisor benefited from giving the promise. Thus, an individual who gives up a job following the promise of a better one could have a case for breach of contract. So would a person who had carried out unpaid work in anticipation of a promised legacy. Even though no consideration is involved in a narrow sense, the courts have for some years treated the sacrifice of the original job or carrying out unpaid work (forms of detrimental reliance) as amounting to consideration. The court may prevent a person from reneging on a promise upon which the promisee has reasonably relied and may complete the gift or the implied contract.

In *Shadwell v. Shadwell* (1862), an uncle promised his nephew a yearly income following the announcement of the young man's wedding. Executors of the older man's estate refused payment. The nephew successfully sued and reference was made in the judgment to his having relied on the promise in incurring expenses, which were viewed as a detriment to him. Also, the knowledge that the younger man was to become settled was viewed as a benefit to the uncle. It is inefficient to allow promisees to incur costs following an unenforceable promise, as this could easily lead to losses from trade, which suggests enforcing well-evidenced gratuitous promises. In *Hamer v. Sidway* (1891), an uncle promised his nephew $5,000 if the nephew would refrain from smoking, drinking alcohol, and gambling until he reached the age of 21. The nephew did this, but the uncle died and the executor of his will refused to honor the promise. The nephew successfully sued for the money: The nephew had forgone opportunities and the uncle could be assumed to have benefited from the behavioral change.

The economists' view that there is a rational basis to law is well supported by the observation that promises are not enforced when they do not change a person's behavior. In *Denney v. Reppert* (1968), employees of the First State Bank in Kentucky were not allowed to recover a reward for help in convicting bank robbers. Three armed men raided their branch in 1963, and the bank workers were particularly vigilant in helping the police to apprehend the villains. The court of appeals in Kentucky cited a version of the rule of preexisting duty to deny them shares of a reward advertised by the Kentucky Bankers' Association. The reasoning was simply that they already owed the duty of helping as part of their normal duties as bank employees.

There is a result similar to *Denney* in the Australian case, *R. v. Clarke* (1927), where the defendant informed upon the murderers of two policemen to escape from an unfounded charge that he committed the murders. Before informing, Clarke had seen a notice from the Government of Western Australia advertising a reward for the information, but had forgotten it. He was not allowed to claim the reward because his information was given to escape prosecution and not as consideration for the money. This is totally efficient, as there was indeed no need to create the additional incentive under the circumstances. Failing to give the reward to Clarke would not deter other informers.

There are increasingly more instances of enforceable gratuitous promises. The long list of situations where modern courts will enforce these promises has put the common law close to a situation where it may be assumed that enforcement will routinely follow. It may be argued that enforcement is efficient because gift promises are presumptively beneficial to the promisor at the time the promise is made. It may be that early law reflected a misplaced paternalism that failed to recognize benefits to the promisor from being able to make enforceable promises.

Moving away from issues of contractual revision, it would seem absurd not to enforce a simple promise when the courts can easily judge that both parties would have wished for enforcement at the time it was made. Even if a simple promise was made without consideration, it might be to the benefit of both businesses if a promise by *A* of certain business terms were enforceable by *B*. The most obvious case fitting this bill is the firm offer, which is a useful business device. It encourages the buyer to devote resources to considering an offer seriously and enables the seller to signal terms clearly.

A firm offer is enforceable in American courts following the UCC §2-205, providing it is in writing. The position is not always as clear in other common-law jurisdictions, but one must not rush to condemn the practice of failing to enforce firm offers. In other common-law jurisdictions such as England, a firm offer is no different from any other gratuitous promise but can always be turned into an enforceable option contract by charging for the right to hold the offer (selling an option to buy, possibly for a token price). Option contracts are a key feature of many markets, particularly financial ones, and have all the efficiency advantages of enforceable firm offers. The difference may be a case of the law achieving the same objective through slightly different approaches.

UNILATERAL CONTRACTS

The examples given earlier are all of bilateral contracting, in which buyers and sellers are in direct contact with each other. As long as the terms of a contract are clear and apply to anyone who accepts them, unilateral contracts are also possible. In the famous case of *Carlill v. Carbolic Smoke Ball Co.* (1893), the defendant had advertised a smoke ball as a preventative against influenza and had promised to pay approximately $400 compensation to anyone catching influenza after buying and using it. The plaintiff had complied with all terms and had still caught influenza. She successfully obtained an award of the $400 (worth over $50,000 in today's money). The company sought to be excused from its promise to pay on the basis that the offer was mere "advertising puff." The court enforced the contract on the basis that an offer had been made to the whole world and that Mrs Carlill's *behavior* in buying and lighting the smoke ball indicated her clear acceptance.

From an economic perspective, enforcing this type of contract has advantages. Firms may often wish to signal the reliability of their products by advertising compensation schemes that apply if things go wrong. These signals would become impossible to use to any effect if it were known that such offers were unenforceable and could not be taken seriously. Once again, there is an important principle here: Contracts are used to insure against adverse events, and this insurance use tends to imply that firm enforcement is desirable. Unstable contracts would be of much less value to people who would otherwise use them.

Unilateral contracts often crop up in curious guises. In *Davis v. Jacoby* (1934), the Supreme Court of California enforced a promise to bequeath money and property. An elderly couple had encouraged a younger couple to move from Canada to take care of them, promising that the will would favor them. This turned out to be untrue. The court adopted the argument that a unilateral offer may be accepted by performing the conditions of the offer. Like *Carlill*, this enforceability is useful. In inheritance cases, it means people can credibly commit themselves to compensate caregivers who may make considerable sacrifices. Performance as acceptance also means that modest price or quality changes for regular supplies, such as natural gas to a firm, need only be notified "on the hoof," with continued use of the supplies acting as acceptance to avoid the need to rewrite contracts.

HARD BARGAINS AND UNCONSCIONABILITY

The law has often enforced a wide range of hard bargains, preferring not to inquire into the adequacy of consideration. The traditional outlook reflects a nineteenth-century approach that is still valid in principle, but has given way in practice as U.S. courts have increasingly interfered with individual choice. Often, interference and setting aside of contracts occurs because judges deem them to be unconscionable, that is, consider them to be unfair owing to perceived bargaining inequalities between the parties. Indeed, some observers consider erosion of the enforcement of private bargains as heralding the death of contract. It is worth remembering that unconscionability is not the traditional doctrine in relation to hard bargains and has not taken root to anything like the same extent outside of the United States.

Disputes over contracts in show business are very common. This is because artists are subject to large, unpredictable changes in their market value, and the stakes can be high. The contracts often come to be seen as hard bargains by the artists. The boxed example refers to one high-profile case.

The Development of the Unconscionability Doctrine

In the United States, the unconscionability doctrine is well grounded but remains controversial. As long ago as 1889, the U.S. Supreme Court in *Hume v. United States* defined as unconscionable "a contract which no man in his senses, not under delusion, would make, on the one hand, and which no fair and honest man would accept on the other . . . ." The court considered such contracts to be based on "fraud, accident, mistake, folly, or ignorance" and to be void at common law, as "against the public policy of honesty, fair dealing, and good morals."

Hard Bargains in the World of Entertainment

In *Georgios Panayiotou v. Sony* (1994), the pop singer George Michael (under his real name) failed in an attempt to have his contract with his record company, Sony, declared void. The singer claimed the contract to be one-sided and a restraint of trade. His particular concern was with the persistence of royalty rates for him of approximately 50 cents per recording on compact discs, even though the rate had been agreed originally for lower-valued vinyl discs. The court in England (where he had signed his contract), taking a traditional view of hard bargains, required George Michael to stick by his original promises or renegotiate terms. In fact, he subsequently renegotiated terms with Sony.

Critics of the unconscionability doctrine would regard the judgment in George Michael's case as efficient. Historically though, not all cases of this type have resulted in firm enforcement of the original terms, not even in traditionally inclined England. In considering earlier entertainment cases that were not firmly enforced, such as *Schroeder v. Macaulay* (1974), critics tended to point to the discouragement given to record companies to gamble on encouraging unknown artists and songwriters. Promotional expenditure on a range of new artists can easily become irretrievable if contracts become insecure with the few artists who manage to become famous. An unintended consequence of setting aside one-sided, unconscionable contracts for stars is that new songwriters might find they must pay to publish their early songs.

Unconscionability is one of the grounds for declaring a contract void in UCC §2-302. It requires (a) conditions to be *grossly* unfairly weighted against one party, and (b) there to be no evidence that the weighting was deliberately selected as a desired allocation of risk by the parties. The court may find evidence of procedural unconscionability, where the bargaining process—although falling short of violating case law or statutory rules covering duress or fraud—is shown to be shady. There may also be evidence of substantive unconscionability, where the basis of the argument is usually a substantial difference between the contract price and the market price.

Early concern over unconscionability originated with add-on clauses used in hire–purchase agreements (agreements for purchase through installments) commonly used between stores and poor people. Add-on clauses allowed the lender to retain the collateral on an older loan when issuing a new loan. This practice could result in defaulting borrowers losing more than the value of the new goods on hire purchase, because they could lose other goods that were substantially paid for but had been required by the lender as additional security for the loan. This form of unconscionability is substantive in relation to the collateral required rather than the price of the goods.

In *Williams v. Walker-Thomas Furniture Co.* (1965), the plaintiff obtained a ruling that an add-on making all previous furniture purchases (worth $1,800) collateral for a new sale (a stereo worth $515) was illegal. The court argued that poor people were unlikely to understand such a clause and that it worked a particular hardship. However, an efficiency consequence of the unconscionability doctrine could be that the poor could find it harder to get credit (and might pay higher interest) if they have a high risk of default. The add-on clause may be a low-cost way of widening collateral to reassure lenders given the high probability of default.

The unconscionability doctrine now covers wider issues than add-ons. A case illustrating its wider application and bringing in procedural unconscionability is *Graham v. Scissor-Tail* (1981), in which a musician was able to withdraw from the last two of a series of four concerts. Scissor-Tail, a music promotion agency, wanted to offset its losses from an earlier concert against profits on later ones before paying Graham, in accordance with a standard contract they had used. The contract also gave details of an arbitration procedure, which Graham lost. The court allowed Graham to rescind on the grounds that it considered the arbitration procedure to be inadequate and therefore to be procedurally unconscionable. The issues here are similar to the ones considered in relation to the George Michael case; there is a risk that judgments like the one in *Graham* will make it harder for new performers to obtain performing contracts. In George Michael's case, the contract was enforced and that decision did not threaten contract stability.

Most commentators point to the adverse implications of the unconscionability doctrine. The arguments tend to focus on the loss of benefits from freely entered transactions. If courts nullify contracts they consider to be one-sided, the principle of encouraging market transactions rather than legal surrogates wherever there are low trading costs is compromised. Many authors have argued strongly that courts should enforce all contracts that do not generate negative externalities. The presence of significant externalities, that is, large spillover effects, would allow the argument that the contracting parties had ignored welfare effects on others, where these outweighed the benefits they expected from the contract.

Special Cases of Efficient Unconscionability

In special circumstances, the unconscionability doctrine may not be inefficient as has been suggested so far. The special cases where it could make sense to set aside hard bargains are mostly based on the impossibility of one contracting partner having been fully aware of the implications of actions. It may also be the case that the unconscionability doctrine favors the interests of subgroups in society, in particular serving the interests of taxpayers.

The efficient special cases that have been suggested are best considered first. A party might be transactionally incapable and this would make enforcement of the associated contract unconscionable. This case is distinct from incapacity, which is a standard excuse for breach of contract, where the party is a minor or is infirm. In transactional incapacity, an intelligent person is confused by a particular transaction, such as when a contract is written in particularly complex terms. Nullifying such contracts puts those drafting legal documents on notice to use simple language, which will reduce transaction costs and could increase efficiency. An obvious criticism here is that an intelligent person could pay a specialist to interpret documents.

It could also be efficient to nullify contracts where the buyer, out of ignorance, has paid a price much greater than the normal market rate, which could be regarded as substantively unconscionable. Such purchases could not happen in a perfectly competitive market, where information is readily available and prices are uniform. This is effectively an argument against enforcing contracts associated with imperfectly competitive conditions and is open to criticism on several grounds. First, the argument suggests nullifying all contracts in the imperfectly competitive industry, not just the one before the court, which would lower social welfare if all other buyers were happy with their terms of purchase. Also, there could be an undesirable reduction of the incentive for buyers to search carefully for the best prices. If these search costs are

lower than the costs of using the court system to assess the reasonableness of contracts, it is best to enforce the "unfair" contract along traditional lines.

It may also be efficient to refuse to enforce contracts where the buyer has been subjected to heavy persuasion. There is often suspicion that some companies exert high-
pressure sales techniques over products like time-share vacation properties. If someone's
willingness to buy was a temporary phenomenon, we cannot be sure that there are gains
from trade from the transaction. However, courts would need to distinguish between
buyers who were merely fickle and those on whom high-pressure tactics had been used.
In some jurisdictions, a cooling-off period is specified for contracts signed in the home,
consistent with regarding heavy persuasion as unconscionable. During the cooling-off
period, of perhaps several days, the buyer is free to declare the contract void.

Economic analysis does not generally support the unconscionability doctrine. If
one takes the view that voluntary exchange only occurs when there are gains from
trade, there is no basis for overturning contracts at some later date. It is possible to
argue (paternalistically) that weaker members of society may ignorantly enter into
contracts that do not then have the characteristics of fully informed voluntary trade,
or that they may become impoverished, and that these contracts might be struck
down by the courts. However, the law does not generally seek to protect people from
unwise bargains, and moving in that direction raises many problems. How do we
know where to draw the line over the protection?

Interest-Group Approaches to Unconscionability

It is difficult to justify the unconscionability doctrine from the point of view of general economic efficiency, but it may be easier to explain how the doctrine has come to
influence the courts. Recent research notes that restrictions on freedom of contract
counteract distortions of the incentive to bear risk that result from the activities of the
modern state in providing minimum welfare levels for its citizens. In particular, this
line of inquiry addresses use of the unconscionability doctrine when courts strike
down contracts that were apparently entered into voluntarily and that do not involve
price disparities or procedural imbalances.

Williams v. Walker Thomas did not involve procedural or substantive unconscionability (the value of the collateral was unconscionable, not the price of the stereo).
Cases like this invariably reveal a poor person (usually a welfare claimant) defaulting on
a credit agreement. We have already noted that voiding contracts like *Williams* will
reduce the availability of credit to the poor. This may be precisely the result required
by the welfare state if the availability of welfare benefits is not to create a major problem
of moral hazard. There is a danger that people might become careless about borrowing
money because any impoverishment that arises from a combination of indebtedness and
unwise expenditure would be partly relieved by welfare benefits. There is a risk that poor
people will then become even poorer and need even more support unless the supply of
credit is restricted. Restrictions on freedom of contract such as the unconscionability
doctrine make lending less attractive to lenders and could control this possible extension
of the liabilities of the state.

This private-interest approach to unconscionability is a useful line of inquiry,
although still in its early stages. Much remains to be explained: in particular, how the
courts have come to oblige the modern state in this way. The general argument is
intriguing: If we accept that the unconscionability doctrine is generally inefficient,
then we need to explain how the inefficiency persists.

LONG-TERM, RELATIONAL CONTRACTS

The existence of long-term contracts has radically altered the way in which businesses and the courts view contractual relationships. Legal scholars and courts have become more aware of the industrial context within which contracts operate. Adjustments to changing economic conditions may often occur without explicit reference to the written terms of an agreement and may be based more on the long-run value to the parties of maintaining their business relationship. It has become normal to distinguish three forms of contract: classical, neoclassical, and relational contracts.

Classical forms of contract have evolved over time, through an intermediate neoclassical stage to a relational stage that reflects much more than just the original terms. The study of relational contracting develops observations made by lawyers and economists on the *incomplete* nature of contracts. It is impossible in all but the simplest (classical) cases to specify all contingencies in a formal agreement. Many aspects of a relationship will need to be sorted out as events unfold. Indeed, this is precisely how courts often come to be involved in contracts. As contracts became more complex following economic development in the twentieth century, they inevitably became more prone to containing gaps. In turn, courts became increasingly involved in intervening in them as a form of third-party governance used to fill gaps—reflecting the intermediate stage known as *neoclassical contracting*.

If a contractual relationship reaches a high level of complexity, perhaps involving a very long association and frequent interaction between parties, even neoclassical governance may prove inadequate. The parties then have an incentive to set up their own private governance system, perhaps using specialist arbitrators to settle disputes. Arbitration is very common in franchise, procurement, and engineering contracts. Relational contracting relies predominantly on the value of the long-term economic association for governance of the parties. Interestingly, the practices of relational contracting often show up well in activities like organized crime, where the participants cannot rely on the legal system.

In relational contracting, the emphasis is on overcoming short-term problems to preserve a valuable continuing relationship. An implication is that courts should look at the whole relationship as it has evolved over time rather than just the original agreement, if they become involved in the governance of a long-term contract. This rather sociological view of contract contrasts strongly with the traditional view that, since the parties chose the original terms of an agreement to condition subsequent renegotiations, the courts should enforce terms that are subject to foreseeable information flows.

The material in this section does not imply that the study of classical contracting rules, from an economic or indeed any perspective, has somehow lost its relevance. The classical rules, with their piecemeal amendments, represent a starting point in studying contracts. There are still many short-term contracts, in which repeat business is not an issue and the identity of parties is largely irrelevant. However, the idea of relational contracting alerts us to the fact that long-term contracts are different and raise many additional issues. There is empirical evidence that businesses do not resort to the law to nearly the extent that might be expected when contracts begin to fail.

Trust in Relational Contracts

Some of the complex issues surrounding relational contracts may be understood with the aid of a little game theory. Relational contractors may be thought of as being bound together in a sequence of moves in a game that offers returns from cooperation. At any time they might stop trusting each other and lose the gains from trade. Table 4.2 illustrates the benefits from one such game. Party A decides whether to trust B, who in turn decides whether to respect or abuse A's trust. Neither party knows what the other has chosen but does know the pattern of benefits shown in Table 4.2. The payoffs reflect money gains, showing the greatest individual benefit if A is trusting and some benefit to B from abusing A's trust.

If the game in Table 4.2 were played just once, trust would never emerge. Abusing A's trust is a dominant strategy that makes B better off if A is trusting ($30 > 20$) and at least as well off if A is distrusting (0 either way). Given this prediction, A would distrust B, which gives a payoff of 0 to A rather than -10. Both of them end up in the bottom-right cell with a zero payoff.

Trust can emerge if the game in Table 4.2 is repeated. Individual A needs a mechanism to punish abuse of trust by B. Using a carrot-and-stick approach, A could punish B at least long enough to wipe out any opportunistic gains B made (for example, by not cooperating for two rounds, A deprives B of a possible 40 payoff). For a strategy based on punishment to work, it is important that the number of repetitions of the game not be known with certainty, or punishment is not a credible threat in the endgame. If they know there is no credible threat in the last period, then the immediately preceding period also becomes unstable and, by backward induction, so will all others.

Transactions-Cost Analysis

The new institutional economics places a great deal of emphasis on problems of trust in relational contracting. The focus is normally on the manner in which the costs of contracting may be influenced by the need to protect contracts from opportunistic behavior. An organization, such as the business firm, is a nexus of contractual relationships between owners, workers, and customers. Organizations develop to minimize the costs of transacting, assuming for simplicity that production costs and revenues are similar across different organizational arrangements. The formation of organizations based on long-term, relational contracts takes place in an environment characterized by uncertainty. Transactions-cost analysis draws attention to three further phenomena that must be present before significant contracting problems can arise. These are bounded rationality, opportunism, and asset specificity. If any one of these three were removed, contractual problems disappear.

TABLE 4.2	Trust in a Relational Contract	
	B	
	Respect A's Trust	**Abuse A's Trust**
Trust B	20, 20	−10, 30
Distrust B	0, 0	0, 0

(Payoffs: A, B)

People suffer from bounded rationality when there are limits on either the information at their disposal or on their capacity to process it. Bounded rationality implies that contracting will be incomplete. Opportunism has already been discussed in this book but may now be defined precisely as the propensity that people have to pursue self-interest with guile, or cunning. Asset specificity has also already been encountered and refers to investment that cannot be moved to alternative uses, reflecting sunk costs. As we already know, asset specificity makes individuals vulnerable to hold-up strategies. Bounded rationality makes it difficult to deter opportunism over sunk costs.

Without bounded rationality, contracting is simple because parties have full information and are able to write fully contingent contracts. Opportunism does not matter because the contracts can be written to ensure that it always pays for a party to behave honestly. Similarly, a cleverly written contract would ensure that nobody would want to take advantage of asset specificity. The world without bounded rationality would be the one beloved of high theorists in economics: self-enforcing contract mechanisms would govern behavior.

If we assume there is no asset specificity, it does not matter that people are opportunistic, or that they are boundedly rational. No party is locked into a contract, and, if someone begins to cheat, it is easy to find an alternative trading partner. This would be a world of competition. Interesting contracting questions only arise, therefore, in small-numbers bargaining situations that are not associated with competitive industries.

Taking away opportunism means that parties can simply agree to adapt to all contingencies in a jointly profit-maximizing fashion when required. It is then easy to cope with bounded rationality and asset specificity in a world of promise.

The world is characterized by complex transactions and by bounded rationality, opportunism, and asset specificity. Modern transactions-cost analysis emphasizes the need to protect specific assets from opportunism while economizing on bounded rationality. The focus is very much on the costs of controlling hold-up problems, as these are seen as the main driving force in creating transaction costs. Contracts will consequently reflect the need to protect parties from the risk of holdup.

Hostages in Contracts

The economic equivalents of hostages are widely used to effect credible commitments in long-term contracts. The simplest example of a hostage arises when a firm undertakes to pay a penalty (liquidated damages) if it fails to complete work on time. The penalty reassures a buyer that money would be available to offset disruption costs if the contractor failed to deliver on its promise. Without the penalty, the contractor might be tempted to try to increase contract charges, claiming costs had risen, knowing that the buyer faced the disruption of either finding another contractor or enforcing the original contract in the courts. Hostages can be more implicit than in the example just considered; for example, one party may be reassured over making a highly specific investment just by knowing that the other party is also incurring sunk costs. Hostages lower the costs of contracting by reassuring parties that contractual performance is more likely.

It is possible to state some rules as to what makes a good hostage. Principally, the hostage should be of no direct value to the hostage taker, who might otherwise be tempted simply to abscond with the hostage. In practical terms, a business is best advised to offer in-kind (implicit) hostages, which are less vulnerable to opportunistic appropriation by trading partners compared with monetary bonds.

Franchise contracts, such as those used by McDonald's or by automobile retailers, often show developed use of hostage arrangements. Franchising increases the specificity of investment for the satellite business, compared with independent operation. As an example, improvements to the trading premises are trademarked and therefore difficult to adapt to other uses. Also, there are lump-sum fees paid to the franchiser, and other contract-specific expenditures are incurred upon starting the franchise. These expenditures are incurred in anticipation of staying with the business for a period of time and will signal to a franchiser that there is no intention to just learn the ropes and then set up business on one's own. At the same time, most of the expenditure of the franchisee is of no direct benefit to the franchiser, who should not be tempted to abscond with early-paid fees.

There is a danger that courts will be inhospitable to the type of arrangements seen in franchise contracts, interpreting them as unconscionable on the grounds that small businesses are offered standard contracts on a take-it-or-leave-it basis by more established franchisers. It is important to recognize the efficiency role of some apparently unfair contract terms that seem to be one-sided in signaling commitment.

Summary and Conclusions

In this chapter, we have examined a series of issues concerning the nature of contracts. Beginning with the traditional bargain approach to understanding contract formation, we examined the requirements for enforcing promises in terms of offer, acceptance, and consideration. We then quickly saw that contract law has evolved, with the courts becoming more interventionist over time. Furthermore, intervention—for example, over hard bargains—has strong economic implications. We also examined the economics of long-term contracts, particularly in terms of transactions-cost analysis, which is useful in examining a wide variety of organizational and contractual questions.

Questions for Review

1. On November 21, 2000, the *Washington Times* reported the case of 18-year-old Grammy Award–winning singer, LeAnn Rimes, who filed a federal lawsuit seeking to void a contract with Curb Records, Inc., of Nashville, TN. The contract had been entered into under the guardianship of her parents some years previously. She regarded the terms as unfavorable to her relative to the record company, because her career had blossomed since her first big hit in 1996. State courts had enforced the contract. What are the consequences of enforcing such a contract?

2. Does the traditional requirement for fresh consideration for enforceable contract modifications make economic sense?

3. An oil company has received promises of low land rents and low taxes for 10 years, if it will develop a refinery in a newly established country. The country has a poor record regarding observance of the rule of law. What advice would you give to the oil company's executives, based on the theory of long-term contracts?

4. Road construction companies often deposit monetary bonds against their possible failure to complete a road improvement on time. Does money make a good hostage in this case? Does it make a good hostage in general?

5.   Examine the extent to which there is any economic logic behind the unconscionability doctrine.

NOTES ON THE LITERATURE

- Trebilcock (1993) gives an excellent assessment of the welfare properties of freedom of contract. Another important strand in the literature, associated with the "new institutional economics" (Williamson, 1985, 2000) examines long-term contracts that often have self-enforcement characteristics.

- An excellent detailed account of contractual practices in diamond trading is in Bernstein (1992).

- The general arguments on consideration are drawn from Kull (1992), Posner (1977), and Halson (1991). The special cases where contract modifications appear to be safely supportable are discussed in Aivazian, Trebilcock, and Penny (1984) and Dnes (1995). Miceli (2002) suggests that limiting the value of enforceable modifications to the cost of the adjustment would remove incentives for opportunism.

- Gilmore (1986) regards modern developments in the courts as so extensively undermining contract enforceability that he has written of the death of contract. Recent work has come to the defense of contract, claiming that reports of its death are greatly exaggerated. See the essays collected in Buckley (1999).

- Trebilcock and Dewees (1981) give a good statement of the argument that setting aside contracts as unconscionable may harm the very people regarded as in need of protection, as established businesses could refuse to trade with them. If courts nullify contracts they consider one-sided, the principle of encouraging market transactions rather than legal surrogates wherever there are low trading costs is undermined. The authors most associated with the argument that courts should enforce all contracts that do not generate negative externalities are Epstein (1975), Schwartz (1977), Posner (2002), and Trebilcock (1993, pp. 97–101). Eisenberg (1982) has made the strongest claim that there may be efficiency grounds for the unconscionability doctrine. Eisenberg's findings form the basis of the special cases in the text. The interest-group approach to unconscionability is from Eric Posner (1995), whose argument also extends to such things as ceilings on interest rates.

- Kull (1992) has argued that there are few modern instances of unenforceable gratuitous promises. He considers a long list of situations where modern courts will enforce these promises.

- Macneil (1974; 1978) argues that classical contract has evolved through a neoclassical stage to a relational stage but recognizes that the definition of relational contracts is not very precise. Schwartz (1992, p. 317) put forward the contrary view discussed in the text, arguing against the irrelevance of courts in long-term contracts.

- Organized crime is well documented by Gambetta (1993; 2000).

- The game-theoretic example in Table 4.2 uses an iterated-dominant strategy equilibrium (a trial-and-error solution). See the references in Hviid (2000) for more on the game-theoretic approach to relational contracts.

- Williamson (1985; 1993; 2000) recognizes Macneil's work on relational contracting as a major influence on his development of transactions-cost analysis. Williamson follows Coase (1937) in arguing that organizations develop to minimize the costs of transacting and gives an account of the factors affecting transactions costs. He develops work of Simon (1957) in connection with bounded rationality. Williamson places a great deal of emphasis on problems of trust in relational contracting.

- The literature on hostages is examined further in Dnes (1993; 2003) and Klein (1978; 1997). In his recent work, Klein has emphasized that the outstanding net benefits on a contract (the rents) motivate behavior rather than sunk costs.

- The unconscionability doctrine is most developed in the United States. For England and other common-law jurisdictions, the doctrine is less well established.

BREACH OF CONTRACT

If someone fails to honor a contractual undertaking, the courts tend to award the promisee compensation for breach of contract. If a seller fails to deliver a product, for example, compensation would be aimed at enabling the disappointed purchaser to buy the product from another supplier. A less-commonly used alternative approach would be to require specific performance of the promised service. In this chapter, we examine the remedies available to courts in dealing with breach of contract. We also consider the economic implications of standard defenses against actions for breach.

OPTIMAL BREACH

Lawyers and economists agree that it is not a suitable purpose of law to enforce the terms of an agreement rigidly. The legal convention is to allow breach of contract providing the contract breaker pays damages to the promisee, which generally makes economic sense. Monetary compensation is intended to place the victim of breach in the position that would have been obtained had the contract been completed. Only in very special circumstances do courts require specific performance of a contract. The economic justification for this approach is that the law should encourage efficient adjustments. If circumstances changed after the contract had been agreed, it may be desirable to allow breach (with compensation for losses) so that resources can be moved to higher valued uses.

Suppose that an auto manufacturer orders 5,000 pressed-steel bodies for a new model but, after taking delivery of 500 bodies, realizes that demand is poor and it would be best to close down production. The manufacturer contacts the supplier and cancels the order, apologizing for the breach of contract. It would be wasteful if the supplier could insist on specific performance, which requires the delivery of the original order for the agreed price. Resources would be used to make products that were not in demand. It is better that the auto manufacturer be allowed to withdraw from the contract (buyer's breach) but be required to compensate the supplier for any lost profit. The resources saved by not producing the bodies can be used elsewhere in the economy. Interestingly, under the doctrine of mitigated damages the law will not compensate the supplier for losses incurred after notice of breach is received, which helps create the correct incentives.

It is tempting to argue at this point in favor of *uncompensated* breach. In terms of the previous example, is it enough that the car maker could in principle compensate the supplier and still be better off from the breach, without actually requiring the payment to be made? The same efficiency gain occurs with uncompensated breach. However, this argument overlooks the fact that we cannot be sure that a given sum of money creates the same utility for different individuals. A net gain in money terms for the defaulter need not reflect a net welfare gain. We can only be sure that there is a net gain from breach if the car maker actually compensates the supplier. The car maker is better off from the breach and, because the supplier is as well off as before, there must be a net welfare gain. The legal doctrine that adherence to contracts is typically not compelled, but that compensation must be paid for breach, is generally efficient.

In special cases, courts order specific performance by the breaching party. This normally arises when the good or service under contract is unique, implying that money compensation would be very difficult to calculate and might not be adequate. For example, a contract may relate to antique furniture or to an original oil painting, for which a disappointed buyer could find no market alternatives. Courts avoid ordering specific performance if doing so would involve high costs of monitoring performance.

DEFENSES AGAINST ACTIONS FOR BREACH OF CONTRACT

Defenses against actions for breach of contract fall into the formation or performance categories. A formation defense is a claim that the contract was improperly constructed at the start and is therefore void, or—in some cases—voidable by the adversely affected party. A performance defense claims that the contract cannot be completed for some reason and is therefore voidable. An economic commentary is possible for both formation and performance defenses.

Duress

Courts do not enforce contracts based on threats of physical, mental, or economic harm. This is sensible from an economic perspective, since gains from trade can only arise for sure on voluntary trade, and duress is consequently a defense for breach of contract. Originally, the doctrine was confined to threats of physical harm but of most interest from an economic perspective is the doctrine of economic duress that has developed more recently. The boxed example focuses on an international case, once more involving seafarers' contracts.

Continuing with a nautical theme, the legal principle that duress cannot be the basis for contract lies behind the *Admiralty and Maritime Law Guide* rules of salvage that apply to high-seas activities. A contract made after a ship gets into trouble, usually for saving the whole ship or cargo, is held not to be binding. A rescuing ship cannot extort a high fee based on its monopoly power as the only towing rope available. If the master of the sinking vessel disputes the fee later, the courts can revise the figure downward. If rescuers were permitted to extract very high fees, it would deter travelers and adventurers from their activities. A traveler of any kind balances the expected benefits of the trip against its costs, including the risk of total loss (of life, or a ship, or other property). The costs are reduced if rescuers receive reasonable fees rather than extortionate ones. There is a clear economic justification for the duress defense in rescue cases.

As noted in the previous chapter, the doctrine of economic duress has become more important in recent years since the courts have become more sympathetic to enforcing contract modifications. This move requires courts to develop the ability to distinguish hold-up situations from cases of genuine mistake, which may be very difficult as a practical matter. The doctrine of economic duress supports the nullification of opportunistic revision.

> ### *Dimskal Shipping v. International Transport Workers' Federation* (1991)
>
> Dimskal owned the merchant ship known as the *Evia Luck*, which stopped in the port of Uddevalla, Sweden, during a voyage in 1983. She was then boarded by officials of the International Transport Workers' Federation (ITF), who threatened to stop members of the union from working on the ship, unless the *Evia's* owners entered into ITF contracts with the crew and gave them back pay totaling $75,000. The union also required payment of ITF entrance and membership fees, payments to its welfare fund, and certain costly bank guarantees, which together added up to a further $30,000.
>
> The *Evia*, which had a Filipino crew made up of nonunion labor, would have been unable to continue its voyage if its owners had resisted the demands, because union labor at the port was needed for towage and berthing. The union was concerned about nonunion ships undercutting the costs of vessels that used more expensive union labor, indirectly undermining the union's monopoly power. The *Evia's* owners agreed to the contractual revisions, continued the voyage, and then sought to have the revisions overruled in the courts and to reclaim the additional expenditure. The court nullified the contractual revisions owing to economic duress.

Incapacity

The courts do not enforce contracts entered into by mentally infirm persons who are incapable of making carefully considered economic decisions. They may be unable to understand the full extent of their contractual obligations or the true nature of the benefits to them. Again, economic reasoning supports nonenforcement, because we cannot be sure that such contracts generate gains from trade for both parties. Juveniles are also regarded as incapable of entering contracts, although in their case there is an exception allowed for necessaries, for which parents will be charged. Incapacity is another formation defense against a claim for breach of contract.

In *Dexter v. Hall* (1872), the U.S. Supreme Court stated that "a lunatic, or a person *non compos mentis*, has nothing which the law recognizes as a mind." Contracts entered into by such people are regarded as voidable, a position summarized in the *Restatement (Second) of Contracts* §15. In *Faber v. Sweet Style Manufacturing* (1963), Faber was receiving psychiatric care (in relation to well-documented symptoms of a manic-depressive psychosis) at the time he entered into a contract to purchase land. The court did not enforce his promise to purchase the land. *Halbman v. Lemke* (1980) shows that a minor who purchased and subsequently damaged an automobile was not held liable for the (nonmalicious) damage to the vehicle. The same infancy doctrine protecting the minor from his improvidence over purchases also operated to protect him from any obligation to pay restitution for damage to the car, regarded as the fault of the careless trader in allowing the contract to arise. The court in *Halbman* made it clear that liability would exist (possibly as a part of parental responsibility) for malicious damage, which is a tort.

Because the courts routinely do not enforce such contracts, competent traders are put on notice to check the contracting credentials of buyers. The doctrine of incapacity encourages the least-cost checking of ability to contract intelligently. Finally, there is a deterrent to those who would take advantage of the infirm, as they might worry about incurring costs only to have contracts routinely set aside by the courts. Liability of minors for tortuous acts puts parents on notice to supervise children, and the doctrine of parental liability for necessaries helps to ensure that children are cared for correctly.

Mistake

Courts allow the use of a limited doctrine of mistake as a formation defense against an action for breach of contract. Judicial excuse for mistake is rare, and there is some confusion over the circumstances in which it is allowed. There is a tendency for writers to generalize by claiming that mutual mistakes are more readily accepted as excuses for breach of contract compared with cases where one party made the mistake. In fact, economic analysis suggests that this distinction is spurious and that the minimization of the cost of mistakes should be of paramount concern. The study of mistake is a complicated area in contract law.

Cross-Purpose and Mutual Mistake. The courts will declare a contract void if it can be shown that each party thought differently at the time of contract formation about the nature of the contract obligations, that is, if they were at cross-purposes and there was no meeting of minds. This type of problem is not strictly a form of mutual mistake, as each party thought differently, but it is a classic form of misunderstanding. We shall use the term *cross-purpose mistake* to describe it. From an economic perspective, if both parties misunderstand the nature of what is being traded, we cannot be certain that gains from trade exist.

In *Raffles v. Wichelhaus* (1864), the plaintiff sold the defendant 125 bales of cotton to arrive on the ship *Peerless* from Bombay. The ship departed in December and when it arrived, the defendant refused to take delivery. It emerged that the defendant thought his cotton would have been on a ship called *Peerless* departing from Bombay in October. It seems the ships were not peerless after all. The defendant obtained judgment on the grounds that there was no meeting of minds. One party thought the sale was for cotton arriving by one ship in October; the other though it was for cotton arriving in December. The judgment in *Raffles* illustrates the approach taken toward cross-purpose mistake for most common-law courts. The position is summarized in the *Restatement (Second) of Contracts* §20, which recognizes a lack of mutual consent in cases where the parties attach different meanings to the contract, regardless of whether there is any perception of the other's meaning.

We can be fairly sure that basing the contract around the later voyage would generate a net loss from trade. The defendant did not simply take the bales but preferred to end up in court. This preference implies that taking the bales would have resulted in a significant loss. There is effectively an "accidental" delivery of cotton to clear up at lowest cost. The supplier was almost certainly better placed to sell the bales, as he was in regular contact with many potential buyers. This is not to argue that the agent faced no losses from the need to sell the cotton, because he also preferred to go to court. However, assuming that the agent was better placed to sell the consignment, the court ruling led to the minimization of losses.

Even if the agent was not the lowest-cost seller, the ruling may still have been efficient because the judgment defined obligations, which needed to be settled before a bargaining solution to the accidental delivery could occur. Once liability was assigned, the agent could offer to pay the defendant a fee to sell the cotton if this were the least-cost option. However, prior to the ruling, neither party had much incentive to bargain. The ruling also puts shipping agents on notice to take the utmost care in getting the details of their shipments right. This notice will reduce the number of cases of cross-purpose mistake. Cases of mistake reflect costly errors, and deterring the underlying negligence is probably the strongest support for the ruling in *Raffles*.

Sherwood v. Walker (1877)

A much commented-upon case is *Sherwood v. Walker*, in which both seller and buyer believed an Aberdeen Angus cow, "Rose of Aberlone," was barren. Walker was a farmer in Wayne County, Michigan. Sherwood agreed to buy the cow for its value as beef. After the contract was entered into, it became clear to Walker that Rose was in fact pregnant and worth 10 times the selling price. Walker refused to allow delivery of Rose to Sherwood, refusing also to take the latter's money. The seller effectively canceled the sale. The Michigan Supreme Court upheld the cancelation on the grounds that the mutual mistake "went to the heart of the contract" and was not a mere matter of valuation differences. A barren cow was a substantially different creature from one able to breed, and this difference gave an excuse for nonperformance.

Courts also recognize common mistake where the parties share the same misconception, for which they reserve the term *mutual mistake*, as an excuse for breach of contract. Providing the mistake strikes at the heart of the contract, the adversely affected party may treat the contract as voidable, unless the party can be shown to have assumed the risks associated with the mistake. The boxed example gives details for a famous case of mutual mistake concerning a cow.

The ruling can be seen as efficient, although it is tempting to argue that a distributional issue is at the heart of the case. Given the appreciation in the value of the cow, the buyer could resell to a higher-valuing user, which could also include selling back to the original seller, who might have the highest valuation. Clearly, the resource can move to its highest-valuing user. It seems to be a question of who appropriates the gains from trade. Similarly, with depreciation in value, the buyer might object to the contract, and the main question seems to be who suffers the unforeseen loss.

How would the parties have allocated the risk of common mistake had they foreseen it? If the seller were able to assess the characteristics of the cow at the lowest cost, which is likely to be the case, then the seller would be the best bearer of the risk. If that was the case, then the judgement in the *Sherwood* case is inefficient: Leaving liability with the seller in these cases would encourage adjustments to be made earlier and would save court costs. The parties might have taken more care over the allocation of the risk in the contract, which could have given the seller the right to extra payments if Rose turned out not to be barren. The court appears to have focused on the impossibility of transferring a barren cow who was not in reality barren.

Unilateral Mistake. Unilateral mistake, which refers to a mistaken belief by one party, is not generally a valid defense against an action for breach. As a general rule, courts allow people to trade on superior information when this is entrepreneurial in nature and increases wealth. For example, a person who discovers a cheaper production process is allowed to continue selling at the old product price, and nobody inquires into the understanding of costs held by the buyer. We would not expect the courts to interfere with such highly profitable contracts, because intervention would destroy the incentive for innovation.

Where one party is mistaken and the other knows it at the time of entering into the contract, courts will not enforce contracts. The *Restatement (Second) of Contracts* §153 holds that unilateral mistake allows the disadvantaged party to avoid a contract if the other party could be expected to know of the mistake, or if it would be unconscionable to enforce the contract. It is difficult to obtain release from a contract owing to unilateral mistake, unless it seems that the other party has actually invested in obtaining unproductive distributional advantages. There is a disincentive to opportunism as a result of this treatment of asymmetric information.

Insider trading in stocks relates to a form of unilateral mistake. The insider in a company or in a consulting group of financial specialists may have advanced knowledge of a takeover that might affect the share prices for the target and bidding firms, and cannot legally buy shares until that information has become public. It is difficult to criticize insider trading on efficiency grounds. The very fact that someone begins to trade in stocks will communicate to others the fact that some development is occurring and cause adjustments to happen more quickly than would otherwise be the case. Concerns over insider trading focus on gains enjoyed by some rather than others.

A famous case illustrating unilateral mistake is *Laidlaw v. Organ* (1817). The case refers to one of those little misunderstandings that occasionally characterized American–British relations in the aftermath of the American Revolution—the British sent gunboats into New Orleans! This unfortunate restriction on marine transport unsettled the tobacco trade. The defendant (Organ) learned ahead of others that the British had ended their blockade and bought tobacco at a war-depressed price from Laidlaw. The next day, the treaty became public knowledge and tobacco prices increased. The lower court set the contract aside, but the higher court reversed this and enforced the contract. It is hard to draw a line in this case between trading on superior knowledge and trading knowing the other person is mistaken. Particularly because the main issue was price, it seems the issues in *Laidlaw v. Organ* were distributional rather than allocative. However, it could be argued in Organ's defense that he was communicating useful information.

There is no real economic logic behind the distinction that courts draw between mutual and unilateral mistake. There may be a tendency for courts to use the distinction as an ex-post rationalization of their decisions: calling a case "mutual mistake" if the general facts lead them to excuse the defendant from performance of the contract. Some writers have suggested drawing a distinction between productive and redistributive information: If trading on asymmetric information would allow more productive use to be made of resources, then the contract should be enforced. However, if the mistake merely redistributes wealth, it should be grounds for the disadvantaged party to treat the contract as voidable. This approach would deter people from investing resources in acquiring information that gives them a trading advantage but does not lead to increased production: a form of rent seeking.

In cases of unilateral mistake, the mistaken party may be the person who can avoid the mistake at least cost. Thus, someone who is mistaken about the suitability of a car for long-distance driving could have rectified this easily by researching the relevant consumer reports before buying. It is more costly to correct the mistake afterward by using the courts. Mistaken buyers, for example, would be given a better incentive to do a bit of research prior to purchasing, if courts routinely follow the approach of enforcing contracts in cases of unilateral mistake.

Recent game-theoretic work applies two principles to questions about setting aside contracts owing to mutual or unilateral mistake. First, we should avoid negative gains from trade. Second, we need to follow the principle of creating an incentive for cost-efficient care to avoid mistakes. Whether it is desirable to enforce contracts based on mistake depends on the facts of particular cases, not on whether the mistake was mutual or unilateral in nature. There are some cases of unilateral mistake where enforcement of the contract would lower the joint welfare of the parties.

The case of *M.F. Kemper v. City of Los Angeles* (1951) is an example where unilateral mistake would be best dealt with by rescission of the contract. Kemper successfully bid $780,305 for a contract to build a piping system, having overlooked a cost of $301,769 in the estimates. When the error was discovered, before work had started, Kemper wished to be released from the contract. The city refused on the grounds that a clause stated that bidders would not be released from obligations "on account of errors." The court released Kemper nonetheless. The court's action was efficient because the costs of recontracting were low for the city, which could just turn to the second-highest bidder. The benefits of avoiding losses from trade in this case outweigh the benefits from encouraging greater care among bidders that would follow from enforcing the contract.

Misrepresentation

Misrepresentation allows the victim to treat the contract as voidable and to claim damages for any losses. An economic justification is not hard to find. Misrepresentation requires investment of resources in misleading the other party. It is inefficient to encourage this because the resources could be put to a more productive use. The option of damages instead of nullifying the contract (which is voidable by the victim) gives a penalty for relatively minor misrepresentation where the victim still has positive benefits from the contract.

The common law interprets misrepresentation fairly narrowly. It used to treat it very narrowly indeed, so that only fraudulent misrepresentation—where the liar had recklessly made a statement knowing it to be untrue—counted. Fraud is a serious matter and also carries criminal penalties. The general doctrine is now covered by *Restatement (Second) of Contracts* §159 and requires that misrepresentation involved steps taken to communicate an unambiguously false statement that drew the victim into the contract. This includes active concealment of defects, for example, where a contractor deliberately covered up dry rot in a property. However, mere silence about some problem is not generally misrepresentation. An economic justification for this exclusion is that courts would incur high costs in distinguishing innocent silence from silent misrepresentation. However, in addition to fraudulent misrepresentation, there can be negligent misrepresentation, where there was lack of care in checking facts, and innocent misrepresentation, where the misstatement is made in true ignorance of the facts. All three categories lead to possible rescission of the contract and to a claim for damages aimed at restoring the situation before the contract was entered into, a form of reliance damages. We discuss reliance further in the sections on damages for breach of contract.

An efficiency argument in favor of controlling misrepresentation does not depend upon harm befalling the duped purchaser. The person misrepresenting makes gains from trade when the victim cannot assess the value of the contract. However, even if the victim gains from the fraudulent contract, it is not clear this was the best option at the time. There is no problem as long as the innocent party can choose to void the contract when misrepresentation is discovered. Also, the argument that fraud causes a wasteful devotion of resources to misleading the innocent is quite independent of the true allocation of costs and benefits to each party. Encouraging proper disclosure also allows defects to be remedied as swiftly as possible (think of a defective car that injures an ignorant buyer).

There is a positive duty to disclose possibly unfavorable facts in contracts of utmost good faith. A good example is the insurance contract, where the purchaser must reveal all information likely to have a bearing on the risk borne by the insurer. A questionnaire is an important source of information for the insurer. The duty to disclose keeps the cost of information as low as possible, because disclosure is a low-cost activity for the buyer compared with the insurer's cost of carrying out independent research. Without the penalty for misrepresentation by the buyer, insurers would revise upward their estimates of risks to be on the safe side, which would drive up the price of insurance. It may be that the large values often involved in insurance makes it worthwhile for courts to attempt to distinguish innocent silence from silent misrepresentation. Many states also have statutes requiring the accident history of used automobiles to be reported. There is a positive duty in American common law to reveal known defects when selling houses, as in *Obde v. Schlemyer* (1980). In sales of automobiles and housing, the seller has a far lower cost of gathering and publishing information about the sale compared with the buyer.

Frustration

Frustration is a performance defense against an action for breach of contract. Impossibility of completion is the traditional basis for claiming frustration of the contract. It is well illustrated by *The Isle of Mull* (1921), where Gans Steamship Line, a New York company, chartered a ship, *The Isle of Mull*, from The Isles Steamship Company in Great Britain. The shipping charter contract was rendered completely impossible owing to the ship's being commandeered by the British government for the duration of World War I. The British government had paid compensation to The Isles Steamship Company in excess of the lost charter rental that was to have been paid by the New York company. The U.S. court concluded that the contract was completely frustrated by physical impossibility and that The Isles Steamship Company did not owe the Gans Steamship Line anything toward its lost profits.

The court followed the approach of an older English case, *Taylor v. Caldwell* (1863), in which the leasing of a concert hall became impossible following a fire, by judging impossibility against a physical standard. The courts' emphasis on physical impossibility can be misleading because it is an insurance issue that really lies at the heart of the impossibility doctrine. In the absence of explicit contractual details covering who is to bear risks, the courts should decide who could have insured the risk most cheaply. The defendant (the charter company) in the *Isle of Mull* case could have offered to insure the plaintiff (Gans) but would have found it difficult to assess consequential losses to the New York shipper. Gans could have bought separate insurance and was in the best position to assess the extent of consequential losses. Therefore, allowing the defendant to claim impossibility would encourage efficient insurance arrangements in other cases.

It is common for parties to insert *force majeure* clauses specifying that the contract will terminate on some contingency, which is usually the outbreak of war. This removes all ambiguity about who bears certain risks. Thus, if a driver refuses to continue with a trip without extra payment because war erupts and the journey is more risky, it makes sense to nullify the original contract if it did not explicitly assign this risk to the employee. The employer is probably in the best position to assess such a risk and insure against it. However, if the prospect of war was well-known before departure, it would seem that the risk was implicitly borne by the driver and that the original contract included a reward for this and should be enforced.

Westinghouse: "Who's Got Uranium to Spare?"

In the 1970s, Westinghouse sold nuclear reactors to electricity-generating utilities with an attached fixed-price contract to sell uranium at $10 a pound. By 1975, Westinghouse had a commitment to supply 60,000 tons of uranium but only had supply lines covering 20,000 tons, and the price had risen to $40 a pound. Had it honored the supply contracts, Westinghouse would have incurred losses of over $2 billion. By the end of the year, Westinghouse announced that it would not honor the contracts and claimed commercial impracticability. The price of uranium rose even higher subsequently. Westinghouse had subscribed to a minority view that prices would fall as military stockpiles were sold off.

Interestingly, the UCC would not have supported Westinghouse; the problem resulted from a widely foreseen rise in the market price of uranium. The claims by the utilities for damages for breach were settled out of court with losses on the contracts being shared. The settlements probably reflected the value to the utility companies of the long-term association with Westinghouse and were considered to be lenient on Westinghouse. The utilities were unwilling to push Westinghouse to the limit. Attempting to enforce the letter of the contracts could have been described, in the context of causing huge losses, as opportunistic. As a postscript, note that by 1982 the price of uranium had fallen to $8 a pound.

Commercial Impracticability

The courts have more recently moved to a standard of commercial impracticability rather than impossibility. According to UCC, §2-615, failure to complete is not a breach if it is made impracticable by a contingency that was not a basic assumption in the contract. The sweeping nature of commercial impracticability is limited in practice by three requirements. First, the contingency really must be unforeseen. Second, the party seeking to be excused must not have assumed the risk of failure directly or indirectly. Finally, the defendant cannot be the cause of the events that form the excuse. Nonetheless, the commentary attached to the Uniform Commercial Code emphasizes the flexibility of the impracticability doctrine in relation to its purpose of preventing performance of a contract from leading to business failure.

In practice, severe shortage of raw materials, due to the closure of suppliers, to war, or to crop failure, is accepted as a basis for impracticability. The implication is that replacement materials may be so costly that the contract would make losses. But rising or falling markets are outside of the scope of impracticability. The contracts are presumed to be the means of covering price variation in either inputs or final outputs.

One of the best-known examples of commercial impracticability is that of the Westinghouse Electric Corporation (now Westinghouse Electric Co., LLC). Westinghouse failed to supply uranium under fuel contracts with 27 utility companies running 49 nuclear power plants that it had built. The details of the Westinghouse case are considered in the boxed example.

A traditional view of contract would eschew the doctrine of commercial impracticability, as it is lenient with the insurance aspect of contracts. Courts may be motivated, because of fears of business failure and associated unemployment, to overlook the long-term implications of reallocating resources. Firms get into difficulties because they are unable to adjust to changing economic conditions. If they fail, other firms might make a better use of their assets and workers. However, as in the Westinghouse case, adjusting contracts to overcome problems of a purely short-term nature may make greater sense.

Commercial impracticability creates several problems. First, firms may be tempted to practice creative accounting and claim impracticability when it does not really exist. This opportunism might give some leverage with customers or suppliers in attempts to renegotiate more favorable terms after a contract has been entered. A doctrine of commercial impracticability could therefore encourage the devotion of resources to fraud and to its detection, which would not be necessary absent the doctrine. Also, fear of postcontract opportunism might in itself deter people from entering otherwise efficient contracts. Finally, firms have less incentive to practice careful management if they can always escape from the consequences of their incompetence. Critics of the defense of commercial impracticability ask whether it is really a good idea to keep firms in business regardless of how inefficient they are.

REMEDIES FOR BREACH OF CONTRACT

Broadly, there are three possible remedies for breach of contract. First, the parties may have stipulated remedies in the contract, perhaps specifying an arbitration procedure or a schedule of penalties for delayed delivery. Second, a court may award compensation for damages caused by failure to carry out promises. Finally, the court may make an order for specific performance of contractual duties. All of these devices have clear economic implications.

Party-Designed Remedies

Party-designed remedies can include monetary (liquidated) damages, performance bonds, and arbitration procedures. Courts are reluctant to enforce remedies that encompass a "pure" punitive element, as in the case of *Norwalk Door Closer v. Eagle Lock & Screw Co.* (1966), where no damage actually followed the breach of contract by the lock company. When courts have enforced penalty clauses, as in *Southwest Engineering Co. v. U.S.* (1965), where the government was able to enforce liquidated damages for delayed completion of construction work, it has been because the amount has been reasonable in relation to possible damage foreseen at the start of the contract. The *Restatement (Second) of Contract* §356 notes that damages for breach may be written into an agreement but only for an amount reasonable in the light of anticipated or actual loss. Judges do not try to set an example by punishing those who breach contract. The general principle is that compensation should be limited to the damage caused, which is the basis of liquidated damages.

There are two good economic reasons for supporting punitive clauses. First, someone may have paid well above the market rate for a service to obtain an unusual level of compensation should the service fail. Thus, if someone hires a chauffeur and car to help find long-lost relatives during a short period of annual vacation, the psychic loss is very high if the car breaks down. The vehicle rental company may be the best underwriter for this insurance because it is in a good position to assess the risks of breakdown and to provide backup vehicles. This point does not necessarily conflict with the view in the *Restatement (Second) of Contracts* §356, providing we regard the high willingness to pay as reflecting consumer surplus, the potential loss of which is foreseeable at the start of the contract.

The second example involves signaling. A supplier may be willing to post a high bond (a *hostage*) to signal that the service is reliable. This signal may be especially useful to a new supplier that knows it is the lowest-cost and most reliable firm but must convince a skeptical market. In general the benefit to a buyer from a contract is

$$\text{Expected Net Benefit} = E[B] = p.b + (1 - p)(d - c)$$

where, p = probability of successful completion

b = net benefit from successful completion
c = costs caused by failure
d = penalty payment (bond) from failed supplier

If the buyer believes the firm to be less reliable than others, p is taken to be lower. If d were set equal to c (compensatory damages), the low value for p depresses the expected net benefit. The supplier can compensate for this by increasing d to yield a higher net benefit and win the contract. If the supplier is the most reliable firm, it is desirable that it should win the contract. It needs to be able to offer a punitive bond as part of the stipulated damages in order to do this. Note again that the economic argument does not necessarily conflict with *Restatement (Second) of Contracts* §356 providing we regard the high probability of failure $(1 - p)$ as implying a high expected cost from failure.

An alleged inefficiency of enforcing stipulated damages is that it encourages completion of a contract when breach would be preferable, as when the stipulated penalty is $10,000 but the benefit of completion is just $3,000 to the buyer. The supplier has an incentive to spend up to $10,000 apparently to avoid a cost of failure of just $3,000. But this ignores the risks borne by the buyer. The higher compensation payment reflects a part of the package offered by the supplier to obtain the contract in the first place. The penalty of $10,000 and buyer's loss of $3,000 are compatible with the following contract (in $s):

$$E[B] = 13,500 = 0.5(20,000) + 0.5(10,000 - 3000)$$

where b, the benefit of successful completion to the buyer, is $20,000, and p, the probability of success, is 0.5. We assume that the $13,500 expected net benefit is required to undercut the next-best contract offered to the buyer. If the supplier cannot complete the contract, the bond ($10,000) should be enforced, or the reliability of this type of contract will be undermined. Undermining bonding would imply that efficient new firms would not be able to compete with inefficient established ones by offering higher bonds.

Damages

Three principal approaches are taken in awarding damages to the victim of a breach of contract. But in addition, courts can consider whether to compensate for consequential damage that flows from the breach. There are, therefore, four analytical approaches to consider:

1.   Expectations loss: The lost gain (expectancy) that was anticipated from the contract

Parker v. Twentieth Century Fox (1970)

The plaintiff was better known as the actress Shirley MacLaine. In 1965, she entered into a contract with the studio to make a movie, *Bloomer Girl*, which was a musical. Her compensation was to be a minimum of $750,000 for 14 weeks' work. In early May 1966, the studio decided not to produce the picture. Fox offered MacLaine a part in an alternative picture, which was a western called *Big Country*. The compensation terms were broadly identical.

MacLaine turned down the alternative part and sued for damages. She succeeded in recovering the promised $750,000 compensation for the canceled movie (plus interest), which was the lost expectancy. The court stated the general rule that a wrongfully discharged employee could claim for lost salary agreed upon for the period of service. It would be correct to deduct any money that the employee could have been expected to earn during the period. However, in relation to *Big Country*, the alternative film was not a musical, was to be filmed overseas rather than in Los Angeles, and was not "equivalent to the song-and-dance production." MacLaine could have damaged her career in musical and light comedy work by appearing in a different type of film at that time, so that it was not reasonable to expect her to mitigate the damage in that way.

2. Reliance loss: The unavoidable costs a victim of breach incurred in reasonable anticipation of completion of the contract

3. Restitution damages: The breaching party's profit from the breach

4. Consequential loss: Indirect losses that follow from the breach

In general, the courts award expectation damages, subject to certain qualifications. Nonetheless, each of the approaches to damages may have a role to play in particular cases.

Expectation Damages. The courts normally award expectation damages to a victim of breach. The courts try to place the victim of breach of contract, as far as money can do it, in the same situation as if the contract had been performed. Expectation damages move the victim back to the higher indifference curve in Figure 4.1 in the previous chapter (also see Figure 5.1 on page 112). It will be as if the breach did not occur. A famous case resulting in expectation damages is illustrated in the boxed example.

The following example shows that enforcing the obligation to pay expectation damages encourages a buyer to breach only when it is efficient to do so. A consumer promises to buy a product from a manufacturer at price p but then considers whether to breach the contract. The manufacturer makes specific investments in anticipation of (in reliance upon) the sale, which means sunk costs are incurred; for example, a manufacturer of custom-built furniture would use up tools and materials in making the item.

From the point of view of both parties, completion of the contract is efficient if this leads to a joint surplus:

$$K + P - C - S > - S$$

i.e.,
$$K + P - C > 0 \qquad (5.1)$$

where, K = consumer surplus on the transaction

P = manufacturer's revenue

C = manufacturer's variable costs

S = manufacturer's sunk (unavoidable) costs

Note that $P - C - S$ equals the manufacturer's profits, and that for simplicity the buyer has no costs. Consumer surplus, K, measures the difference between what the consumer pays and the maximum price he would be prepared to pay rather than go without the item. Sunk costs are irrecoverable expenditures on specific assets, such as the manufacturer's tools and materials, known as *detrimental reliance* in law.

Condition (5.1) tells us that completion is efficient if the contract has a surplus over costs, excluding sunk costs, which are incurred with or without completion. For simplicity, prices and costs are assumed to be unchanged from the start of the contract. However, consumer surplus may be lower than expected, as clearly something must have changed to make the consumer contemplate breach, e.g., the product may have become more cheaply available elsewhere.

Courts expect victims of breach to minimize their losses. This is the doctrine that the victim has a duty to mitigate damages as alluded to in the *Parker* case discussed earlier. However, the courts recognize unavoidable (sunk) costs incurred by the victim prior to breach. These sunk costs, or reliance expenditures, are included in an expectation damages assessment. Thus, if a seller expected a price of $10 and had sunk costs of $4 and avoidable costs of $5, the cost of the breach is $5 ($4 sunk cost plus $1 lost profit) and not $1. It would not do just to award lost net profit in the presence of sunk costs, because the seller expected to recover the sunk costs along the way to making the profits. On this basis, it is fair to say that expectation can include recovery of reliance expenditures. The courts sometimes put this as allowing claims for wasted expenditure and lost net profit.

A little algebra shows that the practice of the courts encourages efficient breach only. With expectation damages, the supplier in our example must be made indifferent between the buyer completing the contract and refusing to buy. Therefore, the supplier receives lost profit plus any incurred sunk costs as damages:

$$(P - C - S) + S = P - C = d_e \tag{5.2}$$

where d_e is the expectation damages if the buyer does not buy. It follows that the supplier receives

$$-S + d_e = P - C - S \tag{5.3}$$

if there is breach, which is the same as the profit from completion.

The consumer completes the purchase if

$$K > -d_e \tag{5.4}$$

where the change of sign on d_e reflects the fact that the consumer pays it as a cost if he breaches. It follows that

$$K + d_e > 0$$

implying $\qquad\qquad K + P - C > 0 \qquad\qquad\qquad\qquad (5.5)$

which is the earlier Condition (5.1) for optimal completion. This shows that the customer completes under expectation damages when it is optimal to do so.

A further numerical example also helps to clarify the issues surrounding expectation damages. This time we take a seller's breach and assume for simplicity there are no sunk costs. Suppose a firm agrees to sell a building for $200,000 but suddenly realizes that it will lose $20,000 on the deal. It therefore wishes to breach. However, the buyer cannot find a replacement building for less than $250,000, and consumer surplus therefore equals $50,000. Under the rule of expectation damages, the seller must pay the buyer the extra $50,000 and will be deterred from breaching, preferring to suffer the $20,000 loss. This is efficient because it is cheaper for the seller to lose $20,000 under the rule than for the buyer to lose $50,000 without it.

Courts generally use market prices in calculating the victim's expectation. However, if a job has been partly completed when a contractor stops work, the only way the victim can be given his expectation may be to award the cost of completion by another contractor. The "cost of cure" is a standard procedure in such building cases. However, if the cost of completion is disproportionate to the market value of the work, courts may intervene on a market price basis, awarding diminution of value. In *Jacob and Youngs v. Kent* (1921), the plaintiff specified a particular make of copper for pipework, but the defendant used another of identical quality but lower cost. The court refused to award cost of cure and only gave the nominal difference between the cost of the different makes of pipe. However, courts do not use market prices if a specific benefit is required; for example, if a wall is contracted for, the court does not allow the imposition of a cheaper structure like a fence. The *Restatement (Second) of Contracts* §348 recognizes the customary alternatives of awarding reasonable costs of completion or diminution in value of the property.

From an economic perspective, expectation is probably the best measure of the real loss to the promisee, as it measures the lost opportunity for the victim of breach. There are some problems with awarding expectations damages, however. First, expectation damages may encourage overreliance by the promisee in situations where this is possible. We return to this issue after we have considered reliance as a damage measure. Second, if a promisee experiences risk aversion, i.e., would prefer a certain sum of money to an exactly equal expected value, then expectation damages may overcompensate for loss (the expected value has a lower certainty-equivalent value). The effect of risk aversion is discussed further in the notes on the literature.

Expectation damages can also be too generous if there is an element of monopoly profit in the victim's loss. In that case, the prospective defaulter will compare the benefits from completion with damages including the monopoly profits, rather than with the cost of the breach in a competitive market for the goods or service. A buyer would complete with a monopoly supplier, when he would not if markets were more competitive and profits were lower. Monopoly profits may be monopoly rents that have been gained at the consumer's expense and should not in such cases be counted as an additional loss from the breach. A possible criticism of this view is that not all monopoly profits are pure surpluses but might be necessary to maintain an incentive for high levels of innovation. In that case, it is appropriate to regard lost profit as a real loss.

Anglia Television v. Reed (1971)

Anglia Television made arrangements to produce the television play *Man in the Wood*, about an American man living in England with his English wife. Anglia chose an American actor, Robert Reed, for the leading role and began setting up production on location in England. A director was employed and location costs were incurred. Less than a week before filming was to begin, Reed's agent telephoned to say that an error had occurred and that Reed would have to pull out of the contract. He claimed to be already booked for work in the United States.

The court awarded the costs incurred up to the time of Reed's breach of contract to Anglia. The television company had not sought expectation damages, accepting that its anticipated profits were too speculative to calculate. It claimed reliance damages because it had spent money in anticipation of production and had then been unable to recast the part in time to meet production schedules.

Reliance Damages. Under a reliance rule for damages, the victim is put into the same position that would have been enjoyed if the contract had never taken place. In fact, this definition indicates straight away that reliance damages are unlikely to be appropriate except in special cases of breach of contract. Compensation would only cover any sunk costs incurred and any payments made in reasonable anticipation of completion of the contract. Courts give the victim of breach the option of claiming reliance where the expected net profit from the contract is too speculative to establish, that is, where expectation was effectively limited to recouping sunk costs. A good illustration of the court's awarding reliance damages is given in the boxed example.

If reliance damages were *generally* used to compensate for breach, inefficient breach would be encouraged. Using the example of the previous section, where a buyer might breach, reliance damages can be defined as

$$d_r = S \tag{5.6}$$

which is less than $P - C$, the expectation measure, because $P - C - S > 0$. The reliance measure is therefore generally less than the expectation measure of damages and would encourage an excessive number of breaches of contract.

The algebra also indicates that it is safe to use the reliance measure of damages if net profit $(P - C - S)$ falls to zero, which is how the courts proceed. The rule is to use reliance when net profit is too speculative to calculate, which is to regard it as effectively equal to zero.

Figure 5.1 on page 112 illustrates the impact of reliance and expectation damages on the number of completed contracts. The horizontal axis shows the number of a certain type of supply contract that a manufacturer offers, whereas the vertical axis shows the benefits from them. Each contract has the same price, variable costs, and sunk costs. Consumer surplus falls with each additional contract, which may be regarded as involving separate consumers. The line labeled K' shows the original consumer surplus from the contracts. The original number of completions would have been X', all of which contracts would have been associated with positive profits for the supplier as well as positive consumer surplus for buyers. Some shock then caused benefits to fall to the line labeled K, implying that $X' - X$ of the original contracts could be breached.

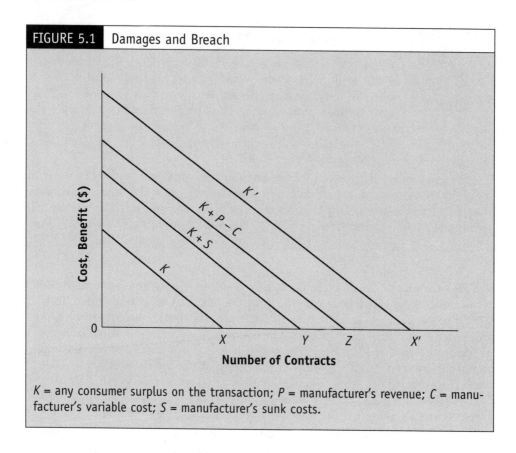

FIGURE 5.1 | Damages and Breach

K = any consumer surplus on the transaction; P = manufacturer's revenue; C = manufacturer's variable cost; S = manufacturer's sunk costs.

With no damages to pay, the buyers would complete X contracts, which is where consumer surplus becomes zero. We then add a constant amount $d_r = S$ onto K to reflect reliance damages, causing Y contracts to be completed. Expectation damages are shown by moving to the line labeled $K + (P - C)$, which causes Z contracts to be completed. The optimal level of breach is $X' - Z$, which we deduced algebraically earlier.

Note again that if net profit $(P - C - S)$ is treated as zero, the line $(K + P - C)$ cannot be established separately from the one labeled $(K + S)$. This corresponds with efficient use of reliance damages as derived earlier, that is, where reliance and expectation are essentially identical.

A Further Comparison. It is useful to compare the general principles of expectation and reliance damages using indifference curves. Figure 5.2 shows the trade-off between damages (on the vertical axis) and gains or losses in a contract for a buyer facing possible breach by the seller. Consider the owner of an unreliable car who hires a mechanic to fix it. Unfortunately, the mechanic makes it worse so that it becomes reliable for only 50 percent of the time on average. Before it was "fixed," the car was reliable 75 percent of the time. The owner was hoping for an improvement to 100 percent.

The indifference curve, labeled I_1, shows the owner's level of welfare before entering the contract. It shows the amount of compensation required for giving up some of the existing reliability level of 75 percent so as to keep the owner's level of welfare constant. The convex shape of the indifference curve reflects diminishing marginal utility for successive increments of money compensation. Compensation has to grow

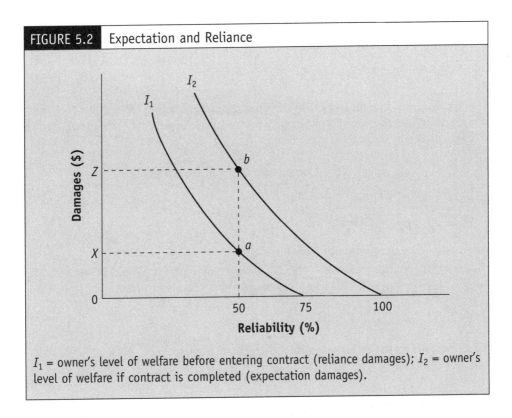

FIGURE 5.2 | Expectation and Reliance

I_1 = owner's level of welfare before entering contract (reliance damages); I_2 = owner's level of welfare if contract is completed (expectation damages).

as more equal losses of reliability occur, if the consumer is to be kept at the same level of welfare. The upper indifference curve, labeled I_2, shows the level of the owner's welfare if the mechanic completes the contract so that reliability increases to 100 percent. I_2 therefore shows the amount of compensation required for giving up some of the improved reliability.

The mechanic makes things worse, giving just 50 percent reliability. A reliance rule of damages puts the owner back to the same level of welfare that he had before the contract. The mechanic pays X in damages to the owner, taking the owner to point a on I_1. The loss of reliability for the owner plays the same role as sunk costs in our earlier examples. An expectation rule requires Z damages to take the owner to point b on I_2, which gives the same level of welfare that would have been enjoyed after the successful completion of the contract.

Restitution Damages. Under the restitution measure, the defaulter returns any payments received before the breach. In a variant of the restitution approach to damages, a contractor who has justifiably ceased performance before completion of a contract may be able to claim for the value of work completed. In *U.S. v. Algernon Blair* (1973), a subcontractor (Coastal Steel Erectors) successfully claimed for part completion of work after the main contractor, Algernon Blair, ceased payment for steel erection and related services. Courts award restitution damages to prevent unjust enrichment when expectation damages may not be available to a plaintiff but where work has been completed.

This form of damages is most easily studied in the case of seller's breach, with payment having been made in advance. An increase in the costs of completing the contract might lead the seller to contemplate breach. This case can be fitted into the analysis used to study reliance and expectation. The damage payment owed by the seller under the restitution rule is

$$d_{re} = P \qquad (5.7)$$

The optimal condition for completion remains the same as before $(K + P - C > 0)$ and is not affected by the fact that payment has been made in advance. In general, having received payment, the seller completes if

Profit from Completion > Profit from Default

i.e $P - C - S > P - S - d$

or $d - C > 0 \qquad (5.8)$

where, d = damage payment of whatever kind.

Under expectations damages, the defaulting manufacturer would be required to compensate the buyer for his lost consumer surplus and also to return the price paid.

$$d_e' = K + P \qquad (5.9)$$

Therefore, under the expectation rule, the seller completes if

$$K + P - C > 0 \qquad (5.10)$$

which is the condition for efficient completion. Expectation damages are also optimal in this case of seller's breach.

Under the restitution rule, $d_{re} = P$, and since:

$$K + P > P \qquad (5.11)$$

damages are too low under restitution (unless $K = 0$) and there will be excessive breach.

Note that restitution damages are relevant whenever courts order the return of money paid prior to the breakdown of a contract. This applies to nullification of contracts for misrepresentation, as discussed in the previous chapter. Restitution may also be part of a damages award that is really based on expectation. For example, in buyer's breach the court may simply return money spent by the seller if profit is too speculative to calculate and may even reduce the payment if the defendant shows that the seller would anyway have made a loss.

Consequential Damages. Consequential damages include compensation for flow-on effects from the breach but are not generally recoverable. The courts generally follow the rule in *Hadley v. Baxendale* (1854), where a mill owner failed to recover lost profits after a mill shaft was delayed while in transit. The court reasoned that the damage was too remote and did not arise naturally. This led to the general rule that consequential damages should not be awarded unless there were special circumstances that were known to both parties at the time that they made the contract.

From an economic point of view, this means the promisee is not permitted to use the promisor as a supplier of insurance without the promisor's consent. Liability for consequential damages requires that a supplier be made aware of any special losses from a delay before being required to promise a delivery date. This ensures that the parties will only select the supplier of a service as insurer if this is indeed the least-cost form of insurance. Otherwise the buyer is assumed to be bearing the risk of consequential loss, which could of course be insured separately, as pointed out in *Kerr Steamship Co. v. Radio Corp. of America* (1927), where Kerr failed to recover for delays caused by a lost telegram.

In terms of the comparisons made for the other rules, and again using seller's breach, liability for consequential damages is defined as

$$d_c = P + Q \tag{5.12}$$

where, Q is the consequential damage, and we assume that the price for the failed service is either not paid or is returned. The supplier completes if

$$d - C > 0 \tag{5.13}$$

as before. This implies that

$$Q + P - C > 0 \tag{5.14}$$

which only corresponds to the condition for optimal completion ($K + P - C > 0$) if $Q = K$.

The consequential loss (Q) could equal consumer surplus (K) if the buyer purchased insurance against consequential loss as an integral part of the contract. This is because the contract price would then include insurance and would indeed save the buyer from bearing all connected risks. Otherwise, consumer surplus is limited to something like the saving of transport costs compared with another contract. If consequential loss exceeds consumer surplus but the supplier is liable for consequential loss, the supplier will complete contracts when this is not optimal.

If consequential losses were awarded to a buyer who had not contracted to cover them, it would be a matter of conferring a windfall gain at the expense of the supplier. Conversely, if they are awarded when contracted for, the buyer obtains the expected gain from the contract and the supplier still gains a return on the insurance side of the business considered over all contracts.

OPTIMAL PRECAUTION AND RELIANCE

We have considered breach of contract and its consequences as if they were completely dependent on factors outside of the control of the parties. In fact, the choice of remedy can affect the promisor's incentive to take precautions against accidents that might encourage breach. Similarly, the remedy can influence the promisee's expenditure in reliance on the promise

The promisor can often take steps to reduce the probability of events likely to encourage breach, balancing the costs against the benefits of this. For example, a builder might put on the roof of a building at an early stage to minimize the risk of bad weather holding up the construction of interior walls. Doing so makes the interior less accessible and increases construction costs. Incentives work efficiently when the promisor receives the full benefit (the value of the associated reduction of risk) of precautionary expenditure. Court remedies are important here. Under the rule of expectation damages, the promisor internalizes the full value of any reduction in risk that is achieved.

Figure 5.3 illustrates optimal precaution. The vertical axis measures the costs and benefits of precautionary expenditure by the promisor. The horizontal axis measures the amount of precaution (this can also be measured in money, if necessary). The horizontal line measures the marginal cost (*MC*) of precaution, which is assumed constant for simplicity. The negatively sloped line shows the marginal benefits (*MB*) of precaution: Moving from left to right, this shows the value to the promisee of additional reductions in the probability of contract failure as the promisor spends on extra units of precaution. The entire area under *MB* (*obY*) equals the expected value of the damage from the breach with no precautionary expenditure (i.e., the sum of all the savings).

An optimum exists at a level of precaution *X*, below point *c*, where marginal benefit and marginal cost intersect. To the left of *c*, the benefit of a unit of precaution exceeds its cost. To the right of *c*, cost exceeds benefit. As long as the courts use the expectation measure of damages, the promisor will be led by self-interest to undertake the optimal level of precaution. This in turn means that the expected damage from breach is reduced to area *XcY*, because the probability of breach falls to the level associated with *X*.

The promisee can also influence the extent of the harm from breach by varying expenditure in reliance on the promise. Suppose a builder is constructing a new gym in a fitness club. The club's profits are higher if the builder performs to schedule so that the gym opens on time. The owner of the club will spend more on staffing and equipping the club if the gym opens on time.

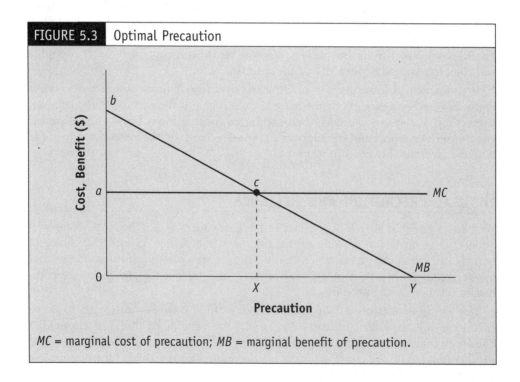

| FIGURE 5.3 | Optimal Precaution |

MC = marginal cost of precaution; *MB* = marginal benefit of precaution.

Figure 5.4 examines the incentives for reliance. It measures revenue and costs on the vertical axis against membership on the horizontal axis. Two total revenue (*TR*) functions are shown depending on whether completion of the gym is certain ($p = 1$) or whether it is certain not to be finished ($p = 0$). Each total revenue function is convex, reflecting the assumption that price must be reduced to attract more members. There is, in fact, a whole family of total revenue curves—one for each value of the probability of completion—but most of them are omitted from Figure 5.4 for simplicity.

Reliance expenditure (equipment and staff) is higher if performance is regarded as certain. We make the simplifying assumption that all costs are sunk for the club (they must be incurred at the start of the year). On the further simplifying assumption that cost per member is constant, total cost (*TC*) is a straight line from the origin. If the club were certain of completion, it would spend R_1 in reliance, as this is where profit (distance *cd*) is maximized (comparing the upper total revenue function with total cost). If it knew for certain that the gym would not be finished, it would only spend R_0 and maximize profit (*ab*) on the lower total revenue function. Any other level of risk of nonperformance will cause the club to spend between R_0 and R_1 in reliance.

The problem is to get the club to take an efficient amount of reliance, given the probability of breach. In particular, if the promisor is liable for all of the promisee's expectation, the promisee will overrely. The promisee may as well spend R_1 and be compensated for the profit and cost difference between membership levels M_1 and M_0. But if the promisor is liable for none of the promisee's expectation, the promisee will carefully assess the probability of failure and only undertake the associated (efficient) level of reliance.

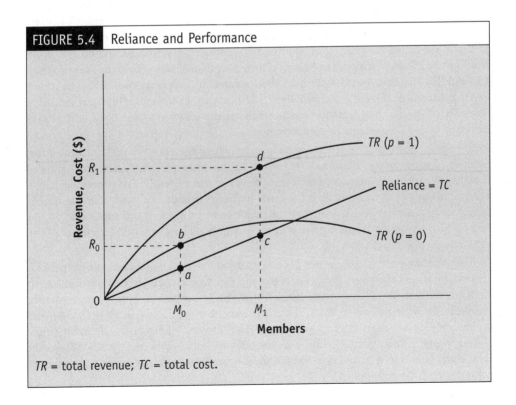

FIGURE 5.4 **Reliance and Performance**

TR = total revenue; *TC* = total cost.

There is a paradox here, but it is one that can be solved. Efficient precaution is obtained by making the promisor liable for all of the promisee's expectation, but efficient reliance is found by making him liable for none of it. The solution is to use the expectation measure of damage in a qualified manner. Courts can impose damages for reasonable expectation, where this includes reasonable reliance. They would state that lost profit (or consumer surplus) plus reliance is the basis for expectation damages, but that reliance expenditures must be appropriate to the probability of failure experienced. The courts can form a judgment about the probability of failure (in an average case) from the precaution undertaken by the promisor when he knows he is liable for reasonable expectation. In principle, the problem can be solved, although the practical difficulties may be severe. Still, courts should be able to approximate this procedure with the careful exercise of judgment.

SPECIFIC PERFORMANCE

An order for specific performance requires the promisor to carry out the obligations of the contract. It is a discretionary remedy that is not commonly used for breach of contract, sometimes taking the form of an injunction preventing breach of a clause in a contract. There is a general presumption in the courts that compensatory damages should be awarded unless there is a particular reason why they are considered inadequate.

Damages are considered inadequate, for example, if it is not possible for the victim of breach to replace the promise. Uniqueness should not be interpreted too literally, as the key fact is whether the good can be replaced. It might be a piece of antique furniture, or an old master, or it could just be that market conditions prevent replacement. In the case of *City Stores v. Ammerman* (1967), the plaintiff was owner of Lansburgh's department store in downtown Washington, DC. The defendant wished to develop retail space at Tyson's Corner, Virginia, and promised Lansburgh's a prime site if the DC store would write letters of support to help overturn a local-authority restriction on rezoning. Lansburgh's did this, but Ammerman then refused to supply a store and took other department stores (Hecht's and Woodward & Lothrop) as tenants. The court held that an order of specific performance was justified, as the location was unique and money damages would be inadequate compensation.

Specific performance is not awarded in cases where the court would encounter difficulties of supervision. The modern version of this principle emphasizes problems of defining the service in the contract, rather than the mere presence of supervision. The economic analysis of this is straightforward. If a court cannot easily ascertain the details of the contracted service, it would incur major costs of inquiry and supervision—not all of which would be borne by the parties—possibly making the welfare effects of the cure worse than the disease.

Also, specific performance is not usually awarded for breach of a contract for personal services, where the court judges that the supplier would then have no option but to perform the services. It is commonly said that this is because to enforce performance would be an infringement of liberty, but there may be more to this. In *Page One Records v. Britton* (1968), the sixties' pop group, "The Troggs" (known for their hit single "Wild Thing"), succeeded in ending its contract with its manager, Page One Records. The court held that it would have been wrong to make the group employ a manager in whom it had lost confidence.

The relationship between The Troggs and their manager was one of principal and agent. The general issue is that an agent may come to pursue subgoals over time instead of properly serving those of the principal, although the precise details of failure may be difficult to pin down. After a pop group has become successful, its manager might be lazy and be content with commission payments from earlier work. This would be manifested in the group losing confidence in the manager. To insist that the contract should hold would give the manager considerable bargaining power to extract a healthy compensation payment for ending the relationship. Bargaining could extract the benefits the group expects from the change as well as the manager's expectation from the contract as an exit fee. If managers are limited to pursuing court-governed compensation for breach, this holdup cannot happen, which makes contracts less valuable for lazy managers, discouraging such behavior. In general, avoiding specific-performance orders in cases involving personal service may reduce agency problems.

Injunctions are often obtained to enforce negative covenants, where courts judge this will not force the defendant to perform a service. Normally, these covenants are highly specific and of short duration. In *Warner Brothers v. Nelson* (1937), the Hollywood star Bette Davis was required to observe an undertaking not to work for another company for a period of one year. In giving the injunction, the court argued it did not force Davis to work for Warner Brothers, because she had the option of not working as an actress. This seems to be a spurious distinction, as individuals are never really forced to perform services by an order for specific performance, since they might buy out the injunction. Clearly, Davis must have been dissatisfied with Warner Brothers as her employer, and the question was how she was to get out of her contract with them. Was she to sacrifice more under an order for specific performance, or less under a court-governed compensation payment? Davis' case had mainly distributional questions because a relationship of principal and agent was not central to the dispute.

The avoidance of specific performance in contract remedies contrasts with the normal rule in cases of nuisance, which is to award an injunction to the victim in cases involving few parties. The normal situation in contract is that there are few parties and, therefore, bargaining costs should be low. An injunction, or order for specific performance, defines entitlement and gives the basis for parties to bargain their way to an optimal solution of their conflict, following the Coase theorem.

A requirement for specific performance might also encourage efficient precaution, because the promisor would save the costs of bribing the victim to forego specific performance. This saving gives an incentive to avoid damages whenever marginal costs of avoidance are below marginal savings of losses. There is no difference between court-awarded damages and negotiated compensation in this respect. Furthermore, if specific performance were the routine remedy, parties could still write conditions into their contract to select court-awarded damages as a remedy for breach whenever special factors suggested doing so.

Would the specific-performance rule provide an incentive for the victim to mitigate losses and undertake only efficient reliance? It is often claimed that specific performance makes the victim indifferent between completion and breach of the contract. The victim may then have taken no steps to mitigate losses, which implies overreliance—especially if some of the steps are best taken in anticipation of a possible breach. This is not the case, however, if the parties have an incentive to bargain around the specific-performance rule, as the following example shows.

Suppose a buyer breaches a contract to take delivery of a boat, and the supplier obtains an order of specific performance. It may seem that the boat dealer has no incentive to mitigate the loss by finding a substitute buyer. This is not so, because, if the dealer is really better placed to resell the boat, the buyer will buy out the order of specific performance by offering the dealer his reselling costs and any difference between net profits on the two sales. The specific-performance remedy may be criticized if hold-up could occur because the dealer may not take compensation on the basis of reselling costs plus expectation. Rather, the dealer may practice holdup and extract a sum equal to the much higher reselling costs faced by the buyer, possibly plus some of the benefits the buyer expects from the breach. There is really a pure bargaining situation here, the outcome of which is difficult to predict. The case for specific performance depends upon an absence of strategic behavior by the victim of breach. The main job that the courts do by favoring expectation damages may well be to avoid strategic bargaining problems.

Specific performance is routinely used as a remedy for breach in cases involving land. Land is treated in the law as necessarily a unique good, and contracts for the transfer of land are strictly enforced. In instances where the seller wishes to default, the buyer can insist upon completion. Specific performance may be efficient in land cases because the buyer probably anticipates consumer surplus on uniquely sited land, particularly in the case of house purchases. If the court were to award damages, it might have difficulty in assessing the loss of expectation to the buyer and would probably be skeptical of claims of a large surplus over market price. Undercompensation might well result.

The case of buyer's breach over land is identical to the case already examined for the buyer's breach over the boat. The seller can force the buyer to complete and thereby extract the buyer's compliance costs—and possibly deter an efficient breach. The use of specific performance remedies for contracts involving land is likely to be efficient only if courts' attempts to assess damages always run into excessively high costs of administration.

Some of the special defenses available to the breaching party when the plaintiff seeks specific performance make sense, although some do not. First, the defendant may claim impossibility. If it really is impossible to complete, without an excuse, the promisor might have to hand over all available wealth to buy out the order for specific performance. This cost may overdeter breach. Second, if there is difficulty of supervision, courts may incur excessively high costs in enforcing the order. If A undertakes to paint B's portrait and the court enforces the contract, how can it be sure that A will paint well? It may very well find the parties back in court with B arguing that A deliberately painted badly. Rather than have a dispute run and run, it may be better to award damages. Contracts for personal services are particularly affected by problems of supervision.

Other special defenses are permitted, such as claiming unilateral mistake or that there was inadequate consideration (implying a hard bargain). It is difficult to give these defenses an economic rationale, and they were considered earlier in connection with defenses for breach of contract and unconscionability.

SUMMARY AND CONCLUSIONS

In this chapter, we have examined defenses against actions for breach of contract and remedies for breach of contract. The approach taken by courts to defining and remedying breach of contract can help in the creation of a reliable trading environment for individuals. For the most part, defenses against actions for breach of contract make economic sense. Defenses based on commercial impracticability and on mistake appear to be exceptions to this. Misrepresentation is another area where legal doctrine could benefit from more attention to economics.

The general procedure of awarding expectation damages for breach of contract is efficient. Exceptions to the general rule represent efficient departures in the main, as courts contend with special factors. However, arguments in favor of greater use of the specific performance remedy should be treated with caution because strategic behavior may cause problems.

QUESTIONS FOR REVIEW

1. In *Hawkins v. McGee*, a surgeon was accused of guaranteeing to make a damaged hand "100 percent perfect." This level of improvement had not occurred. In fact, the hand had become worse. Judged from an economic perspective, what claim could the patient (Hawkins) appropriately make?

2. The courts do not like to use a specific-performance remedy in cases where personal services are involved. Is there an economic rationale behind this avoidance?

3. Does the outcome in *Westinghouse* make economic sense?

NOTES ON THE LITERATURE

*   Fuller and Perdue (1936) functionally distinguished damages based on expectations, reliance, and restitution. Notice the date of the article, which is relatively late in the history of contract law. It took some time for mainstream legal scholarship to disentangle the various strands in breach of contract.

*   Compensated-damage principles underlie the expectations-damages approach to breach of contract. One such principle, the Kaldor-Hicks criterion for a welfare improvement, asks whether the gainers from change can compensate the losers and still have something left over. This criterion was discussed in the introduction to this book.

*   The literature on mistake is well covered in Rasmusen and Ayres (1993), who point out that judicial excuse for mistake is rare and that there is confusion over the circumstances in which it is allowed.

*   There are some differences between the treatment of mistake in the United States and that followed in other common-law countries. In England and other Commonwealth countries, shared or common mistake (where the parties were laboring under a shared mistaken belief, at the time of contract formation, concerning facts affecting the contract) does not make the contract void unless it is impossible to complete. Shared mistake is also sometimes referred to as *mutual mistake*. In this type of case, the parties are not at cross-purposes and clearly understand the contractual obligations. There are therefore two types of mutual mistake in the common law: one where the parties have made different mistakes (cross-purposes) and another where they share the same mistake. This legal distinction is spurious from an economic perspective.

- *Sherwood v. Walker* would have been decided similarly under cross-purposes, as the mistake made it impossible to transfer a *barren* cow.

- Posner (2002) regards the judgment in *Sherwood* as inefficient. Since the seller generally has the lower costs of quality assessment, leaving liability with the seller would encourage adjustments to be made earlier, which would save court costs.

- Bear in mind that the *Restatement (Second) of Contracts* is not a statute, but is an effort by the American Law Institute to give a guide to the practices of the courts.

- Manne (1966) makes a strong case for the efficiency of insider trading based on its communication of information.

- Kronman (1978) argues that in cases of unilateral mistake, the mistaken party is the least-cost avoider of the mistake. It is more costly to correct the mistake afterward by using the courts, which supports the traditional approach of enforcing contracts in cases of unilateral mistake. Also, Kronman's reasoning supports a rule of excusing performance when the mistake was known to the other party, who could easily have pointed it out. The analysis in the text of the *Kemper* case comes from game-theoretic work by Rasmusen and Ayres (1993).

- It is not physical impossibility but an insurance issue that lies at the heart of the impossibility doctrine concerning frustrated contracts (Posner and Rosenfield, 1977; Goldberg, 1988; White, 1988; Posner, 2002). In the absence of explicit contractual details covering who is to bear risks, the courts should decide who would have been the least-cost insurer.

- The move to a standard of commercial impracticability rather than simple impossibility has generated quite a literature (Sykes, 1990). Joskow (1977) analyzes the Westinghouse case in detail.

- Goetz and Scott (1977) make the argument used in the text for enforcing penalties in liquidated damages requirements when particularly high costs are attached to failure. However, Gneezy and Rustichini (2000) dispute whether penal damages would anyway have a deterrence effect on contract breach. They present the result of a field study in a group of day-care centers that contradicts this prediction. A monetary fine was introduced for parents who arrived late to collect their children. As a result, the number of late-coming parents increased significantly, and after the fine was removed no reduction occurred.

- Cooter (1985) explores the similarity between breach of contract and accidents, in that both cause harm and need to be cleared up at the lowest cost, which implies victims and perpetrators need to be encouraged to take cost-effective precautions. Thus, liquidated damages that exclude damages that the victim of breach could avoid give an efficient remedy.

- Friedman (1989) argues that expectation damages can be too generous if there is an element of monopoly profit in the victim's loss. In that case, the prospective defaulter will compare his benefits from completion with damages including the monopoly profits, rather than with the cost of the breach in a competitive market for the goods or service.

- Risk aversion occurs if a person will pay to avoid risk. Suppose that a contract results in an equal chance of obtaining $50 and $100, which has an expected value of $75. The promisee would be happy to give up this gamble for a certain payment of $60. Then the individual probably weights the potential drop down to $50 heavily compared with the extra benefit of possibly ending up with $100. The individual is risk averse and we would overcompensate by giving $75 with certainty if the contract collapsed. We should try to restore the gamble. Expectation damages will be accurate compensation if the individual is risk neutral. The literature mostly proceeds on the basis of risk neutrality.

- An interesting Australian case illustrates reliance damages for breach of contract. In *McRae v. Commonwealth Disposals Commission* (1951), the plaintiff agreed to salvage an oil tanker that turned out not to be at the indicated location. Loss of net profit was not permitted as it was regarded as too speculative, and the compensation was confined to reliance loss.

- Posner (2002) has an example where reliance exceeds expectation. This can occur if the profit (or consumer surplus) has become negative, which is implicit in Posner's example ($60,000 outlay to level land, which then has a market value of $12,000 after land values fall). It is reasonable to regard Posner's example as an unusual one. However, in perfectly competitive markets, pure profits are pushed down to zero, and expectation and reliance damages would converge (Friedman, 1989).

- The indifference curve analysis in the text focuses on repairing a car but actually mirrors the medical case of *Hawkins v. McGee* (1929), in which a surgeon worsened the condition of a patient's hand.

- Ulen (1984) argues for the extension of specific performance as a remedy, claiming it could encourage efficient breach, efficient precaution, and efficient reliance. Also, making an analogy with the treatment of nuisance, he argues that court costs should be avoided by only assessing and awarding money damages where postbreach bargaining costs are high for the parties. Ulen also claims that a requirement for specific performance would encourage efficient precaution, because the promisor would save the costs of bribing the victim to forego specific performance. This saving gives an incentive to avoid damages whenever marginal costs of avoidance are below marginal savings of losses. Finally, Ulen claims that a specific-performance rule would provide an incentive for the victim to mitigate losses and would induce efficient reliance because the parties will have an incentive to bargain around the specific-performance rule. Posner (1998) is critical of these claims for specific performance, arguing that the victim of breach may try to practice holdup.

Chapter 6

TORT

Tort is the part of the common law concerned with the redress of civil wrongs involving injury or damage. It embraces negligence, nuisance, and product liability, as well as intentional torts such as trespass or defamation. Nuisance has already been considered in an earlier chapter. The intentional torts are of considerable interest from a legal point of view but have been subjected to relatively little economic analysis. Therefore, we concentrate in this chapter on negligence, manufacturers' product liability, and related issues.

The victim initiates an action in tort and normally seeks compensation for damages (although, as we have already seen, an injunction is a common remedy in cases of nuisance). In negligence cases, the law of tort deals mainly with accidents and has three main roles. First, liability for damages may encourage a possible initiator of an accident (the tortfeasor) to take precautions. Second, payment of damages compensates the victims of accidents, acting as a form of insurance. Third, the law may encourage potential victims to take care. Historically, tort law tended to be concerned with compensation, a tendency that has reasserted itself in recent years. There has been growing interest in the deterrence of accidents, through encouraging cost-effective prevention, in the economics of law literature.

The modern standard of responsibility in tort law has developed from simple roots. Until the nineteenth century, causing injury implied strict liability for damages. This principle gave way, in most cases, to a negligence standard, in which the tortfeasor became liable for negligent acts. In turn, the treatment of negligence has been refined into standards of contributory and comparative negligence. The traditional view of contributory negligence, in which the victim is held partly to blame for an accident, was that it formed a complete bar to recovery of damages. The courts have moved more recently toward a comparative negligence standard, in which responsibility for the accident is apportioned between the tortfeasor and victim. A comparative-negligence approach implies that damages are reduced for contributory negligence on the part of the victim.

We shall see that economic analysis is highly useful in the area of tort law. It shows that the modern approach of comparative negligence will normally lead to efficient accident avoidance. In addition, economics is helpful as it is often necessary to take an informed view of losses so as to be able to award appropriate damages to a victim of tort.

WHAT CREATES A TORT?

We need some idea of the factors that create a tort so that we may intelligently discuss the economics of tort law. In this section, we examine the principal elements of a tort, again focusing on negligence. A major requirement is that there should be a duty of care owed by the tortfeasor to the victim of negligence. The existence of a duty of care defines the scope of negligence law, telling us which kinds of "neighbors" are expected to take "reasonable" steps to avoid injuring each other. In terms of economics, negligence refers to negative externalities that arise as people go about their normal business; for example, a motorist may inadvertently injure a pedestrian during an auto accident. A duty of care requires the motorist to incorporate the costs of accidents in making decisions about such matters as safe speeds.

The scope of tort law, that is, the imposition of a duty of care, changes over time. Many centuries ago, areas now covered by criminal law such as unlawful killing were matters over which tortfeasors might sometimes be allowed to compensate the victim or relatives for loss without further punishment. In recent decades, the tort boundary has moved to include liability for psychological as well as physical injury following accidents. These examples illustrate the changing nature of tort law over the century and may be explained by economic factors. The emergence of relatively modern methods of policing based on detection made criminal sanctions a more effective way to deter murder compared with private actions for damages. In the case of compensation for accidental injury, modern science made it easier to measure psychological injury so that it may be included in claims without risk of excessively driving up the costs of adjudication.

In general, the courts emphasize proximity of the tortfeasor and victim in establishing a duty of care. Proximity tends to create the circumstances in which injury is foreseeable. In those areas where the courts have accepted that tort law operates, if an injury was foreseeable the tortfeasor will typically be held to have owed a duty of care to the victim. In terms of economics, a duty of care encourages people to consider the value of accidents (externalities) flowing from their activities. Much the same principle operates in the law of nuisance, where landowners are encouraged to internalize externalities through the courts' making comparisons of reasonable uses of land. In the law of negligence, the existence of a duty of care defines a similar link between members of the more general population, not just landowners, who must consider the wider impact of their private activities.

The Duty of Care

Harm need not be intentional to create a tort. Rather, the victim must show that the tortfeasor breached a duty of care, albeit accidentally, for which the principal requirement is that damage to the victim was a foreseeable consequence of either action or inaction by the tortfeasor. A manufacturer of a faulty and consequently dangerous product breaches a duty of care to the user. Similarly, the speeding motorist breaches a duty of care to a pedestrian who is run over. Liability in common law is separate from any liability that may exist under statutes (for example, consumer protection legislation and traffic laws).

In modern law, the standard of negligence is judged in terms of the care to be expected of a "reasonable" person of average characteristics under the circumstances. Lawyers regard this as an objective standard, although it clearly involves no absolute definition of care and requires the court to exercise judgement. Courts are likely to be fairly predictable over what is regarded as reasonable care in particular circumstances; for example, special care would be expected when handling dangerous chemicals. The judgments of the courts in a wide range of cases have given a reasonably clear picture of the circumstances in which a duty of care exists and what the level of care should be. The law of liability became clearer following the decision of Chief Justice Hand in *U.S v. Carroll Towing* (1947), in which he explicitly stated that defendants are expected to take care when the benefits from so doing exceed the costs. Courts interpret the reasonable-care standard in terms of whether the tortfeasor or victim faced the lowest cost of taking care.

One regularity that illustrates least-cost accident avoidance is the courts' requirement that construction work should be managed so as to guard against the special risks to disabled persons, particularly in relation to the blind. The costs to the blind of avoiding an accident might involve staying indoors if there were unguarded holes in the sidewalk. A utility company faces the modest cost of erecting effective barriers around its maintenance work. The reasonable-care standard may also be described as a simplification. It saves the court costs of investigating the defendant's true capacity for care. Accepting what is normal saves costs on balance. Even if normal reasonable practice might not exactly fit every case, on average it will be correct.

The Nature of Damages

There must be measurable damages before there is a cause of action in tort. This requirement is relatively easily met in cases where an individual has suffered a physical injury or damage to property. The injury could be because of negligence or it could be intentional. Things are less straightforward in cases where the victim suffers mental trauma, sometimes referred to as *nervous shock*, which can arise as a result of intentional or reckless action aimed at the victim, or as a result of the victim being present when another person suffers injury.

Tangible and Intangible Damages

The law was traditionally extremely cautious in awarding damages for intangible damage such as mental trauma to the plaintiff, who was required to have incurred a recognizable psychological disorder as the *proximate* result of a personal accident. Courts once completely resisted the award of damages for such injury on the grounds that it could not be judged easily whether the mental damage resulted from an accident or from some other cause. There was fear of inviting fraudulent claims. The position was eased in California in 1968 following *Dillon v. Legg* (1968), which allowed recovery for mental injury to direct victims of accidents *and* those who witness accidents to close personal relations. The ruling in *Dillon* emphasized that courts would determine whether nervous shock was reasonably foreseeable—an attempt to deter possible fraudulent claims.

The position over mental injury is still complex, because some states (such as Illinois) take a more restrictive traditional view and others (such as Massachusetts, which allows recovery for mental injury when arriving after the accident) take a less restrictive view than *Dillon*. In general, a mere bystander, or even a close friend, cannot sue for grief at the sight of an accident. The increased willingness to awarding damages for mental trauma could reflect reductions in the costs of measuring damage as modern psychology has developed and courts have developed experience over time. These two factors lower the costs of assessing claims, which still must encompass recognizable mental illness and cannot simply encompass distress. The boxed case on page 128 draws attention to the economic issues arising in the case-by-case evolution of the law on recovery for nervous shock.

Is it a good idea to award damages for intangible losses? Lack of compensation for pain and suffering is a shortcoming of tort law if it is indeed possible to put a monetary value on nervous injury that is caused by negligent behavior. Ignoring mental trauma could be said to undercompensate the victim and lower the tortfeasor's incentive to take

> ### Potter v. Firestone Tire & Rubber Co., 863 P. 2d 795 (Cal. 1993)
>
> The tire company, Firestone, had permitted employees to dump toxic waste irresponsibly. The toxins found their way into the water supply used by the plaintiffs, who claimed that knowledge of the pollution caused mental trauma. Specifically, the plaintiffs argued that scientific evidence showed that the toxins increased the risk of cancer, of which they were distressingly aware. Firestone claimed that the plaintiffs needed to show some sign of physical injury from the toxins, effectively citing the traditional approach to nervous shock.
>
> The court regarded the traditional view as too restrictive and imprecise. It would effectively allow recovery for mental trauma only whenever it was claimed in association with physical injury—a "hopelessly imprecise screening device." However, the court also recognized the traditionally cited problem of distinguishing genuine from fraudulently claimed nervous injury. The court concluded that each case had to be judged on its merits and needed to show a causal link on the scientific evidence presented. On the merits of the case, Firestone was liable for the mental trauma caused. Its employees had consciously contravened federal and state law in dumping the waste, and the scientific evidence was strong that there were grounds for anxiety over carcinogenic effects.

care. Conversely, if it is impossible to distinguish sound from fraudulent claims or to assess damages accurately, spurious valuation could lead to poor incentives.

Tort law is evolving as courts gain experience of assessing causation and valuation in cases of psychological injury. The mental consequences of experienced or witnessed events, perhaps caused by anxiety over the possible medical results of accidents, are real enough losses—although difficult to measure. The courts may have moved from an objective standard of assessing damages, under which they allowed recovery for a limited range of injuries, to a more subjective standard. It was easier to achieve wide agreement on the scope and value of awards under the older approach, but now cases will lead to more controversy.

Economic Loss. The *Restatement (Second) of Torts* §766c summarizes the general rule of nonrecovery for purely economic losses, in the absence of physical harm. Economic losses, such as loss of earnings or profits, following directly from injury to the victim's property or person, can be recovered. These are damages that follow directly from a tort, as for example when an injured worker cannot work for six months. However, it is not generally possible to recover for more distant economic losses, of which there are several examples, including loss of business revenue following damage to public utility lines or other infrastructure. The courts are also careful to maintain distinctions between other branches of the law such as contract. Therefore, it is not generally possible to recover damages in tort following the breakdown of a contractual relationship, such as when a partner withdraws from a business.

A relatively early case is *Robbins Dry Dock v. Flint* (1927), where the lessee of a boat was required by the lease to take the boat for maintenance every six months. The drydock company negligently damaged the boat while it was being serviced. The lessee was not able to recover damages for loss of business following the damage. The court concluded that "the law does not spread its protection that far" and held that any claim should be in contract law against the boat's owner (who could in turn claim from the negligent dry-dock company). *Robbins* illustrates a general worry that is best described, from an economic perspective, as concern to avoid double counting of claims.

Another example is *Rickards v. Sun Oil Co.* (1945), where the owner of a tourist business that lost revenue after a bridge was damaged could not recover damages. Courts treat such damage as too remote from the original cause and often say they do not wish to open a floodgate of claims. This bar to recovery stood in the way of modern litigants hoping to recover damages following the *Exxon Valdez* oil spill. Note that in Canada the courts are more willing to allow recovery of economic loss on a case-by-case basis, as in *Canadian National Railway v. Norsk Pacific Steamship Co.* (1992), where the plaintiff recovered the additional cost of rerouting trains after the defendants damaged a publicly owned bridge. In *Norsk*, the judge held that by checking for proximity in either physical or causal terms between the plaintiff and defendant, courts could award damages for economic loss without opening a floodgate of claims.

Pure economic loss is often called *relational economic loss*. Commonly, an accident results in an interruption of business, and if the court bars recovery, it leaves the victim bearing the cost of interruption. It may not be possible to impose liability for relational losses upon the tortfeasor without overstating the losses to society. Losses from interruptions to some businesses (such as hotels whose beaches are polluted by an oil spill) will be offset by gains to other businesses (such as increased demand for hotels elsewhere along the coast). This argument is illustrated in Figure 6.1, where the marginal cost of the shrinking (MC) and expanding (MC_1) businesses are equal, and the demand shifts in D_1 and d_1 are identical. The expansion of demand for the second hotel ($q_2 - q_1$) exactly matches the decline in demand for the first hotel ($Q_2 - Q_1$). There is no net effect on welfare: The loss of consumer surplus shown by area *abcd* for the victim is exactly compensated by the gain of area *efgh* for the second business.

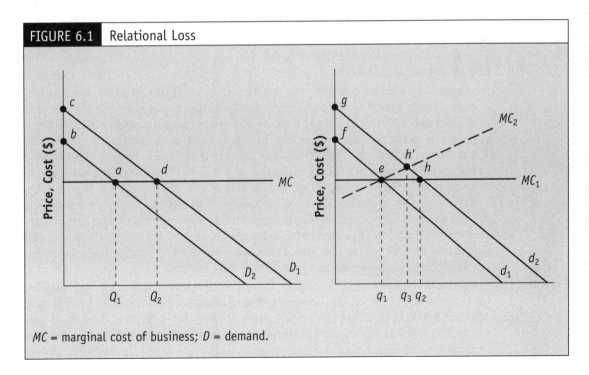

FIGURE 6.1   Relational Loss

MC = marginal cost of business; *D* = demand.

The relational economic loss imposed on the first firm is a *pecuniary* externality (that is, one with purely distributional effects).

The argument for not compensating relational loss is problematic even when gains and losses clearly are offsetting. Requiring compensation to be paid for a pecuniary externality would encourage the tortfeasor to take too high a level of precaution. Conversely, not compensating would lead the victim to take excessive precautions: For example a vulnerable hotel might invest in costly protection against oil spills, whereas liability for relational loss would cause tankers to reroute at lower cost. The argument against compensation also could be carried over more generally because it really applies to all economic loss whether associated with direct injury or not. Consider an accident victim's loss of earnings: If there are unemployed persons who could fill the jobs, there is no social loss. However, courts do compensate the (private) loss of earnings.

If either the marginal costs or demand effects differ between the two businesses, there could be a net relational loss. If marginal cost for the expanding hotel were given by MC_2 in Figure 6.1, the demand shifts would not offset each other. Demand for the expanding hotel grows only to q_3 and the increase in marginal costs reduces the growth in consumer surplus (by $eh'h$ compared with expansion along MC_1).

Net relational loss can be cited as an explanation of an exception to the rule excluding recovery of economic losses. American courts do award damages in cases where fishermen lose some or all of their catch, such as in the oil-spill case of *Union Oil v. Oppen* (1974). Fish cases can be understood as clear examples of net loss. Fish are actually destroyed, and there are no offsetting gains elsewhere. This suggestion makes sense, although it is also possible that the courts simply wish to treat fishermen favorably. The more general exclusion of claims for relational economic loss is probably an imperfect but sensible rule that limits the liability of tortfeasors. Even though offsetting gains may not fully compensate pecuniary losses, to ignore them would overstate the damage to society. On this basis, *Norsk* would appear to have been wrongly decided. Courts cannot make cost-effective detailed enquiries in each case, although fishing may be simpler to assess.

It may simply be the case that courts have yet to sort themselves out over relational losses. Possibly they do not understand the distinction between private transfers and lost real benefits very well. There are many inconsistencies in the area, e.g., a different approach is taken in cases where the economic loss is caused intentionally. The *Restatement (Second) of Torts* §766 also tells us that "one who intentionally and improperly interferes with the performance of a contract" is liable for consequential financial losses. The law here still follows the nineteenth-century case of *Lumley v. Gye* (1853) in imposing a penalty for inducing breach of contract. In *Lumley*, after an opera singer (Wagner) contracted her services to a theater manager (Lumley), another manager (Gye) enticed her to move to his theater. U.S. courts will impose damages upon defendants like Gye, providing the defendants know of the original contract and showed intent to induce the breach.

It should not really matter whether the third party shows intent or not, nor how information was obtained. The normal payment of expectation damages for breach of contract by Wagner would have left Lumley as well off as before the breach (see Chapter 5) and was, in fact, sufficient to deter inefficient breach. In *Lumley*, the judge made this point about regular expectations damages for breach in a spirited dissent from the majority holding, which allowed damages for *inducing* the breach. The court issued an injunction to stop the alternative contract and force either Wagner or Gye to pay compensatory damages to Lumley, so the result was not harmful in the particular case. In many cases involving nonspecialist services, there would be no possibility for the recovery of significant damages for inducement to breach, as the victim (firm) would simply hire identical services at the same price on a competitive market. However, in more specialist cases, the courts may have created an unnecessary alternative route for recovering damages.

Moreover, it is a route allowing for punitive damages, as in a recent oil case. In *Texaco, Inc. v. Pennzoil* (1987), Getty Oil had agreed to sell shares to Pennzoil when Texaco made a better offer and obtained the shares. The court awarded Pennzoil $7.53 billion compensatory damages and $2.5 in punitive damages against Texaco, although the case was eventually settled out of court for $3 billion. The tort action was an alternative to the award of contract damages against the breach of promise, because the court would not have allowed recovery of compensatory damages from *both* Getty and from Texaco.

From an economic point of view, the punitive element in *Texaco* appears overcompensatory. Recovery of compensatory damages from Texaco implies that Pennzoil would be as well off as before the breach. Also, Getty Oil must be at least as well off selling shares to Texaco, which should also experience a net gain if it chooses to proceed with the purchase knowing that it could be made to pay damages. Rationally, Texaco would structure the deal to allow for compensatory damages, removing this amount from the payment it would otherwise be willing to make to Getty. Recovering compensatory damages from both Getty and Texaco then seems to serve no purpose. The Getty assets are likely to be put to better use by the higher-valuing company and, therefore, we would want the ownership of the assets to go to Texaco. The punitive element seems to be unnecessary on a standard reading of the function of expectations damages in cases of breach of contract.

Victim Heterogeneity. The tortfeasor "takes the victim as found." Once a duty of care has been shown, the tortfeasor is liable for the true damage caused and cannot plead that the victim was especially susceptible to injury. This is the "thin-skull" principle: A victim of head injury with an exceptionally thin skull is to be compensated for the unusually severe injuries and not for the injuries the tortfeasor might have expected based on average cases. Such cases can be complex. In the classic case of *Vosburg v. Putney* (1891), the tortfeasor was held to be liable for exacerbating an existing condition of which he was ignorant.

The thin-skull principle encourages economic efficiency. If above-average and below-average damages must be compensated accurately, then expected liability equals actual damage caused in a representative (average) case. This efficient result would also follow if damages were limited to the average, but then all but average victims would find their incentives to take cost-effective steps to avoid accidents becoming distorted. Thin-skulled potential victims would take excessive precautions. They would expect to "lose" on an accident because they would suffer above-average injuries but would receive average damages. Conversely, the thick skulled would not take any cost-effective safety measures because accidents would be "profitable" to them, conjuring up images of a culture of tough guys disregarding safety issues. By awarding damages matching the cost of accidents, the court encourages victims to take avoidance steps when these cost less than the expected value of an accident.

Causality

The victim must show that the tortfeasor breached a duty of care by some action that was a cause of the injury. The courts distinguish between the "cause in fact" and the "cause in law." The cause in fact is sometimes examined in terms of the "but-for" test, which asks whether *A* would have occurred without *B*. If the answer is no, so that *A* could not have occurred without *B*, then *B* is the cause in fact for *A*. The test establishes whether the defendant's act was a *necessary* condition that resulted in the plaintiff's injury, given the circumstances of the case. The but-for test proceeds as follows for a hypothetical accident in which a car hits a pedestrian, causing a leg injury.

"BUT FOR" QUESTION	ANSWER	CONCLUSION
Could the car impact cause the injury?	Yes	Driver may have caused injury.
Are there other possible contemporaneous causes?	No	Driver may have caused injury.
Did the leg injury exist previously?	No	The accident caused the injury.

In the table, the but-for test is passed, making the driver responsible for the injury. Alternatively, if there were another possible cause (perhaps the pedestrian was in the process of tripping just before being struck by the car) or the injury existed prior to the accident, then the case would fail the test.

Unfortunately, the but-for test is not always decisive, because there may be simultaneous candidates for the cause in fact, which could be sufficient conditions for the accident. The test may not always be able to isolate a necessary condition, without which the injury could not have occurred. Two cars may simultaneously hit and kill a pedestrian, in which case each driver could claim under the but-for test not to be the cause in fact: Neither was a necessary condition. Also, the but-for test cannot distinguish between differing degrees of remoteness of causation. A defendant could claim a parental origin for negligence: But for their meeting, the defendant would not have been born to be there to cause the injury. The author could, for example, always blame World War II for his actions, since his father would otherwise never have become a refugee and met his mother at an Allied Services dance! However, in many cases the test will succeed in either ruling out or showing a causal connection without raising problems. For example, if a patient faced certain death due to taking a poison for which there is no antidote, any negligent treatment by a physician would be irrelevant.

If the defendant's action is shown to be a cause in fact, the next question is whether it is a legally significant cause. If so, then it is said to be the *cause in law* and is held to be a sufficient condition for the defendant to be held liable for the damage. The test for causality in law simply asks whether the action was a proximate (i.e., close) cause, or whether it was too remote to be of interest. For the plaintiff to recover damages, the defendant's action must be not only the cause in fact, but also the proximate cause of injury. The classic case is *Palsgraf v. Long Island Railroad Co.*, discussed in the boxed example.

The requirement for a proximate causal link has the effect of suppressing costly legal debate. As in the law of contract, where remote damages are not recoverable, courts

*Palsgraf v. Long Island Railroad Co.,*162 N.E. 99 (1928)

A guard working for the Long Island Railroad Company assisted a passenger to board a moving train. Unfortunately, he dislodged a package of fireworks that the passenger was carrying. Things then went from bad to worse as the fireworks exploded, causing a set of weighing scales to fall on Palsgraf and injuring her. Palsgraf failed to recover damages from the railroad company. Chief Justice Cardozo held that the guard's actions were too remote to be the legal cause of Palsgraf's injuries. No reasonable person could have foreseen the explosive consequences of dropping the unmarked, innocent-looking parcel.

avoid arguments over tenuous links as a matter of public policy. This limitation of long chains of causality can look blunt and harsh from the individual point of view. When, for example, a fire spreads to a property, its owner must prove negligence of the owner of the adjacent source through which it spread. Traditionally, no claim exists against the ultimate source of the fire, except for the immediately proximate properties. This limitation of liability will encourage property owners to take care to avoid the spread of fires.

THE ECONOMIC ANALYSIS OF ACCIDENTS—LEAST-COST AVOIDANCE

The modern approach takes the aim of accident law as being the minimization of the sum of the costs of accidents and the costs of avoiding accidents. Courts should therefore allocate the cost of accidents to the activities that could avoid the accidents most cheaply, which is a form of wealth maximization. This approach is an application of the principle of least-cost avoidance that was discussed in connection with nuisance. It is linked with the Coase theorem, as costs should be allocated to a tortfeasor that a victim would retrospectively have preferred to bribe to take steps to avoid the accident. The economic analysis of accidents reflects considerable normative analysis in seeking to construct guidelines for a rational system of tort law. Whether accident law actually follows wealth maximization is a separate issue.

The approach is illustrated in Figure 6.2 on page 134, which shows the costs and benefits of precaution against a certain type of accident. For simplicity we assume that a single source generates the accidents, and that precaution against accidents is possible at the source. Precaution could refer to something like a bus company taking longer routes on quieter roads to avoid traffic. The marginal cost (MC) of precaution is shown as the constant amount W. The marginal benefits (MB) of precaution refer to the savings in the direct costs of accidents and are assumed to fall as precaution increases. The optimal amount of precaution is X^*, since marginal benefit exceeds marginal cost up to point a. Thus OX^* precaution is taken and X^*X' accidents are incurred. Total cost is $OWaX'$ and is minimized.

The principle of least cost-avoidance suggests that courts should expect people to take only cost-efficient precautions. It really gives us a standard for judging negligence. In the previous example, if a bus company could show that it had lengthened journeys to point X^*, it should not be held liable for the costs of the accidents, X^*X', that do occur. Other forms of avoidance might involve fitting safety equipment, enforcing safety procedures, or stopping a dangerous activity altogether.

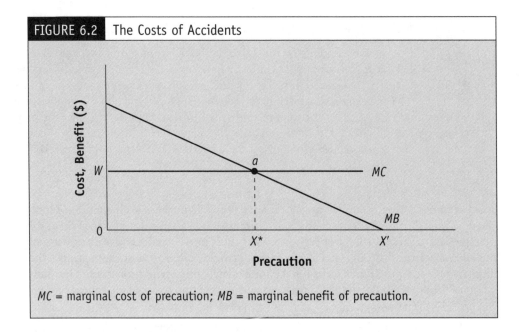

FIGURE 6.2   The Costs of Accidents

MC = marginal cost of precaution; MB = marginal benefit of precaution.

STANDARDS OF RESPONSIBILITY

Standards of responsibility in tort law have developed considerably over time. We now examine the efficiency of the standards under the assumption that the courts have full information concerning the risks faced by and the actions taken by the parties. Broadly, the standard of liability has moved from strict liability for injuries caused to one of shared liability that recognizes victim contributory negligence.

Strict Liability

Until the middle of the nineteenth century, causing injury implied strict liability for damages. The entitlement lay entirely with the victim, who needed to show only that the tortfeasor caused the injury and did not need to prove negligence. Strict liability can be an efficient rule, as shown in Figure 6.3, which has the same benefit and cost functions as Figure 6.2., and where we assume one tortfeasor and one victim for simplicity.

Because damages are shown by the marginal benefit function (MB) for any accidents that occur, the tortfeasor has an incentive to take precautions up to point X^* on the horizontal axis. The tortfeasor then pays X^*aX' damages to the victim, which is cheaper than incurring the cost of additional precaution (X^*acX'). Strict liability can result in least-cost avoidance of accidents.

A standard of strict liability will not encourage efficient precaution in cases where the victim's behavior affects the likelihood of the accident. A fully compensated victim does not care (in principle) whether the accident happens or not. If the victim could take cost-efficient steps to avoid the accident, and bargaining costs are too high for the potential tortfeasor to bribe the victim to take precautions, then strict liability is not an efficient rule. Bargaining costs are likely to be very high in many common situations where the identities of victims are unknown in advance. Victims' incentives can be improved by allowing the injurer the defense of claiming contributory negligence by the victim as a bar to recovery.

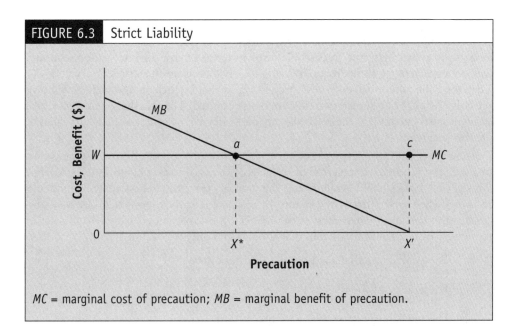

FIGURE 6.3 Strict Liability

MC = marginal cost of precaution; MB = marginal benefit of precaution.

Strict liability persists in three important respects. First, people are strictly liable for the results of hazardous activities (strictly, the consequences of the escape of dangerous materials stored on land) that traditionally encompassed such things as flooding, fire, and explosions. Second, strict liability is imposed upon the owners for any damage caused by dangerous animals. These examples of unusual threats to the ordinary person are dealt with efficiently by strict liability, as it is most unlikely that the victim would be in a position to take cost-effective precautions. For example, if a Black Mamba escapes from its owner's apartment in New York and kills a neighbor, it is unrealistic for the owner to claim that the victim should have made the house snakeproof. Residents would not anticipate waking up to find one of these things sliding down the bedpost in a residential area like Manhattan. It is therefore the owner who is unambiguously the least-cost avoider, or perhaps even the only possible avoider.

The third area of strict liability is in the modern law of product liability, in which manufacturers have been made strictly liable for certain categories of injury caused by defects in their products. The law of strict product liability has provoked a great deal of criticism from economists because of the difficulty in encouraging victim precaution. The American Law Institute's new guide to product liability, the *Restatement (Third) of Torts: Product Liability*, has moved this area of the law back toward general tort law in allowing more scope for manufacturers to use nonnegligence as a defense against a claim. Because this is such an important area, we consider it in a separate section.

Negligence and the "Hand" Formula

Under a negligence standard, a tortfeasor who fails to take reasonable care pays damages. Common-law jurisdictions moved to a negligence standard in the middle of the nineteenth century, probably as a result of the growing importance of railroad accidents. Earlier tort law was little concerned with accidents and was more concerned with intentional harms like assault. The implication of a negligence standard is that at least some costs of accidents will be borne by the victim when the injurer was not negligent.

The negligence standard is efficient. Indeed, it performs better than strict liability in cases where the victim can also take precautions. With reference again to Figure 6.3, as long as the courts interpret "reasonable care" in terms of cost-effective care, the injurer will be expected to compensate for all accidents beyond the efficient level X^*X'. Therefore, the injurer will take OX^* precaution, which is efficient, and victims will bear the cost $(X^* aX')$ of the accidents that are not prevented. The fact that victims may bear accident costs encourages them to take any cost-effective measures available to them to prevent accidents.

The courts tend to interpret reasonable care in terms of cost-effectiveness as shown by the *Hand formula*, which arose from the comments of Justice Hand in *US v. Carroll Towing Co.* (1947). This case illustrates the judicial cost-effectiveness analysis that tends to occur when courts assess the nature of reasonable care in particular cases. In discussing the liability for damages of the owner of an unattended barge that broke its moorings, Justice Hand concluded that the owner's duty was a function of

1. The probability that the boat would break away

2. The gravity of the resulting injury

3. The burden of taking adequate precautions

Algebraically, the three points give the following simple formula, which indicates negligence if

$$B \le pL \tag{6.1}$$

where, B = cost of avoidance (the burden)

p = probability of harm

and L = value of harm (the gravity)

Strictly, the Hand formula should compare the marginal costs of avoidance with the expected value of marginal harm from some action. However, since courts can only identify the effect of discrete changes in precaution by a defendant, the Hand formula is implicitly marginal in its approach.

Several cases provide additional illustration of the Hand formula at work. The defendant in a 1919 case, *Adams v. Bullock*, was not liable for injuring a boy who touched a trolley-car wire, as Justice Cardozo held it would be unreasonably costly to prevent the remote possibility of contact (high B coupled with a low p). Courts in other common law jurisdictions show the same habits of thought: In the much-cited Australian *Wagon Mound (No.2)* (1967) case, the appellate court accepted that a reasonable person would weigh the risk against the difficulty of eliminating it. In *Bolton v. Stone* (1951) a cricketer was not liable for damage from an unusually powerfully hit ball, nor was a golfer similarly liable in *Nussbaum v. Lacopo* (1970): In both cases, the risk was regarded as very small.

If everyone was aware of the duty to take reasonable care under a negligence standard, could there be any accidents for which the victim could win damages? We might expect all cost-effective care to be taken by potential injurers, who would not then be liable for the efficient level of accidents that remained. However, the observation that victims do win damages in court does not discredit the Hand formula. Some tortfeasors may not behave completely rationally. They may be reckless about the consequences of their actions and fail to consider a risk. Others may consider risks but negligently ignore them. There are also issues about nonstandard valuation of damages.

The Hand formula refers to reasonable care by the average person in the circumstances. If an individual is either very risk-taking compared with the average person, or has a tendency to discount future payments heavily, we would find victims recovering damages. To take an example, if the benefits of avoidance are $100 and average avoidance costs are $50, there is a legal duty to avoid an accident. However, if a particular tortfeasor regards the future payment of $100 damages as only equivalent to paying out $40 now, the tortfeasor would impose the injury even though to most of us this would not seem efficient. There could also be cases where an individual has abnormally high costs of avoidance, but the court might expect typical costs to apply.

The law saves costs by concentrating on cost-effective care by an average person in the circumstances and does not generally distinguish differential levels of care in particular cases. However, differential levels of care are distinguished where it is of low cost to do so. A blind person is not held to the normal standard of care, but would be held to the standard appropriate to a reasonable person who was aware of suffering the disability. Similarly, children are not generally held to the adult standard of care. This principle even extends to the intoxicated. In a San Francisco case in 1855, *Robinson v. Pioche Bayerque & Co.*, a drunken man fell into an uncovered hole in the street but this did not excuse the defendant's negligence. Justice Heydenfeldt concluded that "a drunken man is as much entitled to a safe street, as a sober one, and much more in need of it." The view taken of victims in these examples is consistent with the principle of taking one's victim as found, as in the case of the thin-skull.

A negligence standard may provide no incentive for the injurer to limit the scale of an activity. A bus company driving 100,000 miles a year is 10 times more likely to incur an accident compared with one driving 10,000 miles, but if it never drives negligently it always escapes liability for accidents and has no incentive to curtail the scale of its operations. Under strict liability, the tortfeasor is always liable and has an incentive to control all variables that affect the probability or amount of damage. The rule of strict liability is superior to negligence whenever the injurer's activity level is important. However, a negligence standard is better at controlling the victim's activity level because, if the bus company is not negligent, the victim has an incentive to control all factors that could create additional risk.

Contributory Negligence: A Traditional View

The traditional view of contributory negligence, in which the victim is held partly to blame for an accident, was that it formed a complete bar to the recovery of damages. Common-law jurisdictions now generally follow a comparative negligence standard, in which responsibility for an accident is apportioned between the tortfeasor and victim, and damages are reduced for contributory negligence on the part of the victim. This section is concerned with the earlier view, in which contributory negligence was a complete bar to recovery, and which still holds in some states. We examine the modern approach in the next section.

The case of *Leroy Fibre Co. v. Chicago, Milwaukee and St Paul Railway* (1914) illustrates contributory negligence. Sparks from a locomotive had ignited a pile of flax located near the tracks, and the issue was whether the railroad should have taken more care over sparks or whether the owner should have moved the flax. Justice Holmes argued that each party had a right to expect reasonable care from the other. It can be shown that a rule of contributory negligence can cause each party to take cost-effective precautions in a bilateral-care case, which is efficient. We now give a game-theoretic exposition of this conclusion based on the data in Table 6.1, which refer to the costs to the railroad and to the owner of the flax of particular combinations of precautions. The same example will also be used to examine comparative negligence in the next section.

In Table 6.1, the owner can leave the flax by the tracks, move it 50 feet at a cost of $12, or move it 100 feet at a cost of $55. The railway company can exercise no care and allow sparks to fall on the flax, fit a spark guard at a cost of $25, or fit a more effective track guard at a cost of $50. The damage to the flax when there is no care and no movement is worth $100. The track guard will stop all damage regardless of the actions of the owner, but this option is relatively expensive. If the owner moves 100 feet, there will also be no damage, this time regardless of the actions of the railroad, but again this is an expensive solution.

The most efficient solution is for the cheaper spark guard to be fitted at a cost of $25 and for the flax to be moved at a cost of $12, giving a combined cost of $37. This solution is shown in the center of Table 6.1. Both parties will adopt their components of the least-cost method of care providing the courts expect them to do so or be found negligent. Therefore, we can define bilateral reasonable care as that expected when the other party carries out its part of the cost-effective care package. This proposition implies that we expect the flax to be moved 50 feet and for the railway to fit the spark guard.

Consider the first row of the table. In the top left cell, the railway is negligent but pays no damages if the owner did not move the flax, since contributory negligence bars recovery: The owner simply incurs the loss of $100. However, if the owner moved the flax 50 feet, there is no contributory negligence and the railway is liable: The owner paid $12 to move and the railway must pay $100 damages. In the top-right cell, no damage occurs, but the owner paid $55 to move the flax 100 feet. The bottom row of the table has already been explained, as has the least-cost combination in the center cell. In the left cell of the second row, the railway company paid $25 to fit the spark guard and was not negligent: The owner therefore simply incurs $100 damage to the flax. In the right cell of the second row, the $25 cost to the railway combines with a $55 cost incurred by the owner moving 100 feet and there is no damage.

TABLE 6.1	Costs of Bilateral Care ($)		
		OWNER (FLAX)	
		0 Feet	50 Feet	100 Feet
	No Care	0,100	100,12	0,55
RAILROAD	Spark Guard	25,100	**25,12**	25,55
	Track Guard	50,0	50,12	50,55
				(Costs: Railroad, Owner)

More technically, the center cell in Table 6.1 shows the pure-strategy Nash equilibrium. This is named after Nobel Laureate John Nash and is defined as the point from which neither party would choose to move providing the other is expected to stay put. The railroad will not wish to move to the top row, taking no care, because this would make it liable for $100 damages given the location of the flax 50 feet from the tracks (center top cell). Neither will it wish to fit the track guard and move to the third row, as this incurs unnecessarily higher costs of $50 (bottom center). Similarly, the owner will not wish to move to the leftmost column, as $100 uncompensated damage will be suffered, given that the railroad has exercised due care in fitting the spark guard (left center). The owner will not move the flax 100 feet, as this incurs unnecessarily higher costs of $55 (right center). Once at the Nash equilibrium, the parties will not move away.

We can also show that each party will move to the Nash equilibrium, knowing that the courts define due care in terms of least-cost bilateral care. The railway will never fit the track guard as its costs from fitting the spark guard are always lower ($25 < $50). The owner can therefore concentrate on the first two rows of Table 6.1 and will move the flax 50 feet, which is cheaper ($12) than either not moving ($100) or moving 100 feet ($55). The railway then minimizes its costs by fitting the spark guard, as taking no care is more costly given the liability for damage ($100). This iterated-dominant strategy equilibrium for the due-care game moves the owner and railway to the Nash point.

The Last Clear Chance. Contributory negligence came to be seen as a harsh rule in common-law jurisdictions. If the victim were just a little negligent, this would be a complete bar to recovery even though the tortfeasor had been outrageously negligent. In the mid-nineteenth century, the courts tried to mitigate the harshness through the doctrine of the "last clear chance," in which the plaintiff is held to be negligent only if he or she ignored the last clear chance to avoid the accident. In *Davies v. Mann* (1842), the plaintiff was allowed to recover for the loss of a donkey he had negligently tethered in the road, as the defendant, who had been driving negligently at great speed, was judged to have had the last clear chance to avoid the accident. The doctrine of the last clear chance encourages the modification of sequential conduct by placing liability on a second party with knowledge of the actions of the first. If the driver knew of the doctrine and could be presumed to be aware of the tethered animal, he would avoid killing it if this could be avoided at sufficiently low cost. Conversely, negligence as a complete bar to recover leaves liability with the animal's owner and causes the driver to be indifferent over its safety.

In a later case, *Fuller v. Illinois Central Railroad* (1911), a wagon driver was crossing a railroad and appeared to have been unaware of the approaching locomotive. He was killed after the engineer gave a late warning whistle. Justice McClain expressed some impatience with the principle of the last clear chance enunciated in *Davies v. Mann:*

> *It is impossible to follow this case through . . . every jurisdiction subject to Anglo-American jurisprudence. . . . [It] will be sufficient to say that the principle . . . has met with . . . almost universal favor. The groans, ineffably and mournfully sad, of Davies' dying donkey, have resounded around the earth. The last lingering gaze from the soft, mild eyes of this docile animal, like the last parting sunbeams of the softest days in spring, has appealed to and touched the hearts of men. There has girdled the globe a band of sympathy for Davies'*

immortal critter. Its ghost, like Banquo's . . . , will not down at the behest . . . of carping critics. The law . . . has come to stay.

The assessment was partly correct. Contributory negligence persists in some states, and the principle of the last clear chance is still recognized in the *Restatement (Second) of Torts*. In general though, the twentieth-century move has been toward a standard of comparative negligence.

Comparative Negligence

Under a rule of comparative negligence, the courts reduce damages for contributory negligence in proportion to the plaintiff's assessed liability for the accident. Among the common-law jurisdictions, Canada led the way toward comparative negligence as early as 1924. The move to comparative negligence in the United States has occurred more recently, although some states still make use of a traditional rule of contributory negligence. It is relatively straightforward to show that a rule of comparative negligence results in the tortfeasor and victim adopting cost-effective precaution.

We assume for illustration that contributory negligence reduces the victim's recovery of damages by 10 percent and does not act as a total bar to recovery. Using the same underlying data as Table 6.1, the new payoff matrix is shown as Table 6.2. Only the top-left cell has changed to reflect the 90 percent recovery of damages, which implies that fitting the spark guard and moving the flax 50 feet is still the iterated-dominant strategy (and Nash) equilibrium. The owner will still avoid moving 100 feet because it is always cheaper to move just the 50 feet required by the court to remove negligence. Furthermore, the owner can still focus on rows 1 and 2, because the railroad will never fit the track guard, knowing that the court regards fitting the cheaper spark guard as removing all question of negligence and liability for any damages. In fact, the owner can focus on row 2 because the railroad will know that failure to fit the spark guard leaves it negligent and open to a full damages claim ($100 cost) if the owner has moved 50 feet, and a partial damages claim ($90) if the owner has not moved the flax. Choosing along row 2, the owner will move 50 feet (at a cost of $12 to avoid the alternative of losing the $100 crop or paying for a more expensive move). Therefore, we arrive at the center cell, as before when we used a rule of contributory negligence as a complete bar to recovery.

In Table 6.2, the same Nash equilibrium would follow if we were to increase the proportion of recovered damages, e.g. switching the proportions around from 90,10 to 10,90 in the top-left cell. However, the iteration route for establishing the equilib-

TABLE 6.2	Costs of Bilateral Care: Comparative Negligence ($)			
			OWNER (FLAX)	
		0 Feet	**50 Feet**	**100 Feet**
RAILROAD	No Care	90,10	100,12	0,55
	Spark Guard	25,100	**25,12**	25,55
	Track Guard	50,0	50,12	50,55
				(Costs: Railroad, Owner)

rium alters as the proportion is changed. In all comparisons, the railroad never wishes to install the track guard, as the spark guard is adequate and cheaper. Similarly, the owner never wishes to move 100 feet (dominated by 50 feet). So we can focus on the top-left four cells reflecting no care and fitting the spark guard for the railroad, and moving zero or 50 feet for the owner. Notice that a range can be defined starting from a position of where contributory negligence is not a bar to recovery (that is, a top-left cell of 100,0) and increasing the deduction for contributory negligence to $12 (that is, a top-left cell of 88,12). In that range, it is best for the railroad to fit the spark guard ($25) to avoid higher liability for no care (for example, $89, if the deduction were $11 for contributory negligence by the owner). The owner then establishes the equilibrium by choosing to move 50 feet as the best option along the second row (avoiding the possibility of $100 loss if the railroad takes care but the owner does not).

If the deduction for contributory negligence exceeds $12 (for example, a top-left cell of 87,13), the owner will clearly wish to avoid the left column and move 50 feet. The equilibrium is then established by the railroad choosing to fit the spark guard ($25) as the best option along column 2. The railroad's taking due care avoids its possibly paying $100 if it took no care when the owner had moved 50 feet. Our results illustrate the conventional wisdom on comparative negligence. Providing the legal standard of care is set at the efficient level, and given full information for the court, *any* apportioning of damages can provide a full incentive for efficient precaution by both parties. Concern for a more sympathetic treatment for plaintiffs need not incur an efficiency loss.

Comparative negligence has grown in importance relative to other rules for apportioning responsibility for accidents, which implies that the courts emphasize the insurance aspect of the tort system. It is as though they place greatest importance on obtaining compensation for the victim. This is puzzling because separate insurance markets have grown in size and sophistication throughout the twentieth century. The insurance focus may be a result of the courts avoiding the demands the victim would otherwise place on state-run welfare systems, by ensuring that as much private compensation as possible is paid.

Empirical work suggests that the move to comparative negligence has been associated with an increase in the number of road accidents. Studies show more road accidents in states that use comparative negligence than in those still using traditional contributory negligence. There appear to be more road accidents under the comparative rule, after controlling for other influences. It does not follow that comparative negligence is less efficient, as it can be shown that traditional contributory negligence encourages excessive precaution among possible victims when the assumption of full information for the courts is relaxed. Uncertainty about the court's assessment of a party's level of care will lead people to take excessive precautions to avoid risk, as they would give themselves a margin of security to avoid contributory negligence and the bar from recovering a loss. The incentive to overprecaution by potential victims is less under the comparative-negligence rule as losses from courts' mistakes over the proper level of precaution are shared.

DAMAGES AS A REMEDY FOR TORT

An action for damages is the remedy pursued in the majority of tort cases. We concentrate on damages because our focus is primarily on negligence cases. In awarding recovery of damages, the court attempts to place the victim in the same position as though the accident had not occurred [see the comments of Chief Justice Rugg in *Sullivan v. Old Colony Street Railway* (1908)]. This approach is equivalent to the reliance measure of damages discussed earlier (Chapter 5) in relation to the law of contract. The basic task faced by the court is to find a money sum that is equivalent to the loss experienced by the plaintiff. There is normally no attempt to award punitive damages, as punishment of the tortfeasor is not considered relevant. The logic involved in compensation is illustrated by the indifference curves in Figure 6.4.

In Figure 6.4, which measures wealth on the two vertical axes and health status on the horizontal axis, the victim is assumed to suffer personal injury. Health status shows the condition of the injured element of the victim's health (for example, a damaged limb, or perhaps impaired mental health). Before the injury, the victim is faced by budget line *WY*, which reflects his existing wealth and the cost of health improvement (medical and related facilities). The origin *O* shows the individual's health status, before injury, in the absence of any expenditure. Point *a* on indifference curve *U* shows the initial optimal combination of retained wealth and health status.

After the injury, the indifference map in Figure 6.4 must be rescaled. The origin of the figure shifts to *O'*, taking the budget line with it to *W'Y'*. The movement of the origin reflects the lower health status available following injury if there is no expenditure. The movement of the budget line shows that a lower health status (*O'Y'*, at most) results from any given expenditure on health improvement compared with the pre-injury case. Indifference curves do not shift as they show the victim's preferences rather than the feasible possibilities. Faced with budget line *W'Y'*, the new optimum is at point *b* on the lower indifference curve *U'*. The victim's welfare is clearly lowered by injury.

The court must try to estimate the compensation required to restore the victim's previous level of welfare on indifference curve *U*. In Figure 6.4, the required amount is

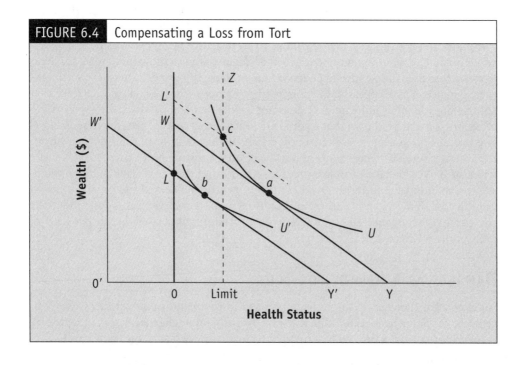

FIGURE 6.4   Compensating a Loss from Tort

shown by the distance *LW*, which is the compensating variation for the injury-induced shift in the budget line. Increasing the victim's wealth by LW will shift the budget line back to its original position and restore the original optimum at point *a*. The analysis so far assumes that expenditure on health care can fully correct an injury.

If expenditure on health care cannot completely restore health, the court needs to award a larger amount of compensation. In Figure 6.4, the vertical line labeled *Z* shows the limit of improvement to the injury that is possible through buying health care. The line cuts through indifference curve *U* at point *c*. Therefore, given the limit on health status, the budget line must be shifted up by *LL'* to make it cut through point *c*. The victim's (corner solution) optimum is then at point *c*, giving the same level of welfare (on indifference curve *U*) as before the accident.

Figure 6.4 illustrates the general principles of awarding compensation for injury. The analysis can easily be used to show compensation for damage to property or for other forms of loss. In practice, the courts cannot operate very precisely as it would be too costly to estimate accurate indifference maps for victims. Over the years, a "tariff" has emerged in which particular frequently encountered injuries attract compensation for suffering based on the assessment of average cases, with adjustments for clear cases of above or below average suffering. Compensation for loss of earnings, which is a *relatively* straightforward calculation, tends to be assessed on more of a case-by-case basis by estimating the capital sum that must be invested to replicate a victim's expected career earnings. Victims may also use expert testimony to quantify their losses.

NO-FAULT ALTERNATIVES TO TORT

Approximately half of the states and most Canadian provinces, along with several overseas countries, have enacted no-fault compensation schemes for road accidents. These schemes provide limited compensation for the victims of road accidents, without requiring proof of fault, and with the money being paid by insurance companies or by a public agency. These insurance mechanisms are strictly liable for damages once a causal connection is shown between the tortfeasor and the victim. The schemes differ in detail and may or may not permit a victim to bring a separate action in tort. The original models for such schemes were workmen's compensation regulations, which also compensate victims without requiring proof of fault and without deducting money for contributory negligence.

An extreme development of the no-fault approach is the Accident Compensation Commission (ACC) in New Zealand, which awards compensation payments for personal injuries from levies on risk creators like employers and motorists and from general taxation. The ACC does not even require that a causal connection be proved between the tortfeasor's actions and the injury: If there is injury, then there is an entitlement to compensation. In the New Zealand case, tort liability for injuries following accidents has been abolished, and the compensation system has effectively become a welfare check. A similar system operates in Sweden covering medical misadventure.

The no-fault alternative to tort is an attempt to provide an insurance scheme incorporating considerable elements of a social-welfare system. The idea is to avoid lengthy and costly litigation and to ensure that victims are not impoverished because they cannot win a case in tort. The downside of this is that a no-fault system may encourage potential victims of accidents to take inadequate precautions. There is an element of moral hazard attached to any insurance system; for example, a car owner is likely to be less careful in locking up if the car is fully insured against theft. Under no-fault accident insurance, less care will be taken to avoid accidents if potential victims regard the compensation payments as adequate.

If a no-fault system is in place, it is necessary to rely on the likely inadequacy of compensation, or the possible simultaneous operation of the tort system, to deter excessive risk taking. Nonetheless, policy makers in many countries appear to believe that the cost savings attached to these schemes make them worthwhile. It is often pointed out that systems of tort law can have operating costs approaching the value of the annual awards paid. However, it is not really appropriate to compare tort law with no-fault systems in terms of the benefit-to-cost ratios, because the tort system also creates deterrence, the value of which is difficult to quantify. Also, many tort cases are settled before going to court, or without full court proceedings, because the system is predictable for both parties. Tortfeasors and victims take approximately just 1 percent of cases to be adjudicated by the courts.

VICARIOUS LIABILITY

Certain categories of people are vicariously liable for the torts of others, known as *vicarious liability*, or *respondeat superior*. The best example of vicarious liability is the employer who is strictly liable for the torts of an employee. The common-law rule is that the employee's actions must be a part of the normal employment for vicarious liability to apply. Cases abound in which employees have caused damage that has become the financial responsibility of their employers. A particularly interesting case is *Bushey*, which is discussed in the boxed example.

Vicarious liability shows that tort law is not simply designed to find a "deep pocket" from which to compensate victims. The employer's vicarious liability is limited to torts inflicted by the employee in the course of the employer's business. The law creates deterrence, as the employer has an incentive to take care in the selection and supervision of employees. Such care is a useful preventative measure that can be interpreted as an aspect of the least-cost avoidance of accidents. However, there is nothing that the employer can do to control negligence outside of working time and away from the job, or strictly personally motivated acts while employed, and so the law does not expect this.

Cases involving the personal acts of employees in working time do not confound this argument. In *Deatons v. Flew* (1949), a bartender threw a glass of beer at the plaintiff during a dispute (an intentional tort of assault rather than a case of negligence). The employer was not held liable, which is reasonable as no employers could be expected to control the temper of employees. However, employers can be expected to enforce procedures to be followed when keeping order on business premises. In *Petterson v. Royal Oak Hotel* (1948), vicarious liability followed the act of a bartender who threw a piece of glass, which hit a bystander, when refusing to serve more drinks to a violent customer.

Similar considerations can be found in vicarious liability cases involving automobiles. In several states, including New York, owners of motor vehicles are vicariously liable for the negligence of drivers using their vehicles with the owner's consent. In these cases, it is not clear whether the driver or the owner would have the deeper pocket. However, it is clear that the owner is put on notice to take care in allowing others to drive the vehicle, which is a low-cost control on the suitability of drivers and the availability of insurance.

Ira S. Bushey & Sons, Inc. v. United States (1968)

The U.S. Coast Guard had placed one of its ships, the *Tamaroa*, in dry dock in Brooklyn. Seaman Lane returned late from shore leave "in the condition for which seamen are famed" and opened the flood valves into the dock. The ship slid off its blocks and was seriously damaged along with the dry dock itself. Remarkably, no person was injured. The court awarded damages against the U.S. government, because Lane was one of its employees and had been engaged in his duties. He was returning to his berth onboard his ship. The court noted that employees do not leave their personal characteristics at home when working. Lane's actions were sufficiently foreseeable to make it fair that the government bear the cost of the resulting damage.

PRODUCT LIABILITY

Product-liability law, which is the area of tort concerned with manufacturers' liability for defective products, has emerged and grown in importance throughout the common-law countries in the late twentieth century. There are two elements to the development of this area of law. First, liability has been extended to the users of products regardless of whether they were the original purchasers. Second, the liability standard has moved from negligence to strict liability.

Before the evolution of modern product-liability law, a buyer had to sue the seller of a faulty product under the law of contract. The seller, in turn, was indemnified through his contract with the manufacturer. This meant that a nonpurchasing (secondary) user of a product had no redress if injured by it. In the United States, manufacturers' liability for negligence was extended beyond the immediate buyer as long ago as 1916, by *MacPherson v. Buick Motor Co.*, in which the plaintiff recovered damages from the car manufacturer rather than the dealer.

From an economic point of view, the inclusion into tort law of liability to secondary users avoids the need for the creation of a complex chain of contractual liability. Without liability, people would not be covered against injury from items that they used but had not purchased unless they could claim negligence or had their own insurance. Also, it may be difficult for nonpurchasing users to obtain information on the product, so that care by the manufacturer would be the least-cost form of accident avoidance.

Strict liability for defects in products emerged in the United States in *Escola v. Coca Cola* (1944). An exploding bottle injured a woman and Coca-Cola was held liable even though no negligence was present. The *Restatement (Second) of Torts* §402A clearly adopted *Escola* principles of strict liability for defects in products in 1965. Strict liability for products is not absolute, since there may be defenses open to a manufacturer, who may claim, for example, that the defect was not present when the product was sold. A most important defense has been that the state of scientific knowledge at the time the product was made and sold did not allow the producer to discover the defect. In particular, the "state of the art" defense removes or reduces liability in some cases where drugs are discovered to have adverse effects long after their initial trials. However, the victim's failure to discover a defect is not contributory negligence.

American law has tended to move in the direction of absolute product liability, in which no defense to liability would be permitted. In *Beshada v. Johns-Manville Products*

(1982), the defendant was held liable for failing to warn of the dangers of asbestos even though they were not known at the time (the 1950s). *Beshada* undermined the state-of-the-art defense, but it has met judicial resistance. Many people interpret cases like *Beshada* as indicating a judicial search for a "deep pocket" to pay damages that amount to a substitute for social welfare payments.

The move toward absolute liability has developed in recent cases against tobacco companies, as in the Florida case of *R.J. Reynolds v. Engle* (1999). Long-term smokers have recovered damages for smoking-related diseases. Tobacco companies have claimed that there was no scientific evidence in the 1950s for a link between cancer and smoking. Courts have found evidence of concealment of adverse scientific evidence as a basis for awarding product-liability damages claims against tobacco companies. No one really denies that smokers also knew of risks from the middle of the 1960s onward, when scientific reports began to link smoking to health problems, but this knowledge has not been a defense. The attorneys general of 40 states sued the major tobacco companies in the late 1990s in an effort to recover for the public costs of caring for sick smokers. The tobacco companies have agreed to a global settlement with the states, which will close off further lawsuits of this kind. Some commentators point to the search for a deep pocket to pay for medical bills in tobacco cases, as suggested by the headline running in the *Miami Herald* that read, "Experts Say Tobacco Firms Can Afford to Pay Billions," which ran during the *Reynolds* case.

The law of product liability is a controversial area. In principle, the introduction of strict liability can be efficient, as long as the manufacturer is the least-cost avoider of accidents, which could be because the user of a product has little or no influence over the safe use of a product. As the twentieth century progressed, increased mechanization and the growing complexity of products may well have raised the costs for consumers of gathering information. If the steps taken by manufacturers at the design and production stage are the dominant influence on product safety, then strict liability does create a full incentive for them to introduce cost-effective safety precautions.

For strict liability to be efficient when the user can influence safety outcomes, it is necessary to allow the manufacturer to cite product misuse or voluntary assumption of the risks as defenses. The first defense rules out claims by consumers who have undertaken inappropriate acts with products, for example, using the electric mower in the pond. The manufacturer cannot prevent accidents from inappropriate use at least cost, and it is most efficient for the consumer to be fully deterred from such practices. The defense of voluntary assumption of the risk allows consumers to be warned of risks. Then, if the user is the least-cost avoider, consumers will buy the product and assume the risk. If the user is not the least-cost avoider, consumers can avoid the risk by paying a premium to buy from a producer prepared to bear the risk.

The American Law Institute's recent revised recommendations for product liability law, the *Restatement (Third) of Torts: Product Liability*, modifies Section §402A of the *Restatement (Second)*'s scheme of liability to reflect concern about weakening defenses in product liability. The *Restatement (Third)* defines the defects for which commercial sellers may be liable as those defects in manufacturing, design, and in warnings given to users. It retains strict liability for manufacturing defects, but abandons true strict liability for design and warning defects. In the latter categories, the *Restatement (Third)* adopts standards of liability that require fault on the part of the sellers. In the case of design defects, there is a requirement of proof of a reasonable alternative design. The *Restatement (Third)* also suggests that failure to warn of risks effectively, unless they are well-known and/or obvious risks, is a form of negligence. *Restatements* tend to be influential in the drafting of state laws and in the development of case law.

SUMMARY AND CONCLUSIONS

We have concentrated on negligence and product liability in examining the economics of tort law. In negligence cases, the choice is between strict liability, contributory negligence, and comparative negligence standards in assessing responsibility for a tort. We showed that, providing the legal standard of care is set at the efficient level, and given full information for the court, any form of negligence rule provides a full incentive for efficient precaution by both parties. Strict liability is also efficient as long as the victim is unable to influence the probability of an accident occurring. Relaxing the assumption of full information over levels of care implies that comparative negligence is the superior negligence standard.

Strict product-liability law has evolved over the late twentieth century, with some evidence of moves toward absolute liability for product defects. Strict liability for product defects can encourage firms to take care and is efficient if victims cannot influence precaution. However, the law of product liability may reflect a search for a deep pocket to compensate victims. The *Restatement (Third) of Torts: Product Liability* has moved back toward a negligence standard over the design and information provision associated with products, in a direction generally in line with economic reasoning.

QUESTIONS FOR REVIEW

1. Give an economic perspective on the approach courts take to compensate monetary losses compared with nervous shock.

2. If a ship breaks its moorings, it can cause damage to neighboring boats amounting to $500,000. Fitting extra-strong mooring cables at a cost of $100,000 will prevent the damage. Should the owner of the ship be expected to fit the extra-strong cables? If so, what would govern the expected duty of care?

3. Give an economic rationale to strict liability for
    a. hazardous activities.
    b. product defects.

4. Rework the example in Table 6.1, using a rule of comparative negligence. What is the optimal strategy for both parties?

NOTES ON THE LITERATURE

- "Tort" comes from the Latin word *tortus*, meaning twisted or crooked.

- Comparative negligence is still called *contributory negligence* in some common-law jurisdictions such as England, Australia, and New Zealand (because those jurisdictions have uniformally adopted comparative negligence and do not need to distinguish it from anything else).

- The position in the Commonwealth countries over duty of care is a little different from that in the United States in relation to causality and is focused more firmly on foreseeability. In England and the Commonwealth, proximity has been ousted as a test for legal causation by the decision in the Australian case *The Wagon Mound (No.1)* (1961), which is also cited in U.S. cases. The defendants had negligently spilled oil into Sydney Harbour from the *SS Wagon Mound*. The oil had spread, causing foreseeable but minor damage to the Sheerlegs Wharf. Later welding operations set fire to the oil, causing considerable damage to the wharf. An appeal by the defendants was upheld on the grounds that the ignition of the oil was not foreseeable. The foreseeability test for legal causation is consistent with the requirement that damage be foreseeable for there to be a duty of care

- Landes and Posner (1987, p. 187) argue that lack of compensation for pain and suffering is a shortcoming of tort law. Schwartz (1988) argues that it is difficult to compensate intangible losses accurately, and that therefore tort law should avoid imposing liability for pain and suffering. Cook and Graham (1977) point out that when preferences depend upon whether or not one is injured, recovery for nonpecuniary loss may be inconsistent with the insurance function carried out by tort law. Product prices will be higher if producers must cover intangible losses, which may reflect insurance that people do not wish to buy. Calfee and Rubin (1992) argue that measurement difficulties can easily lead to overcompensation or undercompensation of pain and suffering and urge a return to the use of contract law to cover this area of liability

- *Potter v. Firestone* appears to open the way for two claims—one for nervous shock (worrying about the carcinogenic effects) and another if the disease appears. In terms of individual subjective assessment of pleasure and pain, this approach is efficient if the law really can assess causes and value anxiety accurately: Anxiety is real enough for those suffering it even if the disease fails to materialize.

- English law is also particularly restrictive over the ability of dispersed victims to claim damages for pure economic loss. In *Spartan Steel v. Martin and Co.* (1973), where the defendants negligently cut through a public-supply power cable, Lord Denning argued that it was most efficient for the likely victims of such accidents to insure themselves against the consequential losses.

- Feldthusen (1989) describes the typical tort case involving pure economic loss as *relational economic loss*. It may not be possible to impose liability for relational losses upon the tortfeasor without overstating the losses to society. Landes and Posner (1987, p. 251) give a good discussion of the common argument in the law and economics literature that compensating relational economic loss leads to excessive compensation. Bishop and Sutton (1986) point out that requiring the tortfeasor to compensate for a pecuniary externality imposes excessive costs and would encourage too high a level of precaution. However, not compensating the victim would also lead to excessive precautions. See Goldberg (1994) for an analysis of the treatment of economic losses in the case of the *Exxon Valdez* oil spill.

- Epstein (1987) notes that courts commonly require notice to have been given of the contract before they will consider awarding damages for the tort of enticing away an employee. This may work to prevent labor being enticed away once it has been committed to a use, which could be an economic rationale for the tort damages. The possible need for notice explains why film and recording studios often prominently announce celebrity contracts.

- Calabresi (1970) put forward the argument that an aim of accident law should be to reduce the sum of the costs of accidents and the costs of avoiding accidents, and links his analysis with the Coase theorem. The principle of least-cost avoidance has already been discussed in connection with nuisance [Calabresi and Melamed (1972)]. Calabresi's approach is formalized by Diamond (1974).

- Some writers argue that the courts operate many tort rules as though economic efficiency were the objective (Posner, 1972, 1973; Landes and Posner, 1987). Conversely, Dworkin (1980, 1986) has argued that economic efficiency is not an appropriate aim for the law, although he has also derived a "market-simulating" approach to accident law based on egalitarian considerations.

- Strict liability for the consequences of a hazardous "thing or activity" follows the rule in *Rylands v. Fletcher* (1868), where a reservoir flooded a mine.

- The observation that a negligence standard may provide no incentive for the injurer to limit the scale of an activity is developed by Shavell (1980b) and Landes and Posner (1987).

- Robert Cooter and Ariel Porat (2000) argue that, as applied by courts, the Hand formula balances the injurer's burden of precaution and the victim's reduction in risk. However, risk to oneself does not increase the duty owed to others, although economists would strictly count risk to one's self in determining the extent of the duty of care. In cases where precaution reduces joint risk (risk to oneself and others), the usual legal interpretation underestimates the reduction in risk relative to the economic interpretation. The consequence is a lower standard of legal care than required to minimize social costs.

- The bilateral care example in Table 6.1 is a development of the treatment of railway cases in Landes and Posner (1987, p. 89) and is a simplification of the approach in Chung (1993).

- White (1989) compares road accidents in the 37 states using comparative negligence with road accidents in the 13 states (plus the District of Columbia) still using traditional contributory negligence. There appear to be more road accidents under the comparative rule, after controlling for other influences. However, Chung (1993) shows that traditional contributory negligence encourages excessive precaution among possible victims when the assumption of full information for the courts is relaxed.

- Carter and Palmer (1991, 1994) have argued that calculations for the loss of an expected future flow of income can be simplified in both principle and practice by recognizing the offset rule. They argue that on average the expected growth (from changes in labor productivity) in a person's income will equal the rate of interest, so that both may be ignored in calculating the equivalent capital sum. If this offset is valid, the present value of a stream of lost earnings is simply a person's current earnings multiplied by the number of years for which the loss occurs. To illustrate the offset rule, assume a simple case in which there is no price or wage inflation. The individual's earnings are expected to grow because of labor productivity growth, but we ignore the effects of possible promotion. To keep the calculation of the present value (PV) simple, assume that the loss occurs over two future time periods. Then

$$PV = D[(1 + w)/(1 + i)] + D[(1 + w)/(1 + i)]^2$$

where

D = current annual earnings
w = annual growth rate of labor productivity
i = rate of interest

If $w = i$, then: $PV = 2D$

In general under the offset rule, the present value will equal current earnings multiplied by the number of years of loss.

Carter and Palmer have presented empirical evidence for the United States (1991) and for Canada (1994) that supports the use of the offset rule. The evidence suggests that interest rates and labor productivity growth cancel out after allowance is made for inflation. Posner (1998) similarly notes that calculations can be simplified by deducting inflation from both earnings growth and nominal interest rates.

- Readers in the United Kingdom should note that the 1932 British case *Donoghue v. Stevenson* (a Scottish case on appeal to the House of Lords and roughly equivalent to the U.S. case of *Escola*) extended the duty of care to include that of manufacturers toward all users of their products for whom possible harm was foreseeable. In *Donoghue*, the plaintiff recovered damages after she drank ginger beer containing a snail, although she had not bought the drink herself.

- It is noticeable that most of the postwar growth in litigation in the United States is in the area of product liability (Markesinis, 1990). Rubin and Bailey (1994) explain this growth in terms of the rent-seeking tendencies of lawyers as a special-interest group. Their explanation of the strict-liability character of modern product-liability law is quite distinct from Landes and Posner's (1987, Chapter 1) efficiency hypothesis and Priest's (1985) ideological explanation. In particular, Rubin and Bailey note that the U.S. legal system operates to the disadvantage of manufacturers. A decision in one state benefits plaintiffs (and their lawyers) in that state but harms manufacturers in all states, as a manufacturer who sells in a state can be sued there. They also note that the American Association of Trial Lawyers was formed as a powerful interest group right in the heart of the period during which pressure began to mount for reforms of product-liability law. There is also statistical evidence in favor of the rent-seeking thesis: Both the number of lawyers per capita (LPC) and the rate of growth of LPC in a state turned out to be statistically significant determinants of revisions to product-liability law.

THE ECONOMICS OF CRIME

There is a considerable body of economic analysis examining crime as a special case of rational maximizing behavior. This literature has developed separately from the economic analysis of law as a part of mainstream applied economics. Economists have mostly concerned themselves with the economics of criminal deterrence. There is a more recent trend toward integrating this work into the modern economic analysis of law by focusing on the way the system of criminal justice operates compared with areas of private law like tort.

THE NATURE OF CRIMINAL ACTIVITY

Usually, a person commits a crime by intentionally carrying out an act prohibited by statute or common law, and for which the coercive power of the state is drawn upon in imposing a penalty. It is not obvious why many injurious acts are regarded as crimes when others are not. Indeed, some noninjurious acts, such as unfinished robberies, can be "victimless" crimes. Also, in the past, many actions now treated as crimes were treated as torts. We need to examine the key features of criminal law that set it apart from its civil counterpart.

The standard of proof is different in the case of crime. First, the prosecution must prove its case beyond reasonable doubt, which is a tougher criterion than the one used in civil disputes. In a tort case, by contrast, it is enough to show that the defendant was negligent—by the standards of a reasonable person—in causing the injury. The tougher criterion in a criminal case reflects the penalties the court may apply, which are potentially severe. Punishment in a criminal case goes beyond compensating the victim and imposes harm on the criminal.

Second, in most cases, the prosecution must show that the criminal intended to commit the crime. There must usually be intent to cause harm. This again contrasts with civil cases: For example, nuisance is defined independently of the state of mind of the tortfeasor. In terms of a spectrum of harm, many injurious acts resulting from negligence are the subject of tort actions. However, intentional harm and severe forms of negligence, like "recklessness" over risk taking or "gross negligence" over professional duties, are dealt with by the potentially more severe sanctions of the criminal law. One explanation of this distinction is that criminal law aims to suppress the criminal frame of mind, which is identified by the demonstration of intent. Recklessness (and gross negligence) are commonly interpreted by the courts as amounting to intent. For example, if a person drops a rock from an overpass onto a car, killing the driver, that person may have ignored a serious obvious risk (advertent recklessness) or not cared at all about it (inadvertent recklessness).

The major exception to the requirement to show intent is the case of the strict-liability crime, such as possession of narcotics. In these instances, possession may reasonably be taken to imply intent to use the items. It would be virtually impossible to distinguish accidental from deliberate possession. Therefore, these examples of strict-liability crimes are not really inconsistent with the general requirement for intent to be proved. A defense in these cases can be that one did not know of the possession, which is consistent with treating possession as indicative of intent absent proof to the contrary.

The third major distinguishing characteristic of criminal law is that the harm has an element of being public. Crime disrupts social codes of behavior that are thought to be beneficial to all. Crimes like murder, assault, or robbery, for example, are disturbing to many people and not just to their victims. There is a wider public interest in prosecuting the criminal than in suing the typical tortfeasor. The victim of a crime (or a relative) has an incentive to sue to reclaim personal losses only. However, this will not obtain compensation for the fear and anxiety experienced by dispersed observers of the crime. Notice that the victim can take an action in tort against a criminal: The criminal law comes in on top of civil remedies. Also, when someone causes an accident through gross negligence, such as an accident caused by driving under the influence of alcohol, the criminal law steps in to prosecute for criminal negligence. Finally in this regard, the prosecution of public nuisance—for example, blocking a public highway—by public authorities also supports the hypothesis that it is mainly the dispersed nature of damage that causes the state to step in.

There is usually a low probability of apprehension in the case of many criminal acts, particularly because the criminal intends to hide the crime. Therefore, relatively severe penalties will be needed to deter the harm. For example, if there is only a 50 percent chance of catching the thief of a car valued at $1,000, the fine must be set at just over $2,000 if the expected value of stealing is to be negative. Action in tort would for the most part succeed only in reclaiming $1,000 in damages. On a related theme, criminals are often poor and would not be able to pay damages, particularly because they often sell stolen property at below market value. Then the only real way to create a deterrent is to impose a custodial or other nonmonetary sanction. These considerations suggest that the coercive power of the state is useful in deterring criminal behavior.

Finally, most crime is socially wasteful and represents a classic form of rent-seeking behavior. Criminals devote resources to pure redistribution of existing goods without creating anything new. Their potential victims devote resources to security devices, to paying insurance companies, and to funding the cost of the police service. Similarly, a thief may value a stolen item at an amount (say, $1) that is below its owner's valuation (of, say, $50). We cannot be sure that resources move to their highest-valued uses when items are stolen. Crime is typically doubly wasteful.

CRIMINAL DETERRENCE

Standard economic analysis has been successfully applied to general criminal behavior. If people are rational maximizing beings, we should find that

1.   Crime rates respond to the costs and benefits of committing crimes.

2.   People respond to deterring incentives such as criminal law.

It follows that devoting resources to detection, conviction, and punishment should influence the level of crime. For this to be true, people need not be rational all the time.

They must, however, be influenced by criminal penalties at the margin of their behavior in order for deterrence to work. The deterrence hypothesis has influenced not only economists, but some sociologists and policy makers as well.

The main alternatives to the deterrence hypothesis are claims that crime results from biological influences like mental illness or from social factors such as unemployment. The policy implications of these alternative explanations are that we need to tackle problems like unemployment and poverty and/or improve the mental health of the population. The alternatives to the deterrence hypothesis are not convincing in explaining rising crime rates, for crimes against either property or persons. We would have to show that poverty was rising or that the mental health of the population suddenly deteriorated, when in reality these factors change slowly.

Strictly biological accounts of crime are also often subject to criticism. If criminals were genetically predisposed toward a life of crime, it would be hard to explain why the original convict population of Australia did not beget a nation of criminals. Furthermore, the common observation that criminals are frequently of below average intelligence is not in itself in conflict with the deterrence hypothesis. Low intelligence may limit criminals' options, leading them rationally to turn to crime unless deterred. With few exceptions, statistical studies fail to give a major role to nondeterrence factors.

Deterrence and the Supply and Demand for Crime

The deterrence hypothesis is illustrated by Figure 7.1. The horizontal axis shows the amount of crime committed by an individual, measured by the number of offenses, and the vertical axis shows costs and benefits. If the marginal costs (MC_1) of criminal activity rises and the marginal benefits (MB) fall, as shown, there is an optimal level of crime (C^*) where marginal cost intersects marginal benefit. Marginal cost shows the minimum return required before an individual would engage in successive units of crime:

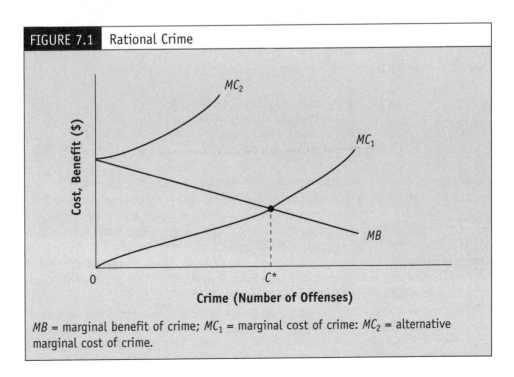

FIGURE 7.1 Rational Crime

MB = marginal benefit of crime; MC_1 = marginal cost of crime: MC_2 = alternative marginal cost of crime.

It is therefore a supply function for crime. Marginal benefit shows the maximum the individual would pay for the opportunity to undertake successive units of crime, ignoring costs, and can be regarded as the demand for crime.

For some people, the intersection of supply and demand gives a corner solution to Figure 7.1, for example, if marginal cost (supply) takes the position MC_2, meaning the individual does not engage in crime. As one example, the higher position of marginal cost could be consistent with worrying about the effect on one's reputation if criminal activities are apparent. The costs of criminal activity are not necessarily monetary ones associated with committing crimes. Similarly, marginal benefits are not limited to monetary gains: For example, some sadistic people obtain direct pleasure from engaging in acts of violence. We would nonetheless need to measure the individual's willingness to pay for the benefits or for avoiding the costs.

Economics suggests that we can influence individuals to reduce their criminal activity by undertaking policies to shift the marginal cost function upward and the marginal benefit function downward. Comparing the costs and benefits of clearing up a particular crime allows us to find an optimum level of crime prevention. It is important to remember that no policies are without cost and it is unlikely to be sensible to try to stop all crime, which would almost certainly be too costly to achieve. The concept of optimal crime and punishment is discussed later in this chapter.

The deterrence approach is not necessarily incompatible with alternative approaches emphasizing wider social factors or apparently noneconomic individual characteristics. For example, in Figure 7.1 a psychological predisposition toward crime might shift the marginal cost function to the right, reflecting lower psychic (conscience-based) costs from engaging in crime. We can fit various shift factors like this into a model of rational crime. The real question is empirical: Which factors influence criminal behavior in a major way?

The deterrence hypothesis can be formulated by using a little calculus. Taking any crime as an example, we can write

$$EU = pU(Y - f) + (1 - p)U(Y)$$

where: p = probability of capture and punishment

$$
\begin{aligned}
U &= \text{utility (assumed measurable)} \\
EU &= \text{expected utility} \\
f &= \text{value of punishment} \\
Y &= \text{income if undetected}
\end{aligned}
$$

Increasing p by a small amount (dp) implies EU changes by $dp[U(Y-f) - U(Y)]$, which must be negative. The cost-benefit calculation of the rational criminal implies that increasing the probability of detection, perhaps by expanding the police force, deters criminal behavior. Similarly, increasing the severity of the punishment (f) by a small amount (df) implies EU changes by $df(p)(\partial U/\partial f)$, which is again negative since $\partial U/\partial f$ (the rate of change of utility with respect to punishment) should be negative. Increasing the probability of capture and punishment, and increasing the severity of the punishment, both reduce the criminal's expected utility and should deter crime.

There are several possible economic reasons why deterrence might not be found. First, private deterrence efforts might fall as public deterrence increases. Individuals may be less vigilant about crime if they felt the authorities had it under control. Second, some crime could be displaced to another offense type, time, or location. Also, if criminals have target incomes, deterrence could imply that more crime would occur: For example, there could be more attempted break-ins that the police managed to halt. Finally, in this respect the deterrence of established criminals could encourage the entry of replacements into the crime "industry": Deterring organized drug traffickers might let in amateur drug mules.

However, statistical work tends to support the deterrence hypothesis in terms of the effect of arrest and conviction rates, and sentence length. Some of the statistical results are studied more closely after a brief examination of the impact of deterrence variables on the behavior of a risk-taking individual.

Risk Taking and Deterrence

A standard result of economic deterrence models is that increasing the probability of capture and punishment is a stronger deterrent to crime than increasing the severity of sentencing. This assumes that criminals are risk takers, which may well be true. This suggestion can be examined with the aid of Figure 7.2, which shows a utility function for a risk taker. Utility is shown on the vertical axis and is assumed to be measurable for purposes of illustration. The money value of payoffs is shown on the horizontal axis. The utility function is convex when viewed from below, which is consistent with risk taking. To keep things simple, we also assume that the crime involves the theft of money and may be punished by imposing a monetary fine.

Figure 7.2 shows four possible levels of money income for a criminal. The highest level, Y, results if a crime is successfully completed without detection. The two lower

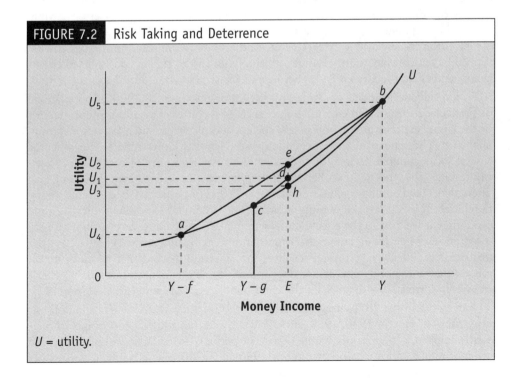

FIGURE 7.2   Risk Taking and Deterrence

U = utility.

levels, $(Y - f)$ and $(Y - g)$, give the post-crime income after the imposition with certainty of either a high fine, f, or a low fine, g. However, detection is not certain. Point e, which is halfway along a line joining points a and b on the utility function, shows the expected outcome if the probability of punishment is 0.5. Reading down from e, the expected money income is given by E (i.e., $[0.5(Y - f) + 0.5Y]$). The expected utility associated with e is shown as U_2 on the vertical axis $(0.5U_4 + 0.5U_5)$. If point e were closer to a, the probability of punishment would be higher.

It follows that point d, directly below e on a line joining c and b and reflecting the lower fine valued at g, results in the same expected income of E. Point d is more than half the distance from b to c. Therefore, d represents a lower fine but higher probability of punishment compared with point e. Since U_1 is less than U_2, the criminal prefers e to d. A low fine coupled with a high probability of punishment is a greater deterrent than a high fine with a low probability, when both packages give the same expected income.

This result depends upon the shape of the utility function, which reflects risk taking by the criminal. Consider an individual at point h with an income of E. The utility from E is U_3. Since e is above h, the individual prefers a gamble in which there is a 0.5 probability of income being either higher or lower by the same amount, and where the expected value of income is unchanged. The shape of the utility function implies the individual is risk loving.

Tests of the Deterrence Hypothesis

Statistical tests tend to support the deterrence hypothesis in terms of the effect of arrest and conviction rates, and of sentence length on the amount of crime. The studies examine the effects of a range of justice and more general variables in determining a variety of types of crime, covering both property and violent crime. Property crime mainly includes burglary and theft, whereas violent crime consists of robberies like muggings, as well as the more obvious categories of murder and assault. Statistical work can be plagued by data problems; for example, it can be difficult to obtain consistent long-run data in studies for the United States because of the separate state jurisdictions.

Typical statistical models of crime link the crime rate (per 100,000 of population) for particular forms of crime to influences such as the arrest rate and sentence length for the crime, expenditure on police, and socioeconomic factors such as the unemployment rate. The influences are independent variables that either reflect deterrence or general socioeconomic factors. Statistical studies have a number of commonly occurring results. First, they tend on balance to support the deterrence hypothesis but give different detailed results for different crimes. Property crime has been found to be more affected by deterrence variables than is violent crime. However, studies typically give different weights to the effects of detection and conviction relative to the severity of sentencing in deterring crime, showing that detection and conviction rates have the greater effect. Finally, a surprising result of the empirical work is that expenditure on police either does not deter crime or does so only weakly. Expenditure on police is not necessarily correlated with arrests if the extra members of the force are desk bound.

Early work in the 1970s using statistical methods to test the deterrence hypothesis using robbery data for 1940, 1950, and 1960 showed that a higher probability of conviction implied a lower robbery rate across all periods. In addition, a higher average sentence implied a lower robbery rate for 1940 and 1960. These results gave support to the deterrence hypothesis and were mostly supported by subsequent research. One

Three Strikes and You're Out!

Many states have enacted "three-strikes and you're out" laws increasing punishment for frequent offenders. To date, California is the only one actively enforcing such legislation. Empirical results indicate that "strike" sentences generally deter crimes: That is to say, they have a statistically significant negative effects on levels of crime. During the first two years of the legislation, approximately eight murders, 3,952 aggravated assaults, 10,672 robberies, and 384,488 burglaries were deterred in California. Petty theft may have increased, which is a possible displacement effect.

SOURCE: Shepherd, Joanna M. 2002. Fear of the first strike: The full deterrent effect of California's two- and three-strikes legislation. *Journal of Legal Studies* 31(1): 159–201.

criticism of this early work was that data on the criminal justice system and crime variables are not fully comparable across different states. Therefore, economists have often turned to the study of crimes for which data are consistent across different states, and to data from unified jurisdictions such as England or from within individual states in the United States. In studies of evasion of the U.S. military draft, for which data are consistently gathered, a greater probability of conviction implied lower evasion of the draft, supporting the deterrence hypothesis. Studies based on English data also tend to support the deterrence hypothesis, with increases in the probability of conviction having a bigger impact on crime than severity of sentence.

Sometimes support for the deterrence hypothesis can be seen in natural experiments as states change laws. Recent work on the effects of increasing penalties for frequent offenders under the "three-strikes" laws in California reveals a deterrence effect, as discussed in the boxed example.

Property crime, in particular, would seem to be highly influenced by deterrence factors. The support found for the deterrence hypothesis is of great academic interest. It shows that criminal behavior is like most forms of behavior and is influenced by costs and benefits. However, it does not follow that public policy should concentrate only on the probability of eventual capture and punishment of criminals. The optimal public policy response to crime depends also upon the costs of creating deterrence. It may still be the case that a technically weak deterrent is very cheap to apply relative to a technically more effective deterrent. Consequently, a country might find it more cost-effective to apply a significant amount of the cheaper deterrent in seeking a given amount of crime reduction. Some studies have shown it to be 30 percent cheaper to reduce, for example, property crime by 1 percent by increasing average sentence length than by increasing the number of offenders imprisoned. It is typically much more costly, by up to a factor of 10, to achieve the 1 percent reduction by increasing general police numbers.

Additionally, the effect on crime rates of changes in unemployment levels has been subject to statistical testing and is currently topical. A possible alternative hypothesis holds that people are driven to crime by deprivation. This hypothesis need not be inconsistent with the economic analysis of crime: The unemployed have a lower opportunity cost attached to their use of time in criminal pursuits. However, the same studies showing support for the deterrence hypothesis tend to show at best a weak impact from changes in unemployment rates. For some crimes, such as auto theft, crime rates can actually fall in a recession and rise in an economic upswing.

There are some fundamental problems in testing theories of crime using cross-sectional data (looking across different regions). A correlation between crime and unemployment, for example, may not show a causal relationship but instead may reflect the influence of a third variable such as poor educational standards. There is a major issue concerning crime spillovers: An area with high unemployment may be less able to raise local taxes to spend on policing and may therefore attract criminals from other areas. The unemployed would not be committing the crimes, but researchers would find a high correlation between unemployment and crime. A similar effect would follow if reduced policing in a poorer area simply encouraged the existing criminals to greater activity. Again, a meaningless correlation would be observed between crime and unemployment.

How Different Is Violent Crime?

Most countries have experienced increases in violent crime in recent decades, although statistics show falls in many major cities in recent years. Violence against the person, including homicide, assault, and rape, amounted to 7.4 million crimes, according to the survey of crime victims carried out by the Federal Bureau of Justice Statistics in 2000. This figure showed a fall of 15 percent from the previous year but was a massive increase on most previous years. According to the Department of Justice, the violent-crime rate never dropped below 675 per 100,000 of population during the period 1992–2002.

Violent crime may be subject to a wider range of influences than property crime. Some statistical studies of the determinants of violent crime show weak significance for deterrence variables such as prison sentences or rates of arrest. Several studies reveal a role for wider influences on violent crime compared with crime against property. However, very recent empirical studies do emphasize deterrence variables and suggest that it may be a more complex matter to study deterrence in the context of violent crime.

Several studies have found a positive correlation between increases in violent crime and upturns in economic activity. The explanation offered is that boom times lead to increased use of leisure facilities and greater interpersonal contact, which results in conflicts and an increase in violent crime. Researchers have also found a positive correlation between the consumption of alcohol and the incidence of violent offenses.

Empirical studies focusing on post-imprisonment experience show that justice variables also deter violent crime. One study tracked 317 youths after they were released following their first custodial sentences. The youths had an average record of 13 arrests each prior to their imprisonment for an average of 10 months. Offenses included homicide, rape, assault, car theft, armed robbery, and burglary. After imprisonment, their repeat arrests fell by two-thirds on average. A comparison group of nonimprisoned juvenile offenders did not show the same reduction in the rate of rearrest. It is unlikely that the imprisoned youths were learning from other prisoners how to avoid arrest to an extent that would account for such a large drop in repeat arrests.

Another study looked at rearrest rates and examined the characteristics of 641 men released over a 3-year period in North Carolina. The higher the probability of conviction for a crime, the lower the number of subsequent arrests per month released. Increases in the severity of prior punishment had a stronger deterrent effect compared with increases in the probability of conviction for violent crime. Increasing the probability of conviction had a stronger deterrent effect on reoffending in the case of crimes against property.

Gun Laws and Crime Rates

A recent study (see "Notes on the Literature" at the end of this chapter) initiated considerable national debate about the deterrence effect of gun laws, focusing on both violent and property crime. There was a general movement after 1985 toward state laws that permit the carrying of concealed handguns, subject to background checks principally meant to exclude criminals and people suffering from mental illness. Right-to-carry laws have now been enacted in over 30 states, often replacing more restrictive laws requiring guns to be visible if carried. The effect of the states passing right-to-carry laws must be carefully disentangled from other developments over recent decades. In particular, the Brady Act tightened background checks on applicants and introduced waiting periods for gun permits from March 1994 until the Supreme Court struck down the law's background check requirements in 1997. A statistically significant negative impact upon crime from the adoption of concealed-handgun laws by the states appears to be evident, after controlling for other possible influences.

The study also analyzed simultaneous effects on crime from background checks, waiting periods, and concealed-handgun laws, using a data set drawn over 16 years from all 3,054 U.S. counties. Possible effects from changes in arrest and conviction rates, changes in prison sentence lengths, and unemployment, income, and poverty levels were also considered. Arrest and conviction rates were the most important influences on crime rates, but laws giving the right to carry concealed handguns were also statistically significant. The study claimed that passing such handgun laws decreased murders by over 8 percent, rapes by 5 percent, and robberies by 3 percent. The reductions were greatest for the most urban and crime-ridden counties. Women benefited more than men from carrying concealed handguns.

In theory, concealed-handgun laws could have a positive or negative effect on violent crime. They make it easier for the criminal *and* the targeted victim to conceal a weapon. The possible negative effect arises partly because of the uncertainty created in the criminal mind: Does the victim have a gun or not? As Ringo explains in the movie *Pulp Fiction*, it may be better to avoid certain targets: "Bars, liquor stores, gas stations—you get your head blown off stickin' up one of them." It is also possible to cite the different international rates for burglaries carried out while a resident is at home, so-called "hot" burglaries. The rate for hot burglary in the United States is 13 percent, whereas in England and Canada, with much tougher gun-control laws, the rate is around 50 percent.

On balance, the effect of right-to-carry laws seems to be negative, with states adopting the concealed-gun law showing a reduction in crime levels. One implication of this result is that violent crime may not be so different from property crime in that violent crime is apparently deterred by risks arising for criminals from citizens' self-defense. Although the relationship between gun laws and violent crime is controversial, the robustness of the early statistical results has been supported by subsequent studies.

PUNISHMENTS

In this section, we examine various economic issues concerning the use of punishment as a means of influencing criminal behavior. Mainly this involves comparing the use of fines with imprisonment. However, there are other sanctions that deserve some attention. Capital punishment, in particular, has generated a considerable amount of literature and is considered separately in its own subsection.

Optimal Punishment

Figure 7.3 illustrates the distinction between cost-effective and optimal levels of deterrence. We assume there are two alternative forms of deterrence, measured as a projected reduction in a crime rate. Marginal cost for the high-cost deterrent (e.g., policing) is shown by MC_2, whereas MC_1 refers to a low-cost alternative (e.g., increasing sentence length). In the case of policing, MC_2 measures the costs of increasing policing hours to achieve an additional unit of deterrence. Similarly, MC_1 shows the marginal cost of increasing average sentence length to achieve the additional unit of deterrence. The marginal benefit of deterrence is assumed to be constant and equal for the two forms of deterrence, as shown by the line labeled MB.

If there are spending constraints, then we maximize deterrence using the available alternatives keeping within the budget constraint. Maximum deterrence for any budget is found by using the cheapest solution (prison) initially and then by switching between policing and prison, depending on which is cheapest to use to obtain an increment of deterrence. For example, Oe prison and Oc policing together give the lowest possible cost for achieving Og deterrence (at a marginal cost of a for either method). We can show the marginal cost of deterrence from combining the two methods by horizontally summing MC_1 and MC_2, giving the line labeled ΣMC in

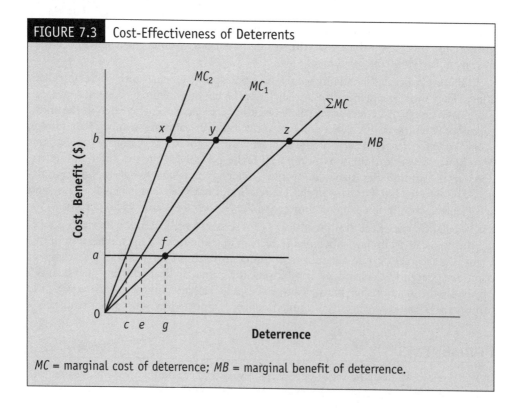

FIGURE 7.3   Cost-Effectiveness of Deterrents

MC = marginal cost of deterrence; MB = marginal benefit of deterrence.

Figure 7.3. The area under ΣMC gives the total cost of particular levels of deterrence: For example, Ofg is the cost of Og deterrence. It follows that a given budget of Ofg should be spent on Oc policing and Oe prison for cost-effective deterrence.

If we had no spending constraints, we would expand deterrence to a level associated with point z, where marginal benefit equals marginal cost. This would place us at point x for expenditure on police and at point y for prison. Notice that in the optimum for both the constrained and unconstrained case, both forms of deterrence have the same marginal cost.

Imprisonment Versus Fines

Imprisoning an offender has one major advantage for the population at large: It incapacitates the criminal and prevents further offenses from being committed against the general public. At the same time, rehabilitation of the criminal is made possible. Also, we know from earlier sections of this chapter that there is a deterrent effect on the incarcerated and on others. A final advantage of imprisonment is that it may gratify a sense of retribution for law-abiding members of society. All of these effects may be regarded as economic benefits.

However, the costs of imprisonment are generally high, which explains why alternatives such as fines are often used. First, there are direct costs of imprisonment: the costs of buildings, meals, and prison guards. The cost of imprisonment can be over $100,000 a year in special category prisons. There are also less obvious costs in the shape of the opportunity costs of prisoners' skills and time, which they cannot use while incarcerated.

Fines have virtually no costs of operation and raise money for the state. They are thus a very attractive option where there are no special reasons to use imprisonment. If offenders were always solvent, the authorities would prefer fines to prison (unless there were noneconomic grounds for jail) as fines are less costly to administer. This is illustrated in Figure 7.4 on page 164, which is based on deterrence indifference curves—for the criminal—between the severity of a fine and of imprisonment. Any deterrence indifference curve (like DI or DI_1) shows the combinations of fine and imprisonment that will produce the same reduction in a particular form of criminal behavior. Higher indifference curves show greater deterrence.

With no constraint on the criminal's wealth, the fine is the least-cost solution. We can reach any level of deterrence, such as Y^* or Y^{**}, simply by imposing a heavy enough fine that the criminal has no problem with paying. With the limit on wealth shown in Figure 7.4, there is a problem. The criminal cannot be made to pay more than Z as a fine. The authorities can only achieve increases in criminal deterrence by moving to points on the indifference curves like a and b, which require X^* and X^{**} years of imprisonment along with a fine of Z, which together will be costly. The existence of a wealth constraint for the criminal may imply that budgetary limits for the authorities restrict deterrence to DI if, for example, X^* is the maximum level of affordable imprisonment. Without the constraint, the authorities could simply set a high fine and achieve deterrence on DI_1 at point Y^{**}.

Other Punishments

Apart from fines and imprisonment, other sanctions include such things as orders for probation or for compulsory community service. Probation involves the close supervision of

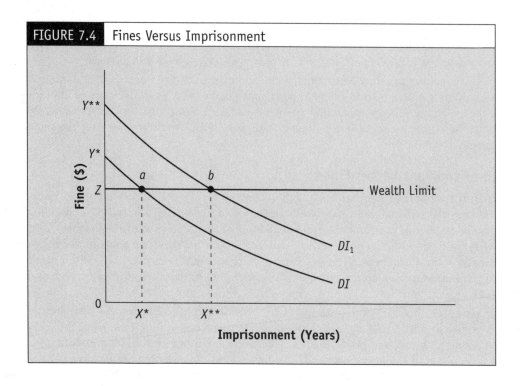

FIGURE 7.4   Fines Versus Imprisonment

a convicted offender and occurs outside of prison. Costs are saved, but there is still the possibility of encouraging rehabilitation. Compulsory community service imposes costs on convicted criminals, but again avoids the costs of imprisonment. The United States, unusual among advanced societies, also allows for the possibility of capital punishment.

Capital Punishment

Capital punishment is still used by 38 states in the United States as a punishment for murder. The use of capital punishment is a continuing issue of public-policy debate. An important question is whether the death penalty has a deterrent effect on homicide.

An early empirical study used a model of deterrence in which the murderer maximizes utility by comparing the costs and benefits of the crime. Technically, this type of study models the "supply" of murder. Time-series data were used for the period 1933 to 1969. Property-crime variables were used to represent the benefits of murder because murder is correlated with property crime, a result found in several studies. The benefits of murder were determined by data on unemployment, levels of wealth, and the age structure and racial composition of the population. The costs of murder (to the murderer) were measured by alternative measures of the hazard of punishment: the probability of arrest for murder; the probability of conviction given arrest; and the probability of execution given conviction. The results of the study showed that the murder rate was negatively and significantly correlated with (in order of deterrence strength) the arrest, conviction, and execution probabilities. One striking conclusion was that one extra execution in a year would deter eight murders, famously quoted by the U.S. Supreme Court in the case of *Gregg v. Georgia* (1976). A less quoted result was that the deterrent effect of improved labor-market conditions was greater than for the justice variables.

The Deterrent Effect of Capital Punishment

Between 1972 and 1976, the Supreme Court imposed a moratorium on capital punishment. Dezhbakhsh, Rubin, and Shepherd construct a linear model (showing proportional effects) of the supply of murder, covering 3,054 counties for the period 1977 to 1996 (a "panel" of data), making use of the natural experiment. A linear model was used partly because it has been found to be the *least* likely to generate a deterrence effect from capital punishment. The data are mostly taken at the county rather than state level.

In carrying out their study, Dezhbakhsh, Rubin, and Shepherd consider an argument that homicide data contain both premeditated acts and crimes of passion, with the latter being insensitive to deterrence. The authors point out that crimes of passion affect statistical models as random events and do not disturb our ability to model the nonrandom, premeditated component of homicide.

Dezhbakhsh, Rubin, and Shepherd construct their model to include the following influences: sentencing and execution data, expenditure on the police and on the judicial system, statewide voting for the Republican presidential candidate (a "get tough" measure), prison admissions (measuring the burden on the justice system), the levels of other violent crimes, labor market conditions, population density and racial mix, and ownership of rifles. The data are used to predict the probabilities of apprehending, sentencing, and executing murderers, which in turn are used to predict the county-level murder rate. They report the results from varying their model across six specifications to reflect the effects on criminals' expectations based on plausible leads and lags in the criminal justice system (they estimate many more versions with different, including nonlinear, specifications as a check on the robustness of results).

Increases in the probability of arrest, sentencing, and execution all have a negative and mostly highly significant impact on murder in all six specifications of their model. The murder rate also increased with measures of aggravated assault and robbery, for which there was a highly significant positive effect. Several other factors are of interest. Increases in the proportion of males increased the murder rate, as did increases in per capita income, whereas youth factors decreased it. Gun ownership, measured by membership of the National Rifle Association (NRA) had a mostly significant positive association with increases in the murder rate. Dezhbakhsh, Rubin, and Shepherd comment that the surprising positive link between NRA membership and murder rates does not necessarily contradict the current crop of results finding a significant negative link between the right to carry concealed guns and murder. NRA membership does not necessarily reflect *concealed* weapons. Further results from the study: the more Republican a state, the more common are death sentences; police expenditure increases the probability of arrest; increases in population density may lower murder rates for ranges indicating suburbs but then raise rates in the inner city. Finally, Dezhbakhsh, Rubin, and Shepherd estimate that, on average for the United States, one execution deters 18 murders with a margin of error of 10—a minimum of eight and a maximum of 28.

SOURCE: Dezhbakhsh, Rubin, and Shepherd. 2003. Does capital punishment have a deterrent effect? *American Law and Economics Review* 5(2).

One possible criticism of the study's findings is that deterrence cannot logically follow unless there is conviction. Capital punishment might make juries less willing to convict, in which case it might not act as a deterrent. A subsequent study reestimated the model and found that an increase in the use of the death penalty decreased the probability of conviction by 17 percent. In the United Kingdom, there was indeed a fall in the number of murderers found not guilty by reason of insanity after the abolition of capital punishment in 1965. However, care must be taken in interpreting this effect of abolition, as the removal of a death penalty may have removed the incentive to plead insanity, which also effectively resulted in a life sentence.

The conclusions of early studies of capital punishment seemed to be sensitive to changes of approach, in particular in relation to the statistical form used as data were aggregated and to the time period chosen. Some later researchers found that omitting the period 1962–1969, during which executions dropped from 47 to zero, had a particularly disturbing effect in removing the deterrent effect of capital punishment. Some researchers found they could remove the deterrent effect by including other crime rates in the murder supply function or by introducing measures of rifle ownership. However, there are several later studies that strongly support the broad conclusions of early work even after controlling for wider factors influencing murder. The boxed example on page 165 gives details of a very carefully carried out piece of research that suggests that on average an execution may deter at least eight murders.

There is a substantial amount of evidence that supports a deterrent effect for capital punishment. It does not follow from this that there is a strong economic argument in favor of using a death penalty for murder. Even if capital punishment is a deterrent, it is not necessarily cost-effective. The financial costs of capital punishment include running an exhaustive appeal system and operating death row, and these costs are high. Also, as Dezhbakhsh, Rubin, and Shepherd point out in their article, the costs of mistaken convictions are very high when an irreversible penalty of this sort is used.

DRUG ENFORCEMENT

Serious drug use has grown in most parts of the world since the 1960s. Most addiction is associated with heroin, although there have been trends toward cocaine use, including crack cocaine. Public concern arises because of perceptions of the debilitating effect of addiction and the association of crime with drug addiction. Addicts seem to be unable to hold regular jobs and therefore support their habits with crime. Much public policy focuses on restricting supplies. There is a possible problem with this policy because if addicts have an inelastic demand for a drug (i.e., one that does not change much in response to price changes), supply restrictions merely increase the price and thus could increase any associated crime. This unintended consequence of government intervention is illustrated by Figure 7.5., where addicts' demand for heroin is given by D_a and that for nonaddicts by D_{na}.

Shifting the supply function to the left in Figure 7.5 causes addicts to pay more but hardly reduces their use of heroin, due to the inelasticity of D_a. Casual users (D_{na}) are more sensitive to changes in price and can be deterred by restrictions, as shown by the large fall in equilibrium sales from Y to X. The supply curve is shifted left by policies that crack down on supplies entering a country, for example, increasing customs inspections.

A policy favored in some countries allows addicts to receive either a particular drug or possibly a substitute for it, but the authorities restrict the supplies to casual users and criminalize possession just as in the United States. The hope is that addicts will be less attracted to crime and may be medically supervised to help them overcome addiction. Clinical supervision of addicts is also useful in controlling needle use and the associated transmission of diseases. The two-track approach to drug control is consistent with the economic analysis of enforcement shown in Figure 7.5.

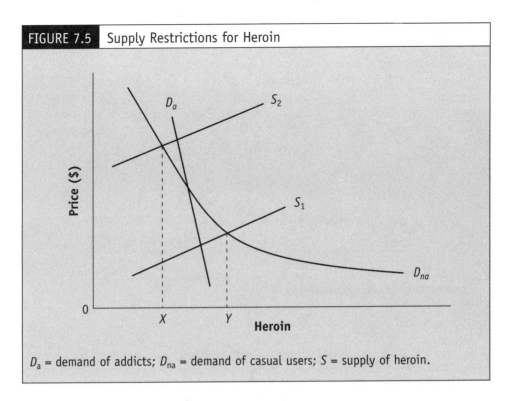

FIGURE 7.5 Supply Restrictions for Heroin

D_a = demand of addicts; D_{na} = demand of casual users; S = supply of heroin.

ASSORTED DEVELOPMENTS IN CRIMINAL JUSTICE

A number of contemporary issues connected with the system of criminal justice are linked by their novelty rather than by anything else. All are amenable to economic analysis.

Plea Bargaining

Plea bargaining is an integral part of the American criminal justice system. Under this arrangement, the accused agrees to plead guilty in exchange for some reduction in the sentence sought by the prosecution. The prosecution, therefore, has a significant influence on sentencing in plea bargaining. A typical pattern might be for the accused to plead guilty to a lesser set of charges than those being brought, in exchange for an agreed sentence that the prosecution will recommend to the judge. Similar, but not identical, arrangements are used in other countries.

Figure 7.6 on page 168 shows the payoffs to a defendant from going to trial. These depend upon whether conviction or acquittal is the result and whether or not the judge is *soft* or *tough*. Figure 7.6 describes a courtroom game in extensive form: That is, we follow all the possible directions a trial could take, beginning at the origin at the left of the diagram. The probability attached to each branch (relative to the preceding node) is printed alongside it. For simplicity, each branch is regarded as equally likely. The defendant is released if acquitted (with probability = 0.5) and incurs no penalty. If guilty, the defendant is equally likely to face a tough or soft judge. A tough judge will impose a sentence of three years, whereas a soft one will impose only one year.

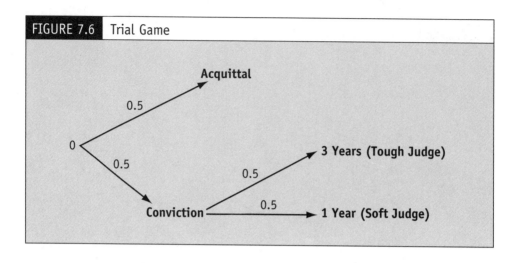

FIGURE 7.6 | Trial Game

Acquittal

0.5

0

0.5

Conviction

0.5

0.5

3 Years (Tough Judge)

1 Year (Soft Judge)

The expected value of punishment is

$$0.5 \, [0.5 \, (3 + 1)] = 1 \text{ year}$$

If the prosecutor and defendant agree on the probabilities, and assuming for simplicity that both are risk neutral, the defendant would plead guilty in exchange for a promised sentence of up to one year. Both sides then save the cost of going to trial. The attraction of plea bargaining is easy to see: Certainty prevails and the parties can save the costs of prosecution and defense. Public prosecutors may be happy with the quantity and level of conviction, which may still create criminal deterrence. Defendants may save the cost of their defense and consider their welfare improved by plea bargaining.

Countries without a system of plea bargaining can have the problem of *cracked trials*. The accused may plead guilty until finally arriving in court, where the plea is changed to not guilty. Observers suggest the accused may wait to see whether the judge is tough or soft before deciding whether or not to attempt a defense. The U.S. experience of plea bargaining has encouraged other countries to follow suit. In the United Kingdom, which was suffering an 83 percent rate of cracked trials, the Royal Commission on Criminal Justice introduced a system of sentence discounts in 1993. The discount is greater the earlier the guilty plea is made, but is subject to procedural rules aimed at ensuring no defendant is pressured into pleading guilty. The judge announces the possible discount at the beginning of a trial so that discretion over sentencing is circumscribed.

Neighborhood Watch

In a neighborhood-watch system, a group of neighbors agree to be vigilant on crime prevention, such as taking care of locking premises and making efforts to report suspicious behavior. The idea is to increase awareness of crime. These methods do not have a good track record and are often found to make little impact on levels of crime. This is not surprising: Economic analysis suggests that a neighborhood watch would be likely to suffer from a free-rider problem. Table 7.1 illustrates this free-rider problem for a simple two-household neighborhood.

The payoffs in Table 7.1 are measured as the value of property lost through theft over a period of time. When both households join the neighborhood watch, both are vigilant

TABLE 7.1	Neighborhood Watch

		HOUSEHOLD B	
		Join	Stay Out
HOUSEHOLD A	Join	5, 5	7, 4
	Stay Out	4, 7	6, 6

(Payoffs to A, B: $000)

in the neighborhood as a whole and each loses $5,000, a total of $10,000 worth of theft. If one stays out but the other joins, total theft increases. However, the free rider can apply more time to protecting separate property and suffers only a $4,000 loss. The household that agrees to watch loses $7,000. If neither joins the program, a total loss of $12,000 occurs through theft and is shared equally.

The rational neighbor would free ride in Table 7.1 and stay out. This is because joining carries the risk that your neighbor might free ride and that you will lose $7,000. By free riding yourself, the worst that could happen is that you would lose $6,000 if your neighbor does the same. Free riding is a dominant strategy (better in every comparison with joining) in Table 7.1 for both parties. Therefore, they both stay out and are driven to the worst possible corner of the table, with joint losses of $12,000.

Privatization of Prisons

There has been a move toward the privatization of prisons in a number of states and also in international systems. Private prisons are not really a new idea: They existed in some southern states until the early nineteenth century. The contemporary move toward the privatization of custodial care is part of a general move toward the contracting out of many services that were traditionally seen as a part of government activity. To a great extent, the federal and state governments have been forced to consider these options because of growing demands on their budgets from areas such as welfare payments. The privatization of prisons raises a number of issues, including those of accountability and propriety, but the cost side is discussed here.

During the 1960s, the U.S. prison population was shrinking, so much so that by 1975 it had fallen to 380,000. The trend was reversed over the following 10 years, by which time the prison population increased to 740,000. By 1995, it was in excess of 1.6 million, and during the 1990s, inmate numbers were increasing by 8 percent per year. It is easy to see that there is strong pressure for budget reduction with such an increase in numbers.

Private companies such as the Wackenhut Corporation and the Corrections Corporation of America play a growing role in the prison system. There is money to be made by private correctional companies from inmates who are often used in a surprising range of commercial activities, such as operating call centers. However, the revenues of the private prison companies mainly come from the fixed prices charged for housing inmates. An example is the Lockhart prison, located 30 miles outside of Austin, Texas. Its inmates make computer circuit boards for global positioning systems for which they receive better wages than standard prison pay, and the companies making the boards benefit from cheap labor. However, Wackenhut is mainly concerned with the daily payment per inmate that it receives from the state of Texas, amounting to $29.50 per day in 2000. This is considerably less than the cost of equivalent state prisons, which run at around $50 a day per inmate.

The scale of private prison operation is by now quite large. The Corrections Corporation of America manages more than 73,000 beds in 82 facilities around the world, including its contracts with 26 U.S. states plus the District of Columbia. The prisoners tend to be low-risk groups such as those on remand or illegal immigrants awaiting deportation. Also, private companies have innovated. Behavioral Systems Southwest, a private custodial business, has achieved cost savings of around 75 percent by incarcerating low-risk prisoners in leased hotels and large houses rather than in conventional prisons.

Contracting out services may not reduce the resource cost of prisons if rent seeking occurs among would-be contractors. Then there may be a great waste of resources. Rent seeking may arise if contractors devote resources to influencing authorities to grant them contracts. Comparing operating costs per prisoner will not show rent-seeking costs, although it should be remembered that some promotional expenditure is clearly required to communicate information to criminal justice authorities. Another worry may be that private-prison companies might lobby for strong law enforcement and stiff sentences to improve their business prospects.

Electronic Tagging

A further modern development in correctional techniques is electronic tagging, which has now spread worldwide. An electronic device is incorporated into an ankle bracelet, and if a person leaves a specified building, the device alerts the authorities. Individuals can be subjected to house arrest, possibly as part of a parole arrangement, which saves a great deal of the costs of a normal custodial sentence.

Experiments in the use of tagging often emerge as a result of financial necessity, as the experience of Tulare County, California, testifies. In the 1990s, the county had filled its juvenile detention center and could not afford to build additional facilities at a cost of $10 million. The county was forced to release offenders because it had no correctional capacity to house them. It turned to electronic monitoring, in which clients wear an ankle cuff that allows them to be supervised 24 hours a day at a much lower cost than incarceration.

The system has several components: a transmitter worn on a strap around the ankle, a receiver attached to the phone in the offender's home, and a computer-based monitoring system. The monitoring software is programmed to know when the offender should be at work or some other location outside the house. Probation officers can use the system to keep track of clients when they are outside the house, such as checking to see if they are actually at work. The county found the cost of electronic tagging to be $10 a day, compared with at least $40 a day to keep offenders in a state-run prison. The cost to the state can be lower because working adults pay $12 a day to be in the program. From a social perspective, the offender can continue to work while still receiving a sentence that restricts freedom and forms a classic nonmonetary sanction.

SUMMARY AND CONCLUSIONS

Economic analysis may be used to aid our understanding of crime and punishment. There is statistical evidence that individuals engage in crime as a rational activity and are deterred by changes in criminal justice variables. This appears to be particularly true in the case of property crime. Increases in the probability of eventual punishment appear to have the strongest deterrent effect. Nonetheless, in cost-effectiveness comparisons, increasing the severity of sentences appears to be the cheapest way to obtain a given reduction in criminal activity. It would appear that if society is serious about tackling modern crime, a toughening of sentencing is likely to be the most successful approach.

Economic analysis is also useful in examining a host of management issues from the criminal justice system. These issues arise mainly as a response to rising costs. The modern trend is toward drawing in investment from the private sector to help in the running of prisons and to examine alternatives to incarceration, such as electronic tagging.

QUESTIONS FOR REVIEW

1. Discuss whether criminals are more concerned about being caught and convicted or with the eventual sentence they may receive.

2. What factors are likely to make criminalizing wrongful acts desirable?

3. Property crime has seemed more amenable to economic analysis than violent crime. Consider whether recent studies support this view.

4. Should the criminal justice system concentrate on using the most technically efficient deterrence mechanisms, or is there a role for cheaper but less efficient approaches?

5. Why is the empirical work carried out in the "guns and crime" debate so important?

NOTES ON THE LITERATURE

*   Articles by Shavell (1985, 1993), Posner (1985), and Dnes and Seaton (1997) explored the incentive structures present in the criminal common law. Note that despite a modern trend toward codification of the criminal law, in several common-law jurisdictions, many serious crimes (such as murder) remain essentially common-law crimes.

*   Tullock's (1968) article on rent seeking used criminal activity as an illustration of wasteful expenditure.

*   As Buchanan and Hartley (1992) point out, for rational choice models to work, people need not be rational all the time but must be so at the margin of their activities. The observation that Australia did not produce generation after generation of criminals belongs to Buchanan and Hartley (who are Australian).

*   Carr-Hill and Stern (1979) began the line of studies finding that expenditure on the police does not appear to deter crime.

- Ehrlich's (1973) pioneering statistical work is the early study discussed in the text. It was based on U.S. robbery data for 1940, 1950, and 1960, and used regression techniques. He found that a higher probability of conviction implied a lower robbery rate. In addition, a higher average sentence implied a lower robbery rate for 1940 and 1960. A study following from and supporting Ehrlich (1973) is Blumstein and Nagin (1977), who used data on evasion of the U.S. military draft in the 1960s and 1970s. Data on the draft are consistent across different states. A greater probability of conviction implied lower evasion of the draft. The studies are summarized in Pyle (2000).

- Wolpin (1978a) used data from England for the period 1894–1967 to test the deterrence hypothesis using statistical time-series analysis. The advantage of English data was that they were compiled on a consistent basis for a long period. Wolpin found evidence of a deterrence effect from both the probability of punishment and from the severity of sentencing, particularly for property crime. The deterrence effect from increasing the probability of punishment exceeded that from increasing the severity of sentencing, consistent with Becker's (1968) prediction for risk-taking criminals.

- Willis (1983) also used English data and the clear-up rate for particular crimes as a measure of the probability of capturing and punishing criminals. The strongest deterrence came from increasing the probability of punishment, although there was also deterrence from increasing the severity of sentences. Willis's study highlighted differences between categories of crime. A 1 percent increase in the clear-up rate:

1. Reduced thefts by 0.8 percent.

2. Reduced sex crimes by 1 percent.

3. Had no effect on violent crime.

These figures describe the *elasticity* (or responsiveness) of crime with respect to the clear-up rate. This elasticity can be defined as the proportional change in the crime variable in response to a 1 percent increase in the clear-up rate, with a higher figure indicating greater responsiveness. Note the complete inelasticity of violent crime (excluding sex crime) in this study, which again raises the question whether violent crime may be in some sense different from property crime.

- Work carried out by Pyle (1983) using several U.K. data sets for the period 1950–1980 also found deterrence from both the probability of conviction and from increases in the severity of sentences. He also found that increasing the probability of conviction had the stronger deterrence effect. The elasticity of offenses with respect to the conviction rate was 0.9, but was only 0.3 with respect to sentence length. Pyle also derived results showing how deterrence differs among property crimes. A 1 percent increase in the clear-up rate reduces

1. Burglaries by 1.6 percent.

2. Robbery by 0.7 percent.

3. Thefts by 0.2 percent.

See Pyle (2000) for further discussion of the different deterrence results for different crimes.

- In a study based on data from Australia, Withers (1984) concluded that the major reliable determinants of crime rates were committal and imprisonment rates. Committal rates reflect the probability of trial, whereas the imprisonment rate is a severity measure. Despite Wither's (1984, p. 182) prior expectation, more attitudinal variables, such as television-viewing habits, were not statistically significant determinants of crime.

- Pyle (1989, 1993) calculated the cost of achieving a 1 percent reduction in property crime by alternative means, discussed in the main text and shown in Table 7.2.

TABLE 7.2	Cost of Reducing Property Crime by 1 Percent
OPTION	**COST (millions £)**
Increased police numbers	51.2
Increased number of offenders imprisoned	4.9
Increased average length of sentence	3.6

SOURCE: Pyle (1989).

The obvious conclusion is that, although the elasticity of deterrence is technically higher for increases in the probability of conviction, increasing the severity of sentences is more cost-effective as a means of beating property crime. Increasing police numbers to increase the probability of conviction looks like particularly poor value.

- Cook and Zarkin (1985) used regression techniques on U.S. data to show that there were small increases in burglaries and robberies during times of recession. However, their results showed there was no effect on homicide rates—and thefts of motor vehicles actually fell in a recession and rose in the upswing. The studies by Wolpin (1978a) and Willis (1983), discussed in connection with the deterrence hypothesis, used data for England and Wales and showed a weak effect on crime from unemployment.

- Field (2000) used changes in consumption levels rather than unemployment to assess the effects of deprivation on crime. The reasoning behind this is that consumption changes have a more immediate motivational impact than becoming unemployed. Field undertook a time-series analysis using data and found evidence of a "bounce-back" effect. Decreases in consumption were initially followed by an increase in property crime, but the crime level returned to its normal trend value in the longer term. Field concluded that there was no real long-run relationship between changes in consumption levels and crime rates.

- Using data for Scotland, Reilly and Witt (1992) estimated several models that all appeared to support a robust link between crime and unemployment.

Their data comprised 15 annual observations from 1974 to 1988 for each of the six regions of Scotland, taking the general crime rate as the dependent variable. Pyle and Deadman (1994) were highly critical of this study, as they could not replicate its results using a data set updated to include 1988–1991. The earlier study ignored a period of falling unemployment from 1987 to 1990, which occurred while crime continued on a rising trend. Adding just three observations to the data set rendereed the unemployment variable statistically insignificant in Reilly and Witt's models. Pyle and Deadman also carried out a separate time-series analysis, using quarterly data to increase the available number of observations, which also failed to find a statistically significant role for unemployment.

- Witte and Tauchen (2000) found a statistically significant (positive) link between unemployment and criminal activity (arrest rates) but not for wages and criminal activity, using a panel of data for Philadelphia.

- Withers (1984) found that deterrence variables were at best weakly significant determinants of violent crimes. Studies of capital punishment sometimes supported the deterrence hypothesis in relation to murder (Ehrlich, 1975, 1977) and sometimes did not (Passell and Taylor, 1977). A number of studies revealed a role for wider influences on violent crime compared with crime against property (Field, 2000; Pyle, 1993).

- The work of Murray and Cox (1979) showed that justice variables also deterred violent crime: They tracked 317 youths after release following a first custodial sentence. The youths had an average record of 13 arrests each prior to their imprisonment for an average of 10 months. Their offenses included homicide, rape, assaults, car theft, armed robbery, and burglary. After imprisonment, their arrest records fell by two-thirds on average. A comparison group of nonimprisoned juvenile offenders did not show the same reduction in the rate of rearrest. It is unlikely that the imprisoned youths were learning from other crooks how to avoid arrest to an extent that would account for such a large drop.

- Witte (1980) looked at rearrest rates and examined the characteristics of 641 men released over a 3-year period in North Carolina. The higher was the probability of conviction for a crime, the lower was the number of subsequent arrests per month released. Increases in the severity of prior punishment had a stronger deterrent effect compared with increases in the probability of conviction for violent crime. Increasing the probability of conviction had a stronger deterrent effect on reoffending in the case of crimes against property.

- One issue is whether punishment reduces crime by deterring criminals or by incapacitating them while they are held in jail. Kessler and Levitt (1999) studied California's Proposition 8, under which sentences have been enhanced for serious crimes. The criminal would have been sentenced to prison without the law change, and so there can be no additional incapacitation effect from the sentence enhancement in the short run. According to Kessler and Levitt, Proposition 8 reduced eligible crimes by 4 percent in the year following its passage and 8 percent three years after passage, consistent with deterrence. Longer term effects suggested that incapacitation may be important as well.

- Lott and Mustard (1997) and Lott (2000) pushed the debate over the determinants of violent crime back toward the view that violent crime has a rational basis and can be deterred. In their case, the deterrence is through the self-defense of the victim based on right-to-carry laws for concealed hand guns.

- Details of the debate between Lott and his critics may be found at http://www.daviddfriedman.com/Lott_v_Teret/Lott_Mustard_Controversy.html, which is a site organized by David Friedman. Articles considering and to some degree resolving statistical issues arising from Lott and Mustard's work are Bartley and Cohen (1998) and Black and Nagin (1998).

- Ehrlich's (1975) work on testing the deterrent effect of capital punishment used a Becker-type model in which the murderer maximized utility by comparing the costs and benefits of the crime. Time-series data were used for the U.S. for the period 1933–1969. Ehrlich represented the benefits of murder by property-crime variables because murder was correlated with property crime. The benefits of murder were determined by data on unemployment, levels of wealth, and the age structure and racial composition of the population. The costs of murder (to the murderer) were measured by alternative measures of the hazard of punishment: the probability of arrest for murder; the probability of conviction given arrest; and the probability of execution given conviction. Ehrlich predicted the relative strength of these deterrents to be in the order just given. Ehrlich's results showed that the murder rate was negatively and significantly correlated with the arrest, conviction, and execution probabilities, with the relative strength of deterrence in this order as predicted. A less-quoted result was that the deterrent effect of improved labor-market conditions was greater than for the justice variables. Ehrlich (1977) also supports these results.

- Some subsequent researchers found it difficult to replicate Ehrlich's results. They seemed to be sensitive to the functional (e.g., log-linear) form used, which if changed can change the results. Also, Ehrlich's results appear to be sensitive to the time period chosen. Passell and Taylor (1977) reestimated Ehrlich's model but excluded data for the period 1962–1969, in which executions dropped from 47 to zero and crime rose sharply. They found no significant relationship between executions and murder for 1933–1961, with the unlikely implication that capital punishment was a deterrent in the United States only for the period after 1962. Leamer (1983) used a model of capital punishment in his demonstrations of how statistics may be misused to support prior beliefs. Hoenack and Weiler (1980) argued that the link between capital punishment and deterrence may not exist if studies have been picking up the response of the criminal justice system to murder. Ehrlich and Zhiqiang Liu (1999) carried out a sensitivity analysis of deterrence results, concluding that the deterrence hypothesis holds for capital punishment and that critics have relied on questionable statistical methods.

- Several studies strongly support Ehrlich's broad conclusions. Wolpin (1978b) replicated Ehrlich (1975) on data for England and Wales for 1929–1968 and concluded that one extra execution in a year would have deterred four murders. In more recent work, Deadman and Pyle (1993) used the modern technique of intervention analysis on time-series data for England and Wales over the period 1880–1989 and for Scotland for 1884–1989. Their hypothesis is that if socioeconomic, demographic, and law enforcement variables change slowly over time, then murder data should show some inertia. The data in fact show evidence of a significant shift in the trend for murder after abolition of the death penalty in 1965. The effect of abolition is equivalent to about 52 extra murders a year for the United Kingdom.

- California is the only state actively enforcing three-strikes legislation. Shepherd's (2002) article is summarized in the main text. She reported that during the first two years of the legislation, approximately 8 murders, 3,952 agravated assaults, 10,672 robberies, and 384,488 burglaries were deterred in California. Petty theft may have increased, which is a possible displacement effect. The paper is an interesting modern test of the deterrence of violent crime.

CONTINGENT FEES, COST RULES, AND LITIGATION

In this chapter, we examine several procedural issues connected with litigation. First, we consider the implications of permitting attorneys to work for contingent fees (on a "no win, no fee" basis). We also examine the impact on the incentive to litigate of following different rules governing the recovery of litigation costs. A further topic is the class action, where an individual commences a suit as a representative of a class of injured individuals. Finally in this chapter, we look at the issue of growing levels of litigation.

CONTINGENT FEES

Attorneys often work for contingent fees, particularly when pursuing claims for negligence. In this system, the attorney's fee depends upon the results gained for a client. The contingent fee is usually a proportion of the client's recovery of money damages, that is, the contract between attorney and client specifies "no win, no fee."

There are several interesting economic questions concerning contingent fees. First, there is great interest in the incentive properties of the system. In particular, contingent fees influence the incentive that attorneys have to represent their client's interests faithfully, rather than to pursue subgoals. A second, and related, major area of interest focuses on the impact of contingent fees on the amount of litigation, measured in terms of the volume of litigation and settlement rates for cases.

Contingent Fees and Principal-Agent Problems

Economic analysis suggests that there can be a major problem of incentive compatibility between a client and an attorney working for an hourly fee. The relationship between client and attorney exhibits classic aspects of the principal–agent problem: The client, as principal in the case, must motivate the attorney, who is the agent, to pursue the client's interests. Hourly fees may not do this, as it is difficult for the client to know how diligently the attorney is working. The attorney may, for example, prolong the case to maximize the hourly fees. There is then a case of moral hazard stemming from the hidden nature of the attorney's actions. A classic solution to the principal's problem in cases where the agent's actions are hidden but output may be observed is to make the agent's rewards contingent on the level of output. By this reasoning, contingent fees for attorneys may be seen as a useful device for ensuring that they deliver services efficiently.

What then determines the level of the contingent fee? The usual assumption made in investigating the determination of the contingent fee is that the attorney is better able than the client to bear the risks of litigation, owing to the attorney's involvement in a wide range of cases over which risks may be diversified. The attorney is therefore treated as risk neutral in not discounting payoffs to reflect risk. The client is regarded as risk averse, which means that a smaller but certain payoff is preferred to a larger but risky one. The client's utility function over the returns to litigation is therefore convex when viewed from above, as illustrated by the function U in Figure 8.1.

In Figure 8.1, the client is assumed to face an equal chance of winning or losing a case. Winning gives an income level of W_1 (with utility level U_1) whereas losing leads to a lower income of W_0 (with utility U_0). Point C, which is halfway along the straight line connecting points A and B on the utility function, shows the expected income from litigation if read in conjunction with the horizontal axis and, reading from the vertical axis, shows the client's expected utility. Note that the point on the utility function directly above C shows a higher level of utility (U_3) because it assumes the same level of income is paid with certainty. Reading across from C to point D, we can deduce that the same utility is obtained from the lower level of income Y, provided that this is available with certainty. Thus, there is scope for risk sharing: A risk-neutral attorney could offer a sum just larger than $Y - W_0$ to buy the case. The client would be better off from shifting the risk in this way, and the attorney would expect to make a profit of $[0.5(W_1 + W_0) - Y]$.

We now show what happens to risk sharing following the introduction of a contingent-fee system. Figure 8.2 shows one effect as a reduction in the income difference between the win and lose states following the change. The spread is between points a and b with hourly fees but is only from a to d with contingent fees: The client no longer pays attorney's fees in the event of losing the case. Still assuming an equal chance of success or failure in litigating, the point of certainty equivalence gives a higher monetary amount and income level for the client in the case of a contingent fee (c_2 compared with c_1).

There are no welfare consequences from introducing contingent fees in an example like the one in Figure 8.2. This is because we implicitly assume that the litigation goes

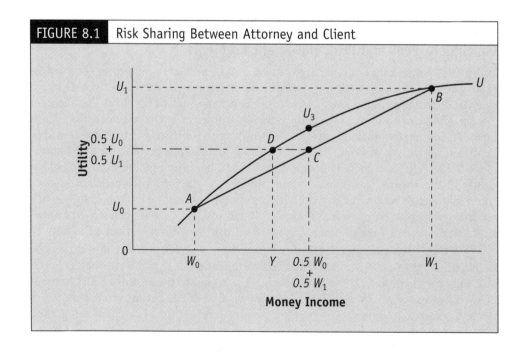

FIGURE 8.1 Risk Sharing Between Attorney and Client

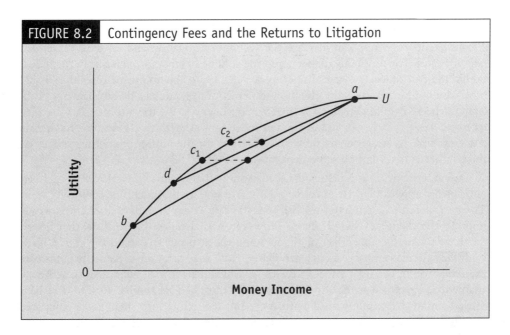

FIGURE 8.2   Contingency Fees and the Returns to Litigation

ahead under either method of paying the attorney, as the expected increase in the client's income is positive. Contingent fees merely redistribute income from the attorney to the client under these circumstances. However, if there are impecunious clients who cannot raise the funds to litigate under hourly fees, then, other things being equal, contingent fees encourage worthwhile litigation. This increase will deter accidents as more tortfeasors would be pursued for damages.

Figures 8.1 and 8.2 imply that attorneys would often wish to buy valuable cases from risk-averse clients in return for contingent fees of 100 percent. In such cases, risk-neutral attorneys would provide full insurance for clients. We do not in fact see this as a general phenomenon because codes of practice and regulations do not permit full trade in legal claims. Figure 8.2 is really a model, based on risk sharing, of the pricing of cases under either hourly or contingent fees in an *unregulated* environment. The position in U.S. jurisdictions is that contract claims are salable because debts are assignable whereas tort claims generally are not.

When clients are restricted to bargaining in terms of the percentage contingent fee, a number of factors influence the size of the percentage fee. The private information held by clients and attorneys is the chief influence on fees. Private information cannot be communicated convincingly to another party. An attorney's confidence (based on skill) in winning the case encourages lower cost-based and higher percentage contingent fees. Conversely, confidence by the client, who may have private information about a defendant, tends to encourage a lower contingent fee. Also, there should be less of a tendency to use contingent fees in cases where the client can easily monitor the efforts of the attorney. Studies show that business organizations used hourly fees in 81 percent of cases in hiring attorneys, compared with a figure of 10 percent for individuals. The monitoring experience of business clients, together with their ability to diversify risk over cases, imply a smaller percentage for the contingent fee.

Contingent Fees and Litigation Levels

A contingent-fee system can increase the volume of litigation and/or alter settlement rates for cases. The possibility of increasing the volume of litigation stems from the reduction in the cost of losing a case. Impecunious clients are able to pursue cases that would otherwise not be litigated. The effect on settlement rates reflects a possible agency problem attached to contingent fees: In one version of the story, the attorney may have an incentive to settle early, obtain the fee, and move on to other cases. However, theoretical and empirical studies generally show mixed results for the impact of contingent fees on the number of cases and on settlement rates.

Taking settlement rates first, some studies show that diminishing returns to an attorney's effort implies that the effective hourly rate under contingent fees falls over time. There is, therefore, a tendency to wish to settle early, even though further effort would improve the client's expected payoff. However, it is also possible to show that hourly fees have the predictable effect of encouraging the attorney to extend the case. Clearly both fee systems can have agency problems. Note that risk-averse clients benefit from the reduction in the risks associated with trials when attorneys' incentives to settle are sharpened. Empirical work also appears to be mixed in its results. Researchers have indeed found that contingent-fee attorneys put less effort into small cases compared with hourly paid attorneys but that difference appears to be reversed for larger cases, which does not support the existence of a conflict of interest. However, other studies find that contingent-fee attorneys settle sooner and for smaller amounts compared with litigants in person in industrial-injury cases, which supports a conflict of interest between client and attorney. Worries over settlement rates may miss the point. Clients use contingent fees to shift risk, which makes them better off, and earlier settlement makes attorneys (and defendants) better off. The implied welfare levels may be as high as possible given the need that impecunious clients have for using contingent fees.

Looking now at the volume of litigation, there is a commonly held view that contingent fees encourage litigation and might be partly responsible for the perceived litigious nature of American society. In fact, there are a number of influences that might explain the difference between high rates of litigation in America and the lower rates in other developed countries. However, the use of contingent fees could, in principle, either increase or decrease litigation rates. There are at least two offsetting influences to the increased incentive to litigate that follow from reducing the risk of loss of legal costs. The first is the increased deterrence of tortfeasors that follows from less costly litigation for victims of accidents. If potential tortfeasors know they will face legal action over accidents, they may be led to act more carefully. Also, attorneys may more carefully screen cases before taking them on under a contingent-fee arrangement. Both of these factors could result in fewer cases reaching the courts. The effects work together rather as in the "raid versus trade" model of property rights formation discussed in Chapter 2, where the discovery of more effective weapons could lead to less fighting.

In Figure 8.3, contingent fees reduce the marginal costs of litigation for a client, but more careful screening by attorneys reduces the client's perception of the marginal benefits of litigation. As drawn, the two effects are completely offsetting so that no change results from introducing contingent fees. The possible offsetting effects of contingent fees can arise both under cost rules where parties bear their own costs and under alternative rules where the loser pays the costs of both parties. Therefore, differences in litigation rates across jurisdictions require a more broadly based explanation than the presence or absence of contingent fees.

FIGURE 8.3	Offsetting Effects from Contingency Fees

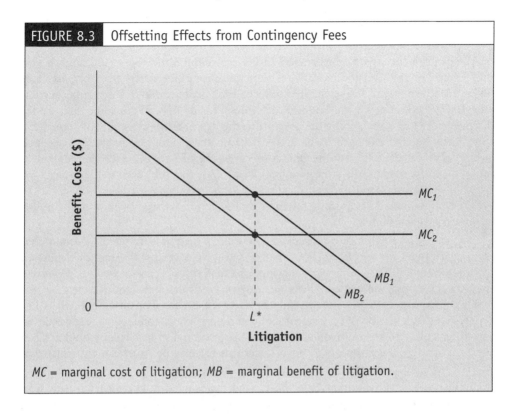

MC = marginal cost of litigation; MB = marginal benefit of litigation.

COST RULES

A distinction may be drawn between two rules governing the recovery of litigation costs in common-law jurisdictions—a distinction between "English" and "American" rules. Both rules have been applied in American jurisdictions, and you also may find English rules referred to as *European* rules. Traditionally in the United States, each party to litigation is responsible for its own attorneys' fees, which are the major costs in a case, although the winner may claim the administrative costs of the case from the loser. At least, this is the broad position: Under Rule 68 of the Federal Rules of Civil Procedure, if the defendant offers a compromise and the plaintiff proceeds to a court action but fails to win more, the plaintiff must pay all of the defendant's costs. Rule 68 provides a limited amount of one-way indemnity over attorney's fees in favor of the defendant.

In England and many other countries, the loser in a civil case pays the legal costs of the winner, including attorneys' fees. There is, in general, indemnity of attorneys' fees, sometimes called *fee shifting*. In England, there is a rule similar to Rule 68 in America. The defendant can protect against liability for costs by registering an early offer of settlement: If the plaintiff proceeds to court and wins, the defendant only pays costs proportional to any positive difference between the offer and the damages awarded by the court. Both of these procedural devices recognize offers of compromise and give the plaintiff an incentive to be careful in considering whether additional court action is worthwhile.

Broadly, the comparison is between litigants meeting most of their own costs (American rules) and "loser pays all" (English rules). Take care not to be confused by names:

Remember that English rules have been also been applied in the United States. There is currently much interest in the incentive structure attached to the two sets of rules.

We can use the model constructed earlier to examine the impact of English and American cost rules on the incentive to litigate. Figure 8.4 shows that the spread of utility from winning or losing a case is reduced for a plaintiff under American cost rules (U_1 to U_2) compared with English cost rules (U_3 to U_0). We assume that under English rules the costs paid by the plaintiff to the defendant on losing (VW) equal the costs received if the plaintiff wins (XY). Because the plaintiff is assumed to be risk averse, the loss of utility from paying costs on losing (U_2 to U_0) exceeds the gain in utility from receiving costs after winning (U_1 to U_3), and the certainty equivalent, or value of the case, falls under English rules (C) compared with American rules (C'). On this reasoning, based on a utility function that is convex viewed from above, English rules tend to deter litigation.

The view that English cost rules deter low-value litigation is frequently encountered among attorneys and legislators. For example, in the "Contract with America" launched by the Republican Party following its winning a majority of seats in the U.S. Congress in 1995, a proposal was made to introduce English cost rules in American courts for precisely this reason. Similarly, in England, the Department for Constitutional Affairs has suggested that a version of contingent fees could be safely introduced. There would be no danger of a growth in frivolous litigation because English cost rules would act as a brake. Therefore there appears to be a concern that it may be American cost rules that explain high litigation rates.

In fact, greater litigation rates in the United States need not result from American cost rules. Just as English rules deter risk-averse plaintiffs from taking action, so too would consequential increases in the spread of outcomes deter defendants from defending cases. It is difficult to make any unambiguous theoretical prediction over the

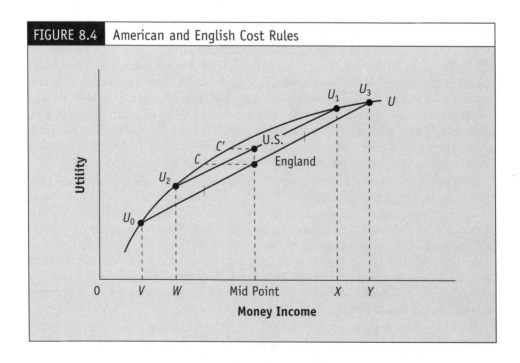

FIGURE 8.4   American and English Cost Rules

impact of English rules. The net result of deterring both plaintiff and defendant depends upon their relative levels of risk aversion and the amount of costs expected by each party from winning or losing a case. Indeed it is possible to apply the Coase theorem to argue that the cost-shifting rule cannot affect the final outcome of a case under the assumption of low bargaining costs. It is therefore an empirical matter whether English rules deter litigation on balance in practice.

There is a shortage of empirical work in this area, but an exception arises in the case of an experiment with English rules carried out by Florida. The rule change was introduced for cases of medical malpractice occurring between 1980 and 1985. The area of medical malpractice contains the type of tort case that many observers consider possibly frivolous. Statistical studies of the experiment with English rules in the Florida system concluded that plaintiffs and defendants were encouraged to be careful and to spend more on legal fees. Plaintiffs who went as far as a trial were more likely to win. Such results are consistent with the clear perception among attorneys and legislators that English rules deter "claim mining," which refers to the practice of suing in the hope that someone will settle rather than incur the costs of defending themselves. If fees can be shifted, spurious suits result in a bill for costs for the claim miner whose bluff is called.

Finally, notice that failure to compensate full attorney's costs in the case of a civil litigant can cause a deviation from principles of optimal compensation. Thus, a tort victim's recovery of damages will not restore the welfare position before an accident, owing to the private burden of attorney's costs. Similarly, the victim of contract breach may end up with expectations damages but minus attorney's fees. Fee shifting is more consistent with economically rational compensation payments.

CLASS ACTIONS

In the United States, individuals may sue on behalf of a class of plaintiffs, providing the court is prepared to certify the claim as a class action. The class action may make it worthwhile for an individual to sue when the individual stakes are small but the aggregate damages may be high, and it is potentially efficiency enhancing because it confronts a tortfeasor with the full costs of damaging activities. If successful in a class action, a plaintiff's attorneys must make attempts to pay damages to the class of victims concerned. However, this is often prohibitively expensive, and the plaintiff and his attorneys typically receive a disproportionately large share of the award. It is the prospect of the large share that motivates plaintiffs in class actions.

If the defendant in a class action settles before trial, the plaintiff's attorney may lack the motivation to press for a settlement in full. Instead, the attorney may settle for a large fee and small award to the plaintiff. American courts regulate attorney fees in settlements of class actions, but attorneys may still be able to persuade judges that they spent a considerable amount of time on a case. There may be a settlement effect, whereby a risk-averse defendant is encouraged to settle just to avoid a possibly higher judgment if the case goes to trial.

SUBSIDIZING LEGAL COSTS

Should the United States subsidize the legal costs of citizens? Such subsidies operate as systems of legal aid in many countries around the world. It is fairly common to find arguments advanced that wide social issues may be involved in litigation, including a value to be placed on preserving access to justice for those with limited financial means, which might support the idea of subsidizing legal costs.

American devices like class actions and contingent fees operate to reduce the plaintiff's costs of pursuing civil legal claims. Introducing public subsidies for litigation by poorer citizens may therefore be unnecessary. It is notable that in countries with legal-aid systems, there has been a recent move toward contingent fees and away from public subsidy. Quite simply, legal-aid systems tend to run up against eventual budget constraints. Alternative means for encouraging access to justice, such as class actions and contingent fees, then look attractive. In such a climate of recent international experience, it is unlikely that the United States will introduce legal-aid subsidies for civil actions. Note however that some subsidy already exists in the shape of court fees that do not fully recover the costs of using courts, which are funded partly from taxation. This implied subsidy is haphazard in operation and not structured to reflect any positive externality from operating the court system.

There may be more of a case for public subsidy in the case of criminal prosecution. Where the state decides to prosecute individuals who turn out to be innocent, it may be of concern that legal fees can literally ruin the individual. There are checks on the state's prosecuting function; for example, an individual could sue to recover damages for the tort of wrongful prosecution. However, the checks may not be that strong, as the individual would have to show that there were clearly no grounds for prosecution, whereas there may well have been a case worth hearing even though the eventual outcome was proven innocence.

One of the necessary checks on state power may well be requiring it to pay the costs of those citizens it unsuccessfully prosecutes. A legal aid system could be structured to ensure that there is a clear obligation for the state to pay reasonable legal costs in criminal cases. Reasonable costs would need defining in terms of some minimum acceptable level of representation and advice. The state could recover litigation costs from those found guilty, assuming that wealth levels permitted this recovery. Our somewhat libertarian argument *does not* reflect the typical basis for criminal legal aid in countries around the world, although there may be some recognition of the principle in the European Convention on Human Rights, which requires signatory countries to provide minimum levels of legal support in criminal cases. Typically, legal aid is paid in criminal cases if a means test indicates that an individual cannot afford an attorney: Wealthy people do not have their legal costs paid if prosecuted but found to be innocent, which would be required by the argument considered here.

An alternative to criminal legal aid is to put in place a system of public defenders, which is broadly the situation in America. Poor people can turn to a public defender if they are unable to hire their own defense attorney. A problem here may be that this system does not give access to high-quality legal representation for poor people. This problem will arise if public-sector pay is low in relation to the private sector, so that recruitment is poor among attorneys for positions as public prosecutors. We might worry that the state would have an incentive to strengthen its hand by keeping the system of public defenders rather poorly financed. The alternative of giving a monetary subsidy to legal costs (recoverable if convicted and wealthy enough to pay) may make it possible for the poor defendant to have access to a high-quality attorney. In this view, legal aid could be seen as a way of *privatizing*, through contracting out, the provision of legal services to the poor.

LITIGATION MANIA?

There is a growing perception in many jurisdictions that individuals are becoming increasingly litigious. There is a further belief that American society is the most litigious in the world. This belief is not well founded as far as general litigation is concerned because the United States is not wildly out of line with many other countries. However, the United States does have an unusually high level of litigation in tort law compared with other common-law countries, particularly for medical malpractice and product liability cases. Nonetheless, even in tort, the rate of litigation is comparable to that in Germany (a civil-law jurisdiction) and may well be comparable to the low rate in other common-law jurisdictions after allowing for income and other socioeconomic differences.

One measure of the amount of private legal action is the total number of civil actions undertaken in a jurisdiction in a given year. Comparisons between countries must be adjusted to allow for different-sized populations. The United States has approximately 60,000 civil actions per million members of the population in a year. In tort cases, the figure is approximately 3,750 per million compared with 1,200 per million in England. Interestingly, Germany has rates of tort litigation that are comparable to U.S. figures. This similarity to German rates seems to rule out an explanation of American litigiousness based on the need to compensate losses in the absence of a generous system of social welfare payments, as has sometimes been suggested. Germany has a well-developed social welfare system and yet has similar levels of tort litigation.

Several explanations have been suggested for the high level of tort litigation in the United States. One is that U.S. judges tend to be fairly innovative and therefore have a commitment to changing the law. This may make litigants optimistic about a judge's treatment of their case. Care needs to be taken with this type of argument, as a great deal of innovation in tort law within the common-law world in fact originated in low-litigation England, e.g., compensation for mental trauma. It is the frequency and scale of application in America that is the issue, which may have more to do with jury behavior than the outlook of judges.

Much modern U.S. private law appears rather pro-plaintiff in nature. The development of strict liability, and then absolute liability, in product-liability torts is an example of this, as is the development of no-fault compensation for auto injuries in some states. Several studies have noted that there are pressure groups likely to have benefited from high levels of litigation. The Association of Trial Attorneys of America (ATLA) has regularly opposed attempts to diminish the effects of pro-plaintiff legislation and judicial decisions. The ATLA also mobilizes to support the election of pro-plaintiff judges. Members of the ATLA are likely to receive higher fees if the entry of attorneys to the bar is limited and the work for them expands: Rents (payments over those necessary to keep the attorneys supplying their services) would be likely to result. Some statistical work shows the strength of the ATLA in a state to be a factor determining adoption of modern (pro-plaintiff) product-liability law, which is a rent-seeking explanation of legal evolution.

We have already noted that contingent fees may make access to law cheaper and encourage more litigation. However, we also noted that contingent-fee attorneys are highly selective in the cases they choose. The overall effect is unclear, as we concluded earlier in this chapter. Apparently, in-house doctors are often used by law firms to advise as to whether to take on a medical-malpractice case, which leads to 85 percent of potential plaintiffs being turned down. We should again note the possible effect of

American cost rules: Empirical work suggests that fee shifting under English rules can deter claim mining and act as a brake on litigation levels.

One legal distinction attached to American legal procedure is the persistence of jury trials for a wide range of civil cases. A judge can try a case as a bench trial, but there remains widespread use of juries in civil trials. In England, juries were progressively abolished for civil trials (but not for criminal trials) from 1833 onward except for cases involving fraud, defamation, malicious prosecution, and false imprisonment. In the United States, no such systematic abolition has occurred, and it is often noted (as it also is in defamation trials in England, where juries remain) that juries tend to take a pro-plaintiff, deep-pocket view of defendants in cases involving medical malpractice or product liability. Government defendants pay 3 times more than private defendants, and corporate defendants pay $4\frac{1}{2}$ times more, in settling such cases. This asymmetry in justice also has the effect of encouraging potential plaintiffs to sue government departments and business corporations.

There is no simple explanation for the high rates of tort litigation in the United States. It appears likely that a combination of plaintiff optimism (focusing on juries) and the absence of fee shifting under American cost rules gives some explanation of high litigation levels.

SUMMARY AND CONCLUSIONS

In this chapter, we have analyzed several, largely procedural, issues connected with litigation. Permitting attorneys to work for contingent fees does not necessarily encourage litigation. Similarly, fee shifting, following an English rather than American cost rule, has an ambiguous effect on the incentive to litigate. Empirical work supports a disincentive for claim mining under English rules. Finally, although differences between American rates of litigation and those overseas are often overstated, the operation of cost rules and plaintiff optimism may partially explain the U.S. experience.

QUESTIONS FOR REVIEW

1.   What kind of evidence would support the idea that contingent fees are primarily a device for controlling the principal–agent problem between the client and an attorney?

2.   Must contingent fees lead to more litigation?

3.   What evidence exists for the proposition that cost rules may be central in explaining "litigation mania"?

NOTES ON THE LITERATURE

- Studies of the theory of contingency fees, focusing on attorneys' incentives to represent their clients' interests faithfully, or to pursue subgoals, include Dana and Spier (1993) and Rubinfeld and Scotchmer (1993). A second, and related, major area of interest focuses on the impact of contingent fees on the amount of litigation, measured in terms of the volume of litigation and settlement rates for cases (Cooter and Rubinfeld, 1989; Rickman, 1999).

- Moral hazard stems from the hidden nature of much of the work (action) done by the attorney. In general, principal–agent relationships may suffer from problems of hidden actions or of hidden information. Hidden information leads to problems of adverse selection: For example, a litigant who is ignorant of the true capacity of individual attorneys will be willing to pay fees based on average ability, which may mean that above-average attorneys leave the profession if their high-quality talents are better rewarded elsewhere.

- Rubinfeld and Scotchmer (1993) argued that private information held by clients and attorneys is the chief influence on fees. Private information cannot be communicated convincingly to another party. An attorney's confidence (based on skill) in winning the case would encourage lower cost-based and higher percentage contingent fees. Conversely, confidence by the client, who may have private information about a defendant, would tend to encourage a lower contingent fee. Also, there is less of a tendency to use contingent fees in cases where the client can easily monitor the efforts of the attorney. Kritzer (1990) showed that business organizations used hourly fees in 81 percent of cases in hiring attorneys, compared with a figure of 10 percent for individuals. The monitoring experience of business clients, together with their ability to diversify risk over cases, would also imply a smaller percentage for the contingent fee whenever one was used.

- Schwartz and Mitchell (1970) showed early on that diminishing returns to an attorney's effort implied that the effective hourly rate under contingent fees falls over time. There is, therefore, a tendency to wish to settle early on, even though further effort would improve the client's expected pay-off. However, Johnson (1981) used a similar model to Schwartz and Mitchell (1970) to show that hourly fees also have the predictable effect of encouraging the attorney to extend the case. Clearly, both fee systems can have agency problems. In general, two possibly offsetting tendencies are set up by contingent fees. The attorney is led to press the client's interests harder, but may also wish to settle earlier, both owing to the attorney's financial interest. Rickman (1999) showed in a game-theoretic setting that cost-bearing contingent-fee lawyers can extract greater settlement offers for clients, using their willingness to sink costs as a bargaining device. In general, the existence of settlement bias is an empirical question.

- Empirical work also appears to be mixed in its results. Kritzer (1990) found that contingent-fee attorneys put less effort into small cases compared to hourly paid attorneys but that the difference was reversed for larger cases, which does not support the existence of a conflict of interest. Thomason (1999) found that contingent-fee attorneys settled sooner and for smaller amounts compared to litigants in person in industrial-injury cases, which supports a conflict of interest.

- Anderson and McChesney's (1994) raid-or-trade model is in fact based on Cooter and Rubinfeld's (1989) analysis of the incentive to litigate or settle cases.

- Marceau and Mongrain (2003) showed that courts determine the damages to be paid in class-action suits by calculating the average of damage to the class. This averaging implies that the individual with least damage has the greatest incentive to initiate the action.

- The literature on the impact of cost rules includes Shavell (1982), Cooter and Rubinfeld (1989), Snyder and Hughes (1990), and Hughes and Snyder (1995). There is no clear theoretical prediction over the impact of English rules as shown by Polinsky and Rubinfeld (1998). The effect of Rule 68 does seem to be to encourage settlement (Farmer and Pecorino, 2000).

- Snyder and Hughes (1990) and Hughes and Snyder (1995) are the studies that use U.S. data from Florida, where English rules were applied in cases of medical malpractice from 1980–1985. Hughes and Snyder concluded that plaintiffs and defendants are encouraged to be careful by English rules and spend more on legal fees. Plaintiffs going to trial were more likely to win.

- Some empirical work supports the existence of a settlement effect under class action (Rosenfeld, 1976). Lynk (1990) noted that the settlement effect may be controlled by the way courts control attorneys' fees and by the existence of contingent-fee litigation. Priest (1997) examined several concerns with class actions, including the adequacy of class representation.

- Helland and Tabarrok (2003) show that when juries are drawn from poorer counties, the average tort award increases, which is consistent with an inclination for juries to favour "little-guy" plaintiffs.

- A good comparative study of U.S., English, and German litigiousness is Markesinis (1990), from which several of the observations used in the text are taken. Curiously, Markesinis has little to say about the impact of American and English cost rules, although he does pick up on arguments about incentives from contingent fees. Posner (1997) showed that controlling for income differences and similar socioeconomic variables across the two countries made England a more, rather than less, litigious country than the United States.

- Rubin and Bailey (1994) make the observations used in the text on the actions of the ATLA as a pressure group in relation to the growth of tort law.

ECONOMICS AND FAMILY LAW

In recent years, economists have paid considerable attention to family life and the extent to which legal change has affected the family. There is no doubt that patterns of family life have changed greatly since the 1960s. In particular, there has been a move away from marriage for life toward unmarried cohabitation and an increase in divorce rates. Between 1960 and 2000 the rate of first marriages fell from approximately 70 per 1,000 to 30 per 1,000 of the male population. The age at which first marriages occur has also risen by three years to 27 for men and 25 for women. The number of unmarried people cohabiting has also risen relative to marriage. Such profound social changes are also reflected by the divorce rate for first marriages, which has increased from 9 per thousand married women to 19 per thousand. Around one-half of all marriages now end in divorce. Late twentieth-century changes in the family have indeed been far-reaching.

Specialists in the economics of law have attempted to answer many questions surrounding these changes in family structures. This type of work may seem like a novel application of economics, but bear in mind that the trends show responses to changing incentive structures. Although economic analysis would not claim the last word on every aspect of the family, it can help us to understand some of the profound changes. The areas of particular concern are the falling marriage rate and delays in marriage; whether increases in divorce may be a response to legal changes making divorce easier, the effects of different settlements on the incentive to divorce; and issues relating to children. Incentives to form families are discussed first.

COMPARATIVE ADVANTAGE AND THE INCENTIVE TO MARRY

An economic basis for the family can be found in the principle of comparative advantage, which tells us to specialize in those activities in which we have the greatest advantage compared with our trading partners. In Table 9.1 on page 190, Cleopatra and Antony each have 40 hours to apply to either domestic or market-based production. Antony can produce $100 worth of either domestic or market production, whereas Cleopatra can produce $75 on the market but just $50 of domestic product (Cleopatra hates domestic duties). Notice that Antony is more efficient than Cleopatra at both activities, in the ratio 4:3 for market work and 2:1 for domestic work. However, Antony is, *comparatively* speaking, best of all at the domestic activities.

Comparative advantage implies that if Antony specializes in the home and Cleopatra goes out to do the market-based work, their combined output will be at a maximum, as shown in Table 9.2 on page 190. No other pattern of specialization produces a higher total household output, that is, switching Cleopatra over to the domestic front and sending Antony out to work would lower total output by $25.

TABLE 9.1	Domestic Comparative Advantage		
POSSIBLE OUTPUT ($)	**ANTONY**	**CLEOPATRA**	**RATIO**
Market Output	100	75	100/75 = 4/3
Domestic Output	100	50	100/50 = 2/1

TABLE 9.2	Household Output Based on Comparative Advantage		
OUTPUT ($)	**ANTONY**	**CLEOPATRA**	**TOTAL**
Market	0	75	75
Domestic	100	0	100

Economists emphasize the gains from specialization and "trade" within marriage as a substantial basis for marriage. This is not to say that other factors, such as pure romance, are unimportant. It is just to say that there is an efficiency impetus to specialized roles within a family unit. Strictly speaking, the story so far implies that individuals might live together rather than separately. An assumption that the sexes are likely to have distinct comparative advantages, e.g., with one more suited to domestic production and the other to work outside the home, is needed to predict that *men* and *women* would live together. Also, to predict *marriage*, a reason would be required to suppose that cohabitation without marriage might be problematic.

A simple explanation of declining marriage rates, and to some extent of rising divorce rates, is that comparative advantage has been eroded by social changes that have caused men and women to become more similar in the labor market and the home. This reduces the incentive to cohabit because if comparative advantage disappears, so that both Antony and Cleopatra produce $100 output either in the home or outside, the basis for their trade disappears. We find a much lower economic incentive to cohabit, implying fewer marriages (unless the economic impetus were swamped by romantic factors). It is indeed true that technical change making paid work less physically taxing, increased control of fertility, and modern patterns of education have combined to make women less dependent on men in the family, in the sense that their output is higher now with less specialization. However, *unmarried* cohabitation has increased relative to marriage. The socioeconomic changes have apparently contributed to reducing the need for a legally governed long-term relationship—marriage—compared with less-obligated cohabitation. Part of the reason for the trend away from marriage may be that legal changes making divorce easier have made marriage less binding as a commitment mechanism.

What of the modern tendency to delay marriage? The erosion of comparative advantage could lead to less cohabitation but could not by itself *delay* marriage. A reason for the delay might be found in observations of assortative mating in society. Studies show that people tend to marry within their own social orbit, probably because the complementarities are more easily found that way. Within any given social orbit, we look for the complementaries signaling comparative advantage. Assortative mating is slowed down by factors hindering economic maturity in the parties. In recent decades, young men have suffered a decline in their ability to be economically independent, and this could be one explanation of later marriage. The median earnings of young men (less than 25 years old) fell by 25 percent in real terms over the period 1975–2000. Women no longer look for a traditional pattern of male financial support so they can concentrate on homemaking, given the increase of 50 percent in the ratio of young female-to-male real earnings over the same period. However, the decline in economic maturity for men makes it harder for women to judge the value of a man's longer-term contribution to the marriage in terms of specialized tasks (involving more sharing of market and domestic tasks in modern marriage). The uncertainty is enough to increase the delay in marriage.

Increased divorce rates might also encourage women to delay marriage and child rearing while they develop skills to fall back on later if a marriage fails: a form of self-insurance. Statistical studies show that between the 1960s and 1980s the growth of no-fault divorce had a significant, depressing effect on the birth rate. These studies controlled for other factors, such as the number of marriages, likely to affect the birth rate. The most compelling interpretation is that lower divorce costs, particularly for men, may encourage married women to be more cautious in having children. Children imply much higher costs for a woman if there is a divorce, making it more difficult for her to work, and sometimes to remarry.

LIFE-PROFILE THEORY OF MARRIAGE

In many respects, the basis in specialization for forming families does not strictly explain the phenomenon of marriage but, rather, suggests cohabitation. Marriage may be explained by a need for stronger signaling of commitment, particularly by the male to the female, because of problems of opportunistic behavior that might otherwise occur. The life-profile theory of marriage that follows draws heavily on ideas from the study of long-term commercial contracts. Traditional marriages involving lifetime support for women are discussed first; later, more egalitarian, modern marriages are considered.

A useful starting point is to think of a marriage as a contract between two parties. Divorce then results from breach of contract, or possibly as mutual agreement to end the contractual obligations. In a traditional marriage, many of the domestic services provided by the wife occur early in the marriage, whereas the support offered by the male will grow in value over the longer term. The opportunities of the parties may change so that one of them has an incentive to breach the contract. Divorce imposes costs on both parties, equal to at least the cost of finding a replacement spouse of equivalent value (in contract terms, this cost is technically a measure of expectation damages, that is, the replacement cost of the anticipated spousal support). The risks and costs of being an unwilling party to divorce are asymmetrically distributed: The husband might be tempted to take the wife's early contributions to the marriage and move out to enjoy his later income without her. There is statistical evidence to suggest that she will find it much harder to remarry in middle age compared with a man.

There are both psychological and instrumental benefits to marriage. The willingness of one to be committed to another is evidence of worthiness of such love, and marriage gives a means of protecting long-term investments in marital assets. The spouses may be regarded as unique inputs in the production of a capital asset, namely the family, and children may be viewed as particularly important shared marital "outputs." Another instrumental gain is the provision of insurance: Parties give up their freedom to seek new partners, should their prospects improve, for a similar commitment from a spouse, which is rational if the gains from marriage exceed the cost of losing freedom to separate. The gains from marriage reflect surpluses and may tempt a spouse into behaving opportunistically.

Traditional marriage is characterized by an asymmetry over the timing of investments made by the man and woman. The woman invests in child rearing and homemaking early on and expects to remain with her husband, enjoying the family income and home over the long term. He is freed of domestic responsibilities to build a career that will yield high earnings later in the life cycle. In contract terminology, the woman has an expectation of long-term support, sharing in her husband's lifestyle. Such marriages are subject to possible "postcontract opportunism" if the husband simply walks away from the marriage with little financial obligation to the wife after he has built up his career and long after she has sunk her investment into child rearing and/or homemaking. There are many natural "hostages" acting to check such a tendency: The couple will have grown together over the years; maintaining contact with children will be an issue; and there will possibly be costs of finding a new partner. Opportunism may not be checked entirely by natural hostages and, therefore, family law has an important role to play.

Alimony and Property Division

Focusing on the asymmetric life profiles of men and women has led to some concern that the moves to make divorce much easier in the 1960s may have created a disadvantage to older women in traditional marriages and may have made marriage less attractive generally. Economic considerations suggest requiring the payment of expectation damages (explained in Chapter 5) by the party breaching the marriage contract to ensure that there would only be "efficient" divorces. Efficiency requires the breached-against party to suffer no loss when the breaching party moves on. The concern is that divorce may often be too cheap. Some U.S. jurisdictions require equal division of assets acquired during marriage, while others require the courts to divide property and award alimony to meet the needs of the divorcing parties. The standard of living of women frequently falls after divorce, suggesting that divorce courts do not award anything like expectation damages. Nor do the courts pay attention to breach of contract because divorce has been based on no-fault grounds since the late 1960s in most states.

After the introduction of no-fault divorce, which does not tie alimony and property division to fault, it becomes possible for the man to tire of his wife and move on to a new relationship without maintaining the promised life style the wife expects. The needs-based approach toward alimony and property division that is followed in some "equitable distribution" jurisdictions also makes divorce too cheap from a woman's perspective. If a financial award is not linked to fault and there are few assets, the parent with care of the children (often the woman) frequently retains all of the assets in the shape of the family home. There could be a problem if she tires of her husband and realizes that she can keep most of the family assets under a no-fault, needs-based settlement. The needs-based form of opportunism cannot operate in states like California, which operate community-property regimes equally dividing assets acquired during the marriage.

Louisiana Covenant Marriage

Economic analysis suggests that the move toward easier divorce ("marriage lite") may have had the unfortunate consequence of undermining an important quality signal in the "marriage market." If marital promises were firmly enforced by tying expectation damages to breach of the marital contract, willingness to marry would be a valuable signal. For example, there would be a separating equilibrium between men who were confidently able to offer marriage and those who would not do so because they would expect to be involved in a later costly divorce. Legislators in Louisiana were so worried about the loss of the signal of commitment that in 1997 they introduced the possibility of a form of marriage that is harder to dissolve (covenant marriage or marriage heavy). They were followed within a year by Arizona.

In covenant marriage, the parties are counseled in terms of the importance of the commitment as they prepare for the ceremony. If they choose a covenant marriage, it cannot be as easily dissolved on a no-fault basis compared with a standard marriage because there must be a 2-year waiting period. The general idea is to return to a firmer set of marriage vows. Some critics have questioned the motives behind couples entering covenant marriage, wondering why they need such a statement of legal "hands tying." However, such comments may miss the point. The covenant form may be of particular value to women, who even in a modern age are likely to incur some sunk costs early on in the marriage—e.g., putting careers on hold while raising children—and may well feel more confident entering marriage if long-term support obligations are more firm. The 2-year waiting period tends to prolong financial support. It is not that women need to tie men down, but that men will happily signal through covenant marriage if they are confident that they will not wish to divorce lightly.

Opportunistic divorce could not happen in a (contract) system based on expectations damages and fault-based divorce, with fault interpreted as breach of contract. Possibly, the parties agree to divorce because the change increases the welfare of one while the other has his or her welfare at least maintained. Alternatively, one party forces a divorce but is required to maintain the value of promises made to the other party, and would only do so in anticipation of being better off as a result. This reflection has caused some economists to argue in favor of what amounts to a specific performance requirement in marriage, i.e., the move to a system allowing divorce, but only by consent. To obtain the consent of the other party, one would have to compensate so as to preserve the expected benefits of the marriage before it failed. Similar considerations underlie the recent moves in some states to resurrect a tougher marital system, as discussed in the boxed example.

It would not be possible to suppress opportunistic divorce by returning to any fault-based divorce system that has yet been seen in the United States. First, there is a difference between fault and breach of contract, and there would need to be a focus on breach: Thus, it could be seen as a breach to file for unilateral termination of marriage, although this is regarded as a no-fault ground in much modern law. Fault would need to be linked to financial settlements with one implication being that a breaching party with no personal financial resources might receive nothing by way of a divorce settlement.

DO NO-FAULT LAWS ENCOURAGE DIVORCE?

It is theoretically possible that the movement to a no-fault divorce system might not affect the level of divorce. If bargaining costs are low, the Coase theorem may apply, and people could then negotiate within marriage to rearrange individual benefits and prevent divorce from occurring whenever there are gains from the marriage. Suppose that two people marry, agreeing that they will share housing and other domestic costs equally but that each will keep any surplus from their own income over and above those costs. There are no children of the marriage. Each spouse would amass savings over the years, assuming that one effect of marriage is to enable the sharing of domestic tasks so that each spouse can increase his or her outside earnings. Suppose further that at the time of marriage, the rule for the divorce courts is to divide property equally upon divorce unless it is covered by a prenuptial agreement. The rule implies that the couple would divide accrued housing assets equally but that each would keep private savings accounts.

Now suppose the divorce settlement rule changes to dividing jointly owned assets to even up the disparity between privately amassed assets More of the housing assets will now go to the spouse with the lower income during the marriage. The rule change might cause the lower-income spouse to expect to be better off divorced. However, this marriage clearly shows a surplus as each earns more when married than when single. The higher-earning spouse might well offer to transfer some earnings to the other to keep the marriage going. It is therefore possible that legal changes covering settlements would have no effect on the divorce rate.

The United States introduced no-fault divorce laws in the late 1960s, and the subsequent experience across states suggests that legal reform is associated with increases in divorce. People divorcing per 1,000 of the American population almost doubled between 1960 and 2000, although the rate has stabilized in recent years, as shown in Figure 9.1. The figures are averages across states and are approximately 0.6 percent higher on average in no-fault states, such as California, compared to states like Virginia, which retains a role for fault in the grounds for divorce or financial settlements. A simple statistical association can be misleading, of course. It could be that legal change followed increased pressure for divorce that was really explained by other factors. Studies have therefore controlled for other factors, particularly those reflecting the greater economic independence of women. Between 1960 and 2000 the proportion of women age 35 to 40 participating in paid employment doubled from 40 percent to 80 percent. Female real wages also increased over the period, as did welfare payments that might cushion the effects of divorce for nonworking women.

Some early statistical studies found that the move to no-fault divorce regimes caused a temporary increase in divorce rates, as though releasing a bottleneck of pent-up demand for divorce. Such early results became controversial as subsequent researchers became much more careful in distinguishing other factors that could affect divorce rates in different states. There currently appears to be a preponderance of results supporting the hypothesis that the move to no-fault divorce did increase the divorce rate permanently, after controlling for a wide range of state-specific and socioeconomic factors. There is further discussion of these results in the "Notes on the Literature" section at the end of this chapter.

One reason that people may be unable to bargain around the legal changes introduced for marriage and divorce is that many of the "products" of marriage are indivisible.

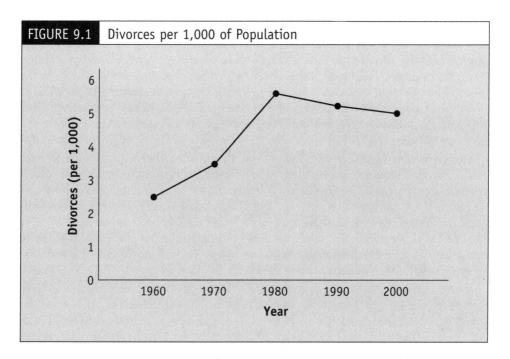

FIGURE 9.1   Divorces per 1,000 of Population

Consider children: Their time might, to some extent, be divisible between parents, but broadly speaking one or the other parent will care for them. The law may itself create some of the indivisibilities in creating a presumption that some assets will always go to one or the other of the spouses. An equitable distribution state tends to award the matrimonial home to the parent with major child-care responsibilities. A community property state divides marital property equally. Such rules may put assets of the marriage beyond bargaining. Even assuming that two parties can bargain at low or zero cost, many family lawyers say that divorcing couples often cannot communicate without huge conflict arising. For these reasons, legal change is likely to have an impact on divorce rates.

From an economic perspective, the expectation is that changes in divorce law affect many aspects of behavior within marriage. Studies have indeed found such links. Typically, the divorce rate does affect the rate of marriage, suggesting the removal of a valuable commitment signal following the easing of divorce laws. Another intriguing finding is that states like California imposing no-fault divorce settlements—where the court pays no attention to behavior during the marriage when dividing property—show higher levels of domestic violence.

RELIANCE AND RESTITUTION

Economic analysis supports the idea of targeting an efficient level of divorce and implies following an expectation-damages approach to marital dissolution. In recent years, courts have become more and more attached to approaches to settling divorce that are likely to compensate divorced spouses inadequately. Apart from the use of needs-based settlements in equitable-distribution jurisdictions, there have been suggestions that economically dependent spouses should be compensated for such matters as giving up careers on entering marriage and for supporting ex-spouses while they completed professional degrees. The suggestions correspond to compensating for the opportunity cost of entering marriage, which is a reliance standard of damages, and preventing "unjust enrichment" of the qualified spouse, which is a restitution approach. In fact, a reliance or restitution approach is likely to give inadequate compensation and encourage nonoptimal levels of breach, as we found in Chapter 5. Nonetheless, lost opportunities and contributions to education and training do feature in cases settling alimony and property division.

Compensation for giving up a career typically gives the abandoned spouse a lower settlement than requiring the compensation of lost expectation. Presumably the spouse entered the marriage because its benefits were expected to exceed the opportunity cost of giving up a previous occupation. Therefore, compensating for opportunity cost (reliance) represents a lower award than expectation damages and would tend to make divorce cheap for the abandoning spouse. Divorce is likely to be encouraged, and investments in homemaking might be discouraged. The reliance standard is not kind to spouses with poor career opportunities prior to marriage.

The classic example illustrating the adverse effect of reliance damages in a divorce settlement is that of the cocktail waitress who marries a millionaire. If they subsequently divorce, she would gain more from enforcing a promise to share in his lifestyle (expectation damages) than from getting back her former lifestyle (reliance damages). Actually, the contrast could be more stark

Under a restitution standard, a divorcing spouse who worked while the other undertook professional training receives a property right entitlement in the earnings of the trained spouse. There is logic to the approach: They both invested time or money in the human capital and should therefore both share the benefits from its employment. Courts do make such awards, and one cannot blame divorcing spouses from increasing a claim on a restitution basis. However, one senses a claim that would be better dealt with under the expectations-damages approach, which would share the lifestyle following from qualification and promised by the trained party. If the court only awards the cost input into the training, it would tend to award too little because the return on the investment is then ignored.

Modern Marriage, Insurance, and Prenuptial Agreements

An implication of the life-cycle theory of marriage is that, under a divorce system awarding expectation damages for breach of the marriage contract, traditional marriages would be associated with the man providing *full* insurance to the woman against marital breakdown. One question that may be asked is whether it remains appropriate for the man to insure the woman fully in modern, more egalitarian marriages. The question is intriguing partly because full insurance is a rarity in more general insurance markets, where we tend to observe copayments by the insured party. Such deductibles are meant to impose some of the costs of accidents on the victim in cases where the victim could influence outcomes. In marriage, full insurance might be one extreme result, but there may be other situations that are also of interest, corresponding loosely to more egalitarian modern marriages characterized by less extreme specialization into domestic and market roles.

The insurance function of marriage needs to be judged in relation to the promises that have actually been made by the spouses. Just as in the case of *Hadley v. Baxendale* of 1854 (the leading case on remoteness of damage in contract, which states that damages should be limited to the natural and foreseeable losses from breach) it is economically undesirable for courts to impose insurance for consequential losses upon promisors unless they have clearly taken on the obligation. Similarly, it is not desirable to vary spousal promises after they are made. The crucial issue in applying the principle of expectation damages to divorcing spouses is the assessment of what was promised to whom and by whom. If both spouses in a modern marriage agreed to maintain their independent careers, perhaps hiring help over childcare, and to divide any commonly acquired assets equally, then self-insurance would seem to dominate. The divorce court should not impose old-fashioned obligations on such couples, or there would be a risk of creating incentives for opportunistic behavior because a financially weaker spouse could agree to self-sufficiency knowing that a divorce settlement would be more generous in reality.

Considerable clarity is given to the intentions of the spouses by the use of a prenuptial agreement. If they are able at the time of marriage to specify the property and income settlement to apply in the event of their divorce, the job of the court is made much easier. A majority of states now follow the Uniform Premarital Agreements Act and recognize prenuptial agreements as long as these result from fully informed consent and are not the result of duress. Courts find prenuptial agreements a great assistance in assessing the nature of the promises made by spouses. It may well be the case that it is only where such agreements prevail that we find divorce courts following something close to the approach of awarding expectations damages.

COHABITATION AND THE LIFE-PROFILE MODEL

There has been movement away from marriage and toward cohabitation in many modern societies. This movement represents a very significant shift in social behavior during the post-war period. Births outside of marriage increased from 5 percent to over 35 percent of all births between 1960 and 2000. In addition, the proportion of cohabiting women between the ages of 20 and 50 trebled. Marriage rates are falling and cohabitation rates are rising, but people are not simply cohabiting as a prelude to marriage. Although cohabiting people often state that cohabitation is a matter of "trying out" prior to marriage, this claim can only be true in the sense that weaker potential marriages may be filtered out, as subsequent marriage appears not to be the typical result. Cohabitation is in reality even less stable than marriage. Many studies point to the much lower stability of cohabitation compared with marriage, even where children are born in the relationship.

A puzzling aspect of the substitution is that cohabitation appears to be against the interests of many women. Marriage is potentially a good mechanism for supporting long-term family investments, according to the life-profile model, and without marriage women might predict their own vulnerability to opportunistic behavior (there might also be men in such a position). It seems unlikely that changes in women's economic activity and in techniques of child rearing have reached a point where the sexes no longer show some asymmetric interdependence over life profiles. Therefore, one would expect a man's

Marvin v. Marvin, 122 Cal. Rptr. 555 (App. 1981)

The case refers to the actor Lee Marvin, who began a cohabitation relationship in 1964. When the relationship between the "Marvins" broke down in 1970, the Californian family court found no evidence of a contract for long-term support. However, the court ordered Lee Marvin to pay $104,000 in financial support as an equitable remedy. The award was reversed on appeal, leaving "Mrs." Marvin with nothing. The ruling has become the leading case illustrating the principle that marriage and cohabitation are not the same thing. The court is not free to stretch equity, trust, or implied contract to duplicate family law for meeting postseparation needs. The claims of cohabiting couples must be based on contract or related doctrines and not on the application of statutory rules used in divorce cases.

willingness to offer marriage to remain a very important signal for a woman. If traditional obligations of spousal support (the promises made) were routinely enforced—implying a considerable cost to the male for later-life opportunistic divorce—willingness to offer marriage would be an important quality signal, giving a "separating equilibrium" that distinguishes committed from uncommitted life partners.

Cohabitation has not generally been subjected to the same kind of settling up regime as marriage in the event of dissolution. There is no equity-based intervention by a family court with powers to reallocate assets between partners or to create maintenance obligations, as shown by the case of *Marvin v. Marvin* (1981), which is examined in the boxed section. Cohabiting couples generally retain individual property rights and have no mutual support obligations in law. Courts can sometimes reallocate property between the former cohabitees or award palimony if there is evidence of an agreement between the parties upon which one has relied. Very often, cohabitees have a perception that they are so close to a married status by living together that they are common-law husband and wife and that divorce law should apply. In fact, few jurisdictions recognize common-law marriage—Montana is one, whereas California is not.

Cohabiting parties must rely largely on natural "hostages" that emerge in the relationship to limit the kind of opportunism described earlier. Such hostages may in fact be the children, with whom a parent may wish to maintain easy contact. Also, the search costs of finding a new partner, or any social stigma that might be attached to living alone, may act to hold people together over a long period of time. In the case of marriage, the hostages are typically bolstered by legal obligations between the ex-spouses to pay child and possibly spousal maintenance and to divide marital property according to statute and case law. Note, however, that recent moves toward treating cohabitation as marriage have led to child-support legislation imposing an obligation on all absent parents, regardless of marital status, to pay child support. Nonetheless, it is clear that it would be rational to choose to cohabit if the parties actually wished to avoid postdissolution obligations toward each other.

Recently, the American Law Institute (ALI) has suggested treating cohabitation more like marriage. The ALI's *Principles of the Law of Family Dissolution, Final Draft* (2001) advises courts to assess cohabitation according to the extent to which it approximates marriage. The court would then follow a formulaic approach to dividing property and awarding maintenance, with a strong presumption of equal property division as with divorce in community property states. The ALI advises courts to minimize the impact of the parties' intentions. Such a policy would treat cohabitation as a status much like marriage.

Treating cohabitation like marriage would remove a valuable individual choice. It would not remove the signal of commitment attached to marriage, because no change would be made to marital obligations. However, the policy could destabilize relationships by causing some people to live apart who might only be prepared to form a more serious relationship if the dissolution obligations were kept light. From a human welfare perspective, worries about the instability of cohabitation are not in themselves a reason for forcing every cohabitee to marry. Cohabitation is not marriage, and a pattern of trying out and deciding to part could be viewed as successful experimentation).

From a life-profile perspective, if there were evidence that women were making early investments in family life with the expectation of lifetime support (a traditional model) and that men were taking advantage of them by imposing cohabitation rather than marriage, there would be the basis for a claim of exploitation. Such reasoning might cause marriage-like obligations to be enforced when cohabitation came to approximate marriage (e.g., after children are born within the union, or after a period of time during which one party becomes highly dependent economically). However, some women and men may be misinformed about the likely outcome of cohabitation and the life-profile problem of making "sunk" investments in homemaking and child rearing, without some guarantee of sharing in other "products" of the relationship later on. In that case, there might be a case for providing information and education but not one for banning a consensual practice. The key issue here is that parties are free to avoid cohabitation because they could choose marriage.

Same-Sex Cohabitation

Some jurisdictions, such as California, Hawaii, and Vermont, and—outside of the United States—others like Canada, Denmark, and Belgium, have instigated "domestic partnership" contracts carrying many of the obligations of marriage. The Netherlands is the only jurisdiction so far to have fully extended marriage to same-sex couples. The issues of property rights connected to same-sex unions are substantially the same as those in heterosexual unions, with the difference that heterosexuals have traditionally had a choice over whether to marry, whereas homosexuals have had no choice but to cohabit. The debate over extending marriage or domestic partnerships serves to cast some of the property-rights issues affecting traditional marriage partners into sharp relief.

The thrust of the life-profile theory of marriage is that the enforcement of long-term support protects reliance investment by the economically vulnerable spouse, thereby creating confidence that commitment is genuine. Marriage enables a man and woman to plan their lives and to avoid turning a sex-based life-profile asymmetry into the basis for exploitation of the weaker party. By this reasoning, it would make sense to extend the status of marriage to homosexual partners if there were evidence of the same life-profile issues that affect heterosexuals. Given the same-sex nature of the relationships, it seems less likely that such asymmetries would arise and at first sight the life-profile approach does not support same-sex marriage. Care must be taken: Just because it seems unlikely that the sunk investments made in same-sex unions will disadvantage one of the partners, it does not mean that we can rule out the life-profile asymmetry that is of concern in considering heterosexual marriage. There may be some homosexual cohabitees who can produce the same life-profile issues affecting heterosexuals.

Extending the choice of whether to marry or cohabit does not force homosexuals into same-sex marriage, but it would give a party to a relationship the opportunity to insist on marriage if *in that party's estimation* the protection of marriage is needed. Thus if two women live together and one develops a career while the other takes care of the home, the possibility of a divorce settlement if the relationship were later dissolved would provide a credible signal of long-term commitment to the economically more vulnerable woman. Indeed, with adoption of children or the use of artificial insemination, it is possible to imagine the duplication of most of the characteristics of a traditional marriage.

The Dutch approach of making marriage available to same-sex couples is like using a property rule (see Chapter 3) to deal with the tort of nuisance—we do not know in advance whether a party will *need* the legal entitlement to make certain costs register with other parties, but in the right circumstances the entitlement supports an efficient bargaining solution. If there are same-sex cohabitees made economically vulnerable over the long term to expropriation of their investment in their relationship, the problem could be solved by extending the possibility of marriage to them. The key feature of that marriage would be the possibility of equitable intervention into property and income entitlements by a divorce court in the event of marital dissolution. However, note that at present the Defense of Marriage Act, 1996, is generally interpreted as making such an extension of marriage impossible. The state has effectively made a demarcation of what may count as marriage based on dominant mores.

At the time of writing, city authorities in several states had begun to issue marriage licenses to same-sex couples, stirring up a huge controversy across the United States. Connecticut and California were particularly embroiled in the controversy, which was sparked by supreme court moves at the state level to declare the limitation of marriage to heterosexual couples as an unconstitutional restriction on liberty. The federal response has included a promise by President George W. Bush to introduce a new possible constitutional amendment limiting marriage to heterosexual unions. It remains to be seen how the public debate will be resolved, but surveys suggest that a majority of Americans are against same-sex marriage at present.

PARENT AND CHILD: ECONOMIC PERSPECTIVES

So far we have discussed marriage and divorce and have not taken an economic perspective on the relationship between parent and child. The relationship is complex, occurs over a long period of time, is characterized by much apparent altruism, and can also be susceptible to opportunistic behavior. Some estimates of the costs of raising a child put the total into millions of dollars (think of college tuition!); there is no obvious financial return to having children. It is not clear in those terms why we continue to focus our lives around homes and children to the extent that we do in the modern age. It was clear that children were a support in old age and were instrumental labor inputs in subsistence farming in earlier periods of history, as they still are in some societies, but this is no longer the case in the United States. The elderly survive on a mixture of savings and social security entitlements in all western societies. There is a powerful motivation toward child rearing that cannot be explained in simple terms. This impetus may be seen very clearly in the strong desire of infertile couples to adopt children: Clearly, the motivation even transcends biological limits.

One school of thought draws on sociobiology to explain our child-rearing instincts in terms of a drive to reproduce our genes. A genetic imperative could lie underneath our

Roe v. Doe, 324 N.Y.S. 2d 71 (1971)

A teenage girl refused to live with her father in New York and sought reimbursement for the rent on an apartment in Louisville, Kentucky, where she was a college student. The court denied that he had an obligation to meet the rent and accepted that the father was not refusing to support his daughter. Rather, he was refusing to be dictated to by the minor daughter over the proper allocation of support. The daughter needed to accept her family's support in the family home or in some alternative setting offered by her parents. Any other approach would be inefficient because the support obligation without a degree of control by the father would be an open-ended recipe for holdup by the daughter.

interest in and satisfaction from raising a family. With this reasoning, other benefits, such as providing for elderly parents, are incidental anyway. Sociobiology finds a genetic imperative behind many aspects of marriage and courtship, where key aspects of attraction are explained by genetic fitness. According to sociobiology, nurturing natural children is substantially concerned with equipping them, in turn, to pass on the genetic code. Adoption, in turn, is emulative behavior: The nurturing and reproductive imperative is so strong that not following it leaves us unfulfilled.

The genetic drive may explain where our wishes and tastes originate, but it may not explain much more. In exercising our preferences, or perhaps having satisfied mother nature and procreated, attention must still be paid to the costs and benefits of alternative behavior in family settings. Economists working to understand the effects of family law come across many examples of how the costs and benefits of alternative behavior do indeed affect parenting. In one extreme example, researchers have found how deadbeat parents tend to gravitate to states where child-support obligations are not firmly enforced.

There are over 4 million child-support cases a year, of which around 1 million involve parents who have migrated across a state line to jurisdictions tolerating their avoidance of family obligations. Statistical studies show that nonpayment of child support is clustered in the low-enforcement states and is increased by the levels of divorce and unmarried births in a state. Measures of contact time spent with children have a positive effect on the payment of support obligations: For example, a joint-custody order applied to the child of divorcees tends to keep both parents involved in raising and financing the child. It seems that when the benefits of parenting (genetically primed satisfaction from contact) fall, parents may be less interested in supporting children. Similarly, more evasion results when the costs of avoiding legal obligations fall.

In intact families, and even in dissolved families where the spouses are able to negotiate their affairs, the courts assume that parents act in the best interests of children. Parents are viewed as acting in a fiduciary manner, rather than in a narrowly defined contracting manner. Historically, this assumption has made courts extremely reluctant to interfere in families. Children have been regarded as firmly under the control of parents and not the state, and they cannot "divorce" their parents (although the courts may, very rarely, grant a minor emancipation status). A corollary is a parental obligation (actually, the common-law obligation is paternal) to support natural or adopted children. The support obligation is interpreted in terms of financing the reasonable needs of the child, within the family, as discussed in the boxed example.

Parental control also extends to medical treatment, reasonable discipline, and to requiring attendance at educational establishments. The required content of education tends to be set by the states, although there has been liberal treatment of home-schooling movements and of religious minorities like the Amish in their pursuit of comparable but different educational programs [see *Wisconsin v. Yoder*, 406 U.S. 205 (1971)]. Interestingly, courts will limit parental freedom if it clearly threatens the welfare of a child in an obvious way. Thus, a court may allow a parent to insist on a child having an operation although the child does not wish it, but it may also order a life-saving operation against the parent's wishes. Therefore, it seems that courts wish to avoid the costs of second-guessing parental choices in raising children unless there is a compelling reason to become involved.

ADOPTION

Adoption of children is an ancient practice that is now covered by legal principles. Adoption gives the adopter and the child all the rights of a natural parent and child and is ordinarily an irreversible event. In recent decades, the supply of adoptable children has declined, because of birth control, a greater acceptance of single parents, and increased protection of parental rights where children have been placed into foster care. It is hardly surprising that a black market in adoptable babies has emerged in such conditions of shortages. Payment of compensation to mothers giving up children for adoption is currently illegal throughout the United States. Would-be adopters sometimes circumvent the normal private and state adoption agencies by entering into questionable or even illegal financial arrangements with overseas agencies or with American agents willing to locate children for them to adopt. Some economists have suggested that an explicit adoption market would work better than the mixture of regulation and black market that currently prevails.

Would a market-based approach cure any of the problems of the adoption system? The supply of adoptable children would logically increase. For a start, some mothers who might terminate pregnancies through abortion under current conditions might give birth if they could be compensated for the disruption to their lives that childbirth implies. It can be argued that the children would move to a parent who values them most, at least as measured by willingness to pay—that is, to give up other things in life. To make such an inquiry is not necessarily an example of people taking economics too literally. One could screen parents for such things as mental deficiency or abusive tendencies before they were allowed to offer compensation to natural mothers so as to protect the adopted children in key respects.

Most state regulation of adoption tries to duplicate in a loose sense what a market process would achieve. That is, the regulatory approach takes children from parents who do not value them enough to keep them (whether they are unable or unwilling) and places them with parents who will endure costs in terms of time and money because they value the children more highly. To note that no parent would give up a child because of financial considerations is actually a poor argument against using markets. Some parents do give up children on black markets, and any parent giving up a child does so in some sense because the costs of keeping the child are too high. Some worry that older and handicapped children would not fare well in a market system, but actually they also do badly at present. Nevertheless, the laws governing adoption place the interests of the child first and the outcome is generally beneficial to the child.

In Re Baby M., 109 N.J. 396 (N.J.Super.Ch. 1988)

Whitehead agreed to bear the child of Stern (through artificial insemination) in exchange for costs plus $10,000 and to terminate her rights as a mother. Upon the birth of the baby (M) and the subsequent handover to the Sterns, she became deeply disturbed by the events and persuaded the Sterns to give her one last week with the child. Whitehead fled to Florida with her husband and the baby. They were eventually ordered to return the child, whereupon the Sterns filed suit, seeking enforcement of the surrogacy contract. The court ordered that sole custody of the child be granted to Stern and also entered an order allowing the adoption of baby M by Stern's wife. Whitehead appealed, and the court held the surrogacy contract to be void as being contrary to laws governing adoption and the public policy of keeping children with both of their natural parents.

The family court eventually determined that Whitehead should be granted liberal visitation rights with baby M. The court treated the matter as a variant on a custody dispute between two natural parents plus an adoption issue. It did not enforce the contract but rather exercised traditional powers in relation to interparental disputes, dividing holiday periods and weekends between the natural parents. Further, the court restrained parties from publicly discussing their relationships, or from selling movie rights in fictional portrayal of their activities, without prior approval of the court.

SURROGACY

Surrogacy raises further questions about the limits of freedom of contract in the family area. Artificial insemination enables a childless couple to have children, providing that one of them is fertile. It is also possible to fertilize human eggs outside of the womb and implant them either in the female partner or into a surrogate. Couples enter into contracts with surrogate mothers as a way to start a family. The legal view of the enforceability of such contracts varies according to jurisdiction. In *In re Baby M.* (1988), which is discussed in the boxed section, the New Jersey court declined to enforce a surrogacy contract. Since then, several states (e.g., Indiana, Louisiana and Kentucky) have decided that surrogate childbearing contracts are legally unenforceable under any circumstances, and some (Michigan and Nebraska) treat them as crimes if they involve compensation other than meeting the mother's medical expenses.

The court in *Baby M* suggested that the legislature resolve the public policy questions attached to surrogacy. The legislative responses of the states to the practice vary from a few that reluctantly accept it to a majority that find such contracts illegal and unenforceable. Several states enforce the contracts when they are regulated if there is no monetary payment for the surrogate's service. One particularly accommodating state is California, where the Supreme Court has held that surrogacy contracts are specifically enforceable, if the egg and the sperm are donated by individuals other than the surrogate mother [*Johnson v. Calvert*, 851 P.2d 776 (Cal. 1993)]. The California court dismissed some of the concerns cited by in *Baby M*, claiming there to be no proof that surrogacy exploits poor women to any greater extent than other occupations open to them.

The court did not accept the claim that surrogacy encourages an attitude regarding children as commodities and did not like the suggestion that a woman cannot give informed consent to deliver a baby since it implied that women lacked personal responsibility. The court noted that a decision not to enforce surrogacy contracts denies intending parents a scarce opportunity of procreating a child of their own genetic stock. It also dismissed the suggestion that surrogacy might be upsetting to the children in later life, regarding it as no worse than other mechanisms transferring children between parents.

An application of the Coase theorem (Chapter 3) tells us that with low bargaining costs, contracts conferring gains from trade on the adults will form whether the law supports enforceability (California) or denies it (New Jersey). The adults should always be able to find a division of the benefits to them that would enable the "trade" to occur. However, the uncertainty surrounding surrogacy contracts will likely cause an increase in bargaining costs and some predictable problems will emerge. The adults will tend to rely on experienced attorneys, who may seem able to secure conformity with the contracts. Also, there will be scope for opportunistic behavior, particularly by the surrogate mother, who may try to extract additional payments close to delivery as an alternative to a later custody dispute. Nonetheless, some surrogate mothers may be very happy with their role and may get satisfaction from helping others, or want additional children without the cost of keeping them. Of course such mothers could carry out the role voluntarily in the absence of enforceable surrogacy contracts.

SUMMARY AND CONCLUSIONS

The economic approach to family law is relatively new, but it gives useful insights into several areas of public concern. Much of the work carried out to explain the growth of divorce and reduction in marriage has an economic focus, due to the need to control for socioeconomic variables in studying the impact of legal change. In addition, the life-profile model has much to say about "settling up" between spouses and can make some issues connected with cohabitation more clear. Economics also illuminates less obvious areas to do with the placement of children and can even be used in understanding such topics as deadbeat parents.

QUESTIONS FOR REVIEW

1. What explains the movement away from marriage since the 1960s?

2. In late 2003, a high-profile Hollywood celebrity ended a short marriage to a professionally accomplished but less wealthy younger husband. What would contractual approaches suggest for the divorce settlement?

3. Examine the extent to which the economic analysis of family law considers the welfare of children.

NOTES ON THE LITERATURE

*   A useful general source on the economic approach to family law is Brinig (2000) and Dnes (2000)—entries in the *Encyclopedia of Law and Economics* on parents and children, and marriage contracts, respectively. See also the articles in Dnes and Rowthorn (2002).

*   Assortative mating is examined by Oppenheimer (1988) and the life-profile theory originates with Cohen (1987, 2002).

- Alan Parkman (2002) favors a specific-performance requirement in marriage, which would be a move to a regime allowing divorce but only by consent.

- Zelder (1993, 2002) examines indivisibilities, particularly the presence of children in a marriage, as obstacles to bargaining. Peters (1986) argued that the Coase theorem might apply to the effects of changes in divorce laws, although her statistical results showing no permanent impact from legal change are not supported by subsequent work (Allen, 2002; Binner and Dnes, 2001).

- Trebilcock (1993, Chapter 2) discusses the difficulties with nonexpectations based approaches to divorce settlement. See also Dnes (1998).

- Brinig and Buckley (1998) look at the effect of no-fault laws on domestic behavior.

- Brinig and Crafton (1994) found that for the period 1965–1987, no-fault divorce laws had a negative and significant relationship on the birth rate, holding time and the number of marriages constant. The result is is consistent with decreased investment by couples in less-secure marriages.

- Divorced women with minor children remarry less frequently than those without them (Becker, Landes, and Michael, 1977).

- Brinig and Buckley (1996) carried out the empirical examination of migration trends in relation to indices of nonpayment of child support.

- Richard Posner (1987) suggested that a market in babies would rectify many of the problems of the adoption system. Posner's critics accuse him of "commodifying" children and mothers. The view in the text is that market mechanisms may help in certain contexts, but that externalities loom very large in relation to children.

- A recent attempt to expand family law and economics in the direction of children's welfare considerations is Bowles and Garoupa (2002).

CASES, STATUTES, AND REFERENCES

Cases

Agricultural Insurance Co. v. Constantine, 58 N.E.2d 658 (Ohio 1944)

Alaska Packers' Association v. Domenico, 117 F. 99 (9th Cir. 1902)

Allied Van Lines v. Bratton, 351 So.2d 344 (S. Ct. of Fl. 1977)

Anglia Television v. Reed, 3 All E.R. 690 (1972)

Re Baby M., 109 N.J. 396 (N.J.Super.Ch. 1988)

Bach v. Longman, Jacob & Alexander 128 (1777, 1993)

Beshada v. Johns-Manville Products, 90 N.J. 191 (1982)

Bolton v. Stone, A.C. 850 (1951)

Boomer v. Atlantic Cement Co., 257 N.E. 2d 870 (C.A. of N.Y. 1970)

Borman v. Board of Supervisors, 584 N.W.2d 309 (Iowa 1998)

Bove v. Donna Hanna Coke Corp., 258 N.Y.S. 229, (N.Y. App. Div. 1932)

Brian Construction & Development Co., Inc. v. Brighenti, 405 A.2d 72 (S. Ct. of Conn. 1978)

Brown v. Voss, 715 P.2d. 514 (Wash. 1986)

Ira S. Bushey & Sons, Inc. v. U.S., 398 F.2d 167 (2d Circ. 1968)

Canadian National Railway v. Norsk Pacific Steamship Co., 1 S.C.R. 1021 (1992)

Carlill v. Carbolic Smoke Ball Co., 1 Q.B. 256 (1893)

City Stores Co. v. Ammerman, 266 F.Supp. 766 (D.C. 1967)

Coffin v. Left Hand Ditch Co., 6 Colo. 443 (1882)

Davies v. Mann, 152 E.R. 588 (1842)

Davis v. Jacoby, 34 P.2d 1026 (1934)

Deatons v. Flew, 79 C.L.R. 370 (1949)

Denney v. Reppert, 432 S.W.2d 647 (C.A. of Ky. 1968)

Dexter v. Hall, 82 U.S. (15 Wall.) 9, 20 (1872)

Dillon v. Legg, 441 P.2d 912 (Cal. 1968)

Dimskal Shipping Co. SA v. International Transport Workers' Federation, 3 W.L.R. 875 (1991)

Donoghue v. Stevenson, AC 562 (1932)

Edgar v. Stevenson, 11 P. 704 (1886)

Escola v. Coca Cola Bottling Co. of Fresno, 150 P.2d 436 (Cal. 1944)

Faber v. Sweet Style Mfg. Corp., 242 N.Y.2d 763 (S. Ct. of N.Y. 1963)

Fletcher v. City of Aberdeen, 338 P.2d 743 (Wash. 1959)

Fuller v. Illinois Central Railroad, 56 So.783 (Miss. 1911)

Georgious Panayiotou v. Sony Entertainment Ltd., All. E.R. 755 (1994)

Graham v. Scissor-Tail Inc., 28 Cal. 3d 807 (1981)

Gregg v. Georgia, 428 U.S. 153, Supreme Court (1976)

Hadley v. Baxendale, 156 ER 145 (1854)

Halbman v. Lemke, 298 N.W.2d 562 (S. Ct. Wisc. 1980)

Hamer v. Sidway, 27 N.E. 256 (Ct. of App. N.Y. 1891)

Harris v. Watson, Peake 102 (1791)

Hawaii Housing Authority v. Midkiff, 467 U.S. 229, Supreme Court (1984)

Hawkins v. McGee, 146 A. 641 (S. Ct. of N.H. 1929)

Hayes v. Aquia Marina, Inc., 414 S.E.2d 820 (Va. 1992)

Hills v. Miller, 3 Paige Ch. 254 (N.Y. 1832)

Hume v. U.S., 132 U.S. 406, Supreme Court (1889)

The Isle of Mull, 278 F. 131 (4th Cir. 1921)

Jacob & Youngs v. Kent, 230 N.Y. 239 (1921)

Johnson v. Calvert, 851 P.2d 776 (Cal. 1993)

M.F. Kemper Construction Co. v. City of Los Angeles et al., 235 P.2d 7 (Cal. 1951)

Keppel v. Bailey, 2 My & K 517 (1834)

Kerr Steamship Co. v. Radio Corp. of America, 157 N.E. 140 (C.A. of N.Y. 1927)

Laidlaw v. Organ, 15 U.S. (2 Wheat) 178 (1817)

Leroy Fibre Co. v. Chicago, Milwaukee and St Paul Railway, 232 U.S. 240 (1914)

Lumley v. Gye, 118 E.R. 749 (K.B. 1853)

Lux v. Haggin, 4 P. 674 (Cal. 1886)

MacPherson v. Buick Motor Co., 111 N.E. 1050 (C.A. of N.Y. 1916)

McRae v. Commonwealth Disposals Commission, 84 C.L.R. 377 (1951)

Mabo & Others v. The State of Queensland, 175 C.L.R. 1 (1992)

Marvin v. Marvin, 122 Cal. Rptr. 555 (C.A. of Cal. 1981)

Miller v. Jackson, 3 All, E.R. 338 (1977)

Morrell v. Rice, 622 A.2d 1156 (Me. 1993)

Nahrstedt v. Lakeside Village Condominium Association, 878 P.2d 1275 (Cal. 1994)

Nollan v. California Coastal Commission, 483 U.S. 825, Supreme Court (1987)

Norwalk Door Closer v. Eagle Lock & Screw Co., 220 A.2d 263 (Conn. 1966)

Obde v. Schlemeyer, 353 P. 2d 672 (Wash. 1960)

Page One Records Ltd v. Britton, 1 W.L.R. 157 (1968)

Palsgraf v. Long Island Railway Co., 162 N.E. 99 (N.Y. 1928)

Parker v. Twentieth Century-Fox Film Corp., 474 P.2d 689, (S.Ct. Cal. 1970)

Pennsylvania Coal Co. v. Mahon, 260 U.S. 393 Supreme Court (1922)

Petterson v. Royal Oak Hotel, N.Z.L.R. 136 (1948)

Poletown Neighborhood Council v. City of Detroit, 304 N.W.2d 455 (Mich. 1981)

Potter v. Firestone Tire & Rubber Co., 863 P.2d 795 (Cal. 1993)

R. v. Clarke, 40 C.L.R. 227 (1927)

R. v. Sparrow, 1 S.C.R. 404 (1990)

Raffles v. Wichelhaus, 2 Hurl. & C. 906, 159 E.R. 375 (Ex) (1864)

R.J. Reynolds Tobacco Co. v. Engle, 751 So.2d 51 Table (Fla. 1999)

Rickards v. Sun Oil Co., 41 A.2d 267 (N.J. 1945)

Robbins Dry Dock & Repair Co. v. Flint, 275 U.S. 303 (1927)

Robinson v. Pioche, Bayerque & Co., 5 Cal. 460 (1855)

Roe v. Doe, 324 N.Y.S. 2d 71 (1971)

Rose v. Mesmer, 75 P. 905 (Cal. 1904)

Rylands v. Fletcher, L.R. 3 H.L. 330 (1868)

Schroeder Music Publishing Co. Ltd v. Macaulay, 3 All. E.R. 616, 1 W.L.R. 1308 (H.L.) (1974)

Shadwell v. Shadwell, 142 E.R. 62 (1860)

Sherwood v. Walker, 33 N.W. 919 (Mich. 1877)

Southwest Engineering Co. v. U.S., 341 F.2d 998 (U.S. Ct. of Appeals, 8th Cir. 1965)

Spartan Steel v. Martin and Co., C.A., Q.B. 27 (1973)

Spur Industries, Inc. v. Del E. Webb Development Co., 49 P.2d 701 (C.A., Ariz. 1972)

Stringfellow v. McCain Foods, R.P.C. 501 (1984)

Sturges v. Bridgman, 11 Ch. 852 (1879)

Sullivan v. Old Colony Street Railway, 83 N.E. 1091 (Mass. 1908)

Taylor v. Caldwell, 3 B&S 826, 122 E.R. 309 (Q.B.) (1863)

Texaco, Inc. v. Pennzoil, 485 U.S. 994 (1988)

Tsakiroglou & Co. v. Noblee Thorl GmbH, A.C. 93 (1962)

Tulk v. Moxhay, 41 E.R. 1143 (1848)

Union Oil Co. v. Oppen, 501 F. 2d 558 (9th Cir. 1974)

U.S. v. Algernon Blair, 479 F.2d 638 (4th Cir. 1973)

U.S. v. Carroll Towing Co., 159 F.2d 169 (2d Cir. 1947)

Victoria Park Racing Ground Co. Ltd. v. Taylor, A.L.R. 597 (1937)

Village of Euclid, Ohio v. Ambler Realty Co., 272 U.S. 365, Supreme Court (1926)

Vosburg v. Putney, 50 N.W. 403 (Wis. 1891)

Wagon Mound (No.1), *Overseas Tankship v. Morts Dock & Engineering*, A.C. 388 (1961)

Wagon Mound (No.2), *Overseas Tankship v. Miller Steamship Pty*, 1 A.C. 617 (1967)

Warner Brothers Pictures Inc. v. Nelson, 1 K.B. 209 (1937)

Williams v. Roffey Brothers & Nicholls (Contractors) Ltd., 1 Q.B. 1 (C.A.) (1991)

Williams v. Walker-Thomas Furniture Co., 350 F. 2d 445 (D.C. Cir. 1965)

Wisconsin v. Yoder, 406 U.S. 205, Supreme Court (1971)

Statutes

California Coastal Act (1976)

Clean Air Act (1970, amended 1990)

Clean Water Act (1972)

Defense of Marriage Act (1996)

Federal Trade Mark Act (1994)

Pollution Prevention Act (1990)

Public Accounting Reform & Investor Protection (Sarbannes-Oxley) Act (2002)

Public Securities Litigation Reform Act (1995)

Racketeer Influenced & Corrupt Organization Act (1970)

Securities Exchange Act (1934)

Sonny Bono Copyright Term Extension Act (1998)

Standard State Zoning Act (1926)

Statute of Monopolies (1623)

References

Agnello, R.J., and Donnelley, L.P. 1975. Property rights and efficiency in the oyster industry. *Journal of Law and Economics* 18: 521–533.

Aivazian, V.A., Trebilcock, M.J., and Penny, M. 1984. The law of contract modifications: The uncertain quest for a benchmark of enforceability. *Osgoode Hall Law Journal* 22: 173–212.

Allen, D.W. 1991. Homesteading and property rights: Or how the West was really won. *Journal of Law and Economics* 34: 1–23.

Allen, D.W. 2002. *The Impact of Legal Reforms on Marriage and Divorce*. In Dnes and Rowthorn (eds.) *op. cit.*

American Law Institute. 2002. *Principles of the Law of Family Dissolution, Analysis and Recommendations*. Philadelphia, PA: ALI.

American Law Institute. 2000. *Restatement (Third) of Property: Servitudes*. Philadelphia, PA: ALI.

American Law Institute. 1998. *Restatement (Third) of Torts: Product Liability*. Philadelphia, PA: ALI.

American Law Institute. 1979. *Restatement (Second) of Torts*. Philadelphia, PA: ALI.

American Law Institute. 1981. *Restatement (Second) of Contracts*. Philadelphia, PA: ALI.

American Law Institute/National Conference of Commissioners on Uniform State Laws. 2003. *Uniform Commercial Code*. Cincinnati, OH: West Legal Studies.

Anderson, T.L. (ed.) 1993. *Property Rights and Indian Economies*. Lanham, MD: Rowman and Littlefield.

Anderson, T.L., and Hill, P.J. 1975. The evolution of property rights: A study of the American West. *Journal of Law and Economics* 18: 163–179.

Anderson, T.L., and Hill, P.J. 2002. Cowboys and contracts. *Journal of Legal Studies* 31: 489–515.

Anderson, T.L., and Simmons, R.T. 1993. *The Political Economy of Customs and Culture: Informal Solutions to the Commons Problem*. Lanham, MD: Rowman and Littlefield.

Anderson, T.L., and McChesney, F.S. 1994. Raid or trade? An economic model of Indian–white relations. *Journal of Law and Economics* 37: 39–74.

Axelrod, R. 1984. *The Evolution of Cooperation*. New York: Basic Books.

Ayres, I., and Goldbart, P.M. 2003. Correlated values in the theory of property and liability rules. *Journal of Legal Studies* 32: 121–152.

Baker, C.E. 1975. The ideology of the economic analysis of law. *Philosophy and Public Affairs* 5: 3–38.

Bartley, W.A., and Cohen, M.A. 1998. The effect of concealed weapon laws: An extreme bounds analysis. *Economic Inquiry* 36: 258–265.

Becker, G. 1968. Crime and punishment: An economic approach. *Journal of Political Economy* 69: 169–217.

Becker, G., Landes, E., and Michael, R. 1977. An economic analysis of marital instability. *Journal of Political Economy* 85: 1141–1187.

Bennett, T. 1989. *Evaluating Neighbourhood Watch*. Aldershot: Gower.

Benson, B.L. 1994. Are public goods really common pools? Consideration of the evolution of policing and highways in England. *Economic Inquiry* 32: 249–271.

Bernstein, L. 1992. Opting out of the legal system: Extra-legal contractual relations in the diamond industry. *Journal of Legal Studies* 21: 115–158.

Besen, S.M., and Raskind, L.J. 1991. An introduction to the law and economics of intellectual property. *Journal of Economic Perspectives* 5: 3–27.

Binner, J., and Dnes. A. 2001. Marriage, divorce and legal change. *Economic Inquiry* 39: 298–306.

Bishop, W., and Sutton, J. 1986. Efficiency and justice in tort damages: The shortcomings of the pecuniary loss rule. *Journal of Legal Studies* 15: 347–370.

Black, D.A., and Nagin, D.S. 1998. Do right-to-carry laws deter violent crime? *Journal of Legal Studies* 27 (1): 209–221.

Blackstone, W. 1766. *Commentaries on the Laws of England*. 1809 edition with notes by Edward Christian, Cardell and Davies, London, reprinted by Professional Books Ltd, Abingdon, 1982.

Blumstein, A., and Nagin, D. 1977. A stronger test of the deterrence hypothesis. *Stanford Law Review* 29: 241–276.

Bouckaert, B., and De Geest, G. (eds.) 2000. *Encyclopedia of Law and Economics*. Northampton, MA: Edward Elgar.

Bowles, R., and Garoupa, N. 2002. Household dissolution, child care and divorce law. *International Review of Law and Economics* 22: 495–510.

Breyer, S. 1970. The uneasy case for copyright: A study of copyright in books, photocopies and computer programs. *Harvard Law Review* 84: 281–351.

Brinig, M. 2000. Parent and child. Entry 1,800 in Bouckaert and De Geest (eds.) *op. cit.*

Brinig, M., and Buckley, F. 1996. The market for deadbeats. *Journal of Legal Studies* 25: 201–232.

Brinig, M., and Buckley, F. 1998. No-fault law and at-fault people. *International Review of Law and Economics* 18: 235–325.

Brinig, M., and Crafton, S. 1994. Marriage and opportunism. *Journal of Legal Studies* 23: 869–894.

Buchanan, C., and Hartley, P.R. 1992. *Criminal Choice: The Economic Theory of Crime and its Implications for Crime Control.* Policy Monograph 24, St. Leonards, New South Wales: Centre for Independent Studies

Buchanan, J.M. 1965. An economic theory of clubs. *Economica* 32: 1–14.

Buchanan, J.M., and Stubblebine, W.M. 1962. Externality. *Economica* 29: 371–384.

Buckley, F. (ed.) 1999. *The Fall and Rise of Freedom of Contract.* Durham, NC: Duke University Press.

Burrows, P., and Veljanovski, C.J. (eds.) 1981. *The Economic Approach to Law.* London: Butterworths.

Calabresi, G. 1970. *The Costs of Accidents: A Legal and Economic Analysis.* New Haven: Yale University Press.

Calabresi, G., and Melamed, A.D. 1972. Property rules, liability rules and inalienability: One view of the cathedral. *Harvard Law Review* 85: 1089–1128.

Calfee, J., and Rubin, P. 1992. Some implications of damage payments for nonpecuniary losses. *Journal of Legal Studies* 21: 371–411.

Cameron, S. 1988. Economics of crime deterrence. *Kyklos* 41: 301–323.

Carr-Hill, R., and Stern, N.H. 1979. *Crime, the Police and Criminal Statistics.* New York: Academic Press.

Carter, R.A.L, and Palmer, J.P. 1991. Real rates, expected rates, and damage awards. *Journal of Legal Studies* 20: 439–462.

Carter, R.A.L, and Palmer, J.P. 1994. Simple calculations to reduce litigation costs in personal injury cases: Additional empirical support for the offset rule. *Osgood Hall Law Journal* 32: 197–223.

Chung, T. 1993. Efficiency of comparative negligence: A game-theoretic analysis. *Journal of Legal Studies* 22: 395–404.

Clarke, A., Fielding, N.G., and W.H.R. 2000. Crime, unemployment and deprivation. In Fielding, Clarke, and Witt (eds.) *The Economic Dimensions of Crime, infra.*

Coase, R.H. 1937. The nature of the firm. *Economica* 4: 386–405.

Coase, R.H. 1960. The problem of social cost. *Journal of Law and Economics* 3: 1–44.

Coase, R.H. 1974. The lighthouse in economics. *Journal of Law and Economics* 17: 357–376.

Coase, R.H. 1988. *The Firm, the Market and the Law.* Chicago: University of Chicago Press.

Coffee, J. 2001. *Testimony Before the Senate Committee on Commerce, Science and Transportation.* December 18, 2001, http://commerce.senate.gov/hearings/121801Coffee.pdf.

Cook, P.J., and Graham, D.A. 1977. The demand for insurance and protection: The case of irreplaceable commodities. *Quarterly Journal of Economics* 91: 143–156.

Cook, P.J., and Zarkin, G.A. 1985. Crime and the business cycle. *Journal of Legal Studies* 14: 115–128.

Cohen, L.R. 1987. Marriage, divorce and quasi-rents: Or, "I gave him the best years of my life." *Journal of Legal Studies* 16: 267–303.

Cohen, L.R. 2002. Marriage: The long-term contract. In Dnes and Rowthorn (eds.) *The Law and Economics of Marriage and Divorce, infra.*

Coleman, J. (ed.) 2002. *Hart's Postscript.* Oxford University Press.

Connell, E.S. 1984. *Son of the Morning Star: Custer and the Little Bighorn,* Harper Collins.

Cooter, R.D. 1985. Unity in tort, contract and property: The model of precaution. *California Law Review* 73: 1–51.

Cooter, R.D., and Porat, A. 2000. Does risk to oneself increase the care owed to others? Law and economics in conflict. *Journal of Legal Studies* 29: 19–34.

Cooter, R.D., and Rubinfeld, R.D. 1989. Economic analysis of legal disputes and their resolution. *Journal of Economic Literature* 27: 1067–1097

Crafts, N. 1998. Forging ahead and falling behind: The rise and relative decline of the first industrial nation. *Journal of Economic Perspectives* 12: 193–210.

Crutchfield, J., and Pontecorvo, G. 1969. *The Pacific Salmon Fisheries: A Study in Irrational Conservation*. Baltimore: John Hopkins University Press.

Dam, K.W. 1994. The economic underpinnings of patent law. *Journal of Legal Studies* 23: 247–272.

Dana, A., and Ramsey, M. 1989. Conservation easements and the common law. *Stanford Environmental Law Journal* 8: 2–45.

Dana, J.D., and Spier, K.E. 1993. Expertise and contingent fees: The role of asymmetric information in attorney compensation. *Journal of Law, Economics and Organization* 9: 349–367.

Deadman, D.F., and Pyle, D.J. 1993. The effect of the abolition of capital punishment in Great Britain: An application of intervention analysis. *Journal of Applied Statistics* 20: 191–206.

De Jasay, A. 1989. *Social Contract, Free Ride*. Oxford: Clarendon Press.

Demsetz, H. 1967. Towards a theory of property rights. *American Economic Review* 57: 347–359.

Demsetz H. 1969. Information and efficiency: Another viewpoint. *Journal of Law and Economics* 12: 1–22.

Demsetz, H. 1970. The private production of public goods. *Journal of Law and Economics* 13: 292–306.

Demsetz, H. 1982. Barriers to entry. *American Economic Review* 72: 47–57.

Demsetz, H. 2002. Towards a theory of property rights II. *Journal of Legal Studies* 31: 653–665.

Dezhbakhsh, H., Rubin, P.H., and Shepherd, J.M. 2003. Does capital punishment have a deterrent effect? New evidence from postmoratorium panel data. *American Law and Economics Review* 5: 344–376.

Diamond, P.A. 1974. Accident law and resource allocation. *Bell Journal of Economics and Management Science* 5: 366–405.

Dnes, A. 1985. Rent seeking behaviour and open-access fishing. *Scottish Journal of Political Economy* 32: 159–170.

Dnes, A. 1993. A case-study analysis of franchise contracts. *Journal of Legal Studies* 22: 367–394.

Dnes, A. 1995. The law and economics of contract modifications: The case of *Williams v. Roffey*. *International Review of Law and Economics* 15: 225–240.

Dnes, A. 1998. The division of marital assets. *Journal of Law and Society* 25: 336–364.

Dnes, A. 2000. Marriage contracts. Entry 5,810 in Bouckaert and De Geest (eds.) *op. cit.*

Dnes, A. 2003. Hostages and marginal deterrence in franchise contracts. *Journal of Corporate Finance* 9: 317–331.

Dnes, A., and Rowthorn, R. (eds.) 2002. *The Law and Economics of Marriage and Divorce*. New York, Cambridge University Press.

Dnes, A., and Seaton, J. 1997. An economic exploration of the tort-criminal boundary using manslaughter and negligence cases. *International Review of Law and Economics* 17: 537–551.

Donohue, J.J. 1991. Opting for the British rule, or if Posner and Shavell can't remember the Coase theorem, who will? *Harvard Law Review* 104: 1094–1119.

Dworkin, R.M. 1980. Is wealth a value? *Journal of Legal Studies* 9: 191–226.

Dworkin, R.M. 1986. *Law's Empire*. Cambridge, MA: Belknap.

Dworkin, R.M. 2000. *Sovereign Virtue*. Cambridge, MA: Harvard University Press.

Eagle, S. 2001. *Property Rights and Regulatory Takings*, 2e. New York: Lexis Law Publishing.

Ehrlich, I. 1973. Participation in illegitimate activities: A theoretical and empirical investigation. *Journal of Political Economy* 81: 521–564.

Ehrlich, I. 1975. The deterrent effect of capital punishment: A question of life and death. *American Economic Review* 65: 397–47.

Ehrlich, I. 1977. Capital punishment and deterrence: Some further thoughts. *Journal of Political Economy* 85: 741–788.

Ehrlich, I., and Liu, Z 1999. Sensitivity analyses of the deterrence hypothesis: Let's keep the econ in econometrics. *Journal of Law and Economics* 42: 459–489.

Eisenberg, J. 1982. The bargain principle and its limits. *Harvard Law Review* 95: 741–752.

Ellickson, R.C. 1973. Alternatives to zoning: Covenants, nuisance rules and, and fines as land use controls. *University of Chicago Law Review* 40: 681–781.

Epstein, R.A. 1975. Unconscionability: A critical appraisal. *Journal of Law and Economics* 18: 293.

Epstein, R.A. 1987. Inducement of breach of contract as a problem of ostensible ownership. *Journal of Legal Studies* 16: 1–23.

Epstein, R.A. 1993. Holdouts, externalities, and the single owner: One more salute to Ronald Coase. *Journal of Law and Economics* 36: 553–587.

Farber, D.A. 1997. Reassessing *Boomer*: Justice efficiency, and nuisance law. *A Property Anthology* (Richard H. Chused, ed.), 387–392.

Farmer, A., and Pecorino, P. 2000. Conditional cost shifting and the incidence of trial: Pretrial bargaining in the face of a Rule 68 offer. *American Law and Economics Review* 2 (2): 318–341.

Farnsworth, W. 1999. Do parties to nuisance cases bargain after judgment? A glimpse inside the cathedral. *University of Chicago Law Review* 66: 373–436.

Farrell, J. 1987. Information and the Coase theorem. *Journal of Economic Perspectives* 1: 113–129.

Feldthusen, B.P. 1989. *Economic Negligence: The Recovery of Pure Economic Loss.* Toronto: Carswell.

Field, S. 2000. Crime and consumption. In Fielding, Clark, and Witt (eds.) *op. cit.*

Fielding, N.G., Clarke, A. and Witt, R. (eds.) 2000. *The Economic Dimensions of Crime.* New York: St Martin's Press.

Fischel, W.A. 1985. *The Economics of Zoning Laws.* Baltimore: John Hopkins University Press.

Fischel, W.A. 1995a. *Regulatory Takings: Law, Economics, and Politics.* Cambridge, MA: Harvard University Press.

Fischel, W.A 1995b. The offer/ask disparity and just compensation for takings. *International Review of Law and Economics* 15: 187–203.

Friedman, D. 1989. An economic analysis of alternative damage rules for breach of contract. *Journal of Law and Economics* 32: 281–310.

Friedman, D. 2000. *Law's Order.* Princeton: Princeton University Press.

Fuller, L., and Perdue, W. 1936. The reliance interest in contract damages. *The Yale Law Journal* 46: 52–98.

Furubotn, E., and Pejovich, S. 1972. Property rights and economic theory: A survey of recent literature. *Journal of Economic Literature* 10: 1137–1163.

Furubotn, E., and Pejovich, S. (eds.) 1974. *The Economics of Property Rights.* Cambridge, MA: Ballinger.

Furubotn, E., and Richter, S. 1997. *The New Institutional Economics.* Ann Arbor: University of Michigan Press.

Galal, A., Jones, L., Tandon, P., and Vogelsant, I. 1992. *Welfare Consequences of Selling Public Enterprise.* Washington: World Bank.

Gambetta, D. 1993. *The Scicillian Mafia: The Business of Private Protection.* Cambridge, MA: Harvard University Press.

Gambetta, D., and Reuter, P. (2000) Conspiracy among the many: The Mafia in legitimate industries. In Fielding, Clark, and Witt (eds.) *op. cit.*

Garoupa, N. 1997. Optimal law enforcement and the economics of the drug market: Some comments on the Schengen agreement. *International Review of Law and Economics* 17: 521–536.

Garoupa, N. 1999. Dishonsty and libel law: The economics of the "chilling" effect. *Journal of Institutional and Theoretical Economics* 155: 284–300.

Gilmore, G. 1986. *The Death of Contract*. Columbus: Ohio State University Press.

Gneezy, U., and Rustichini, A. 2000. A fine is a price. *Journal of Legal Studies* 29: 1–19.

Goetz, C., and Scott, R. 1977. Liquidated damages, penalties and the just compensation principle: Some notes on an enforcement model of efficient breach. *Columbia Law Review* 77: 554–594.

Goldberg, V. 1988. Impossibility and related excuses. *Journal of Institutional and Theoretical Economics* 144: 100–116.

Goldberg, V. 1994. Recovery for economic loss following the *Exxon Valdez* oil spill. *Journal of Legal Studies* 23: 1–41.

Gordon, H.S. 1954. The economic theory of a common-property resource: The fishery. *Journal of Political Economy* 62: 124–142.

Grafton, R.Q., Squires, D., and Fox, K.J. 2000. Private property and economic efficiency: A study of a common-pool resource. *Journal of Law and Economics* 43: 679–714.

Grossman, G.M., and Schapiro, C. 1987. Dynamic R&D competition. *Economic Journal* 97: 372–387.

Haddock, D., and Curran, C. 1985. An economic theory of comparative negligence. *Journal of Legal Studies* 14: 49–72.

Halson, R. 1991. Opportunism, economic duress and contractual modifications. *Law Quarterly Review* 107: 649–678.

Harrison, G.W., and McKee, M. 1985. Experimental evaluation of the Coase theorem. *Journal of Law and Economics* 28: 653–670.

Harrison, G.W., Hoffman, E., Rutström, E.E., and Spitzer, M.L. 1987. Coasian solutions to the externality problem in experimental economics. *Economic Journal* 97: 388–402.

Helland, E., and Tabarrok, A. 2003. Race, poverty, and American tort awards: Evidence from three data sets. *Journal of Legal Studies* 32: 27–58.

Hicks, J.R. 1943. The four consumer surpluses. *Review of Economic Studies* 11: 31–41.

Hobbes, T. 1651. *Leviathan*. Harmondsworth: Penguin (1968).

Hoenack, S.A., and Weiler, W.C. 1980. A structural model of murder behavior and the criminal justice system. *American Economic Review* 70: 327–341.

Hoffman, E., and Spitzer, M.L. 1982. The Coase theorem: Some empirical tests. *Journal of Law and Economics* 25: 73–98.

Holm, H. 1995. The prisoner's dilemma or the jury's dilemma? *Journal of Institutional and Theoretical Economics* 151: 699–702.

Hughes, J.W., and Snyder, E.A. 1995. Litigation under the English and American rules: Theory and evidence. *Journal of Law and Economics* 38: 225–250.

Hulme, S.E.K. 1993. Aspects of the High Court's handling of Mabo. *The High Court of Australia in Mabo*. Papers delivered to the Samuel Griffith Society, Association of Mining and Exploration Companies, Leederville, Western Australia.

Hviid, M. 2000. Long-term contracts and relational contracts. Entry 4200 in Bouckaert and De Geest (eds.) *op. cit.*

Jacob, R., and Alexander, D. 1993. *A Guidebook to Intellectual Property*. London: Sweet & Maxwell.

Johnson, E. 1981. Lawyer's choice: a theoretical appraisal of litigation investment decisions. *Law and Society Review* 15: 567–610.

Johnson, R., Werner, M., and Gisser, M. 1981. The definition of a surface water right and transferability. *Journal of Law and Economics* 24: 273–288.

Joskow, P. 1977. Commercial impossibility: The uranium market and the Westinghouse case. *Journal of Legal Studies* 6: 119–176.

Kahneman, D., Knetsch, J.L., and Thaler, R.H. 1990. Experimental tests of the endowment effect and the Coase theorem. *Journal of Political Economy* 98: 1325–1348.

Kanazawa, M. T. 1998. Efficiency in Western water law: The development of the California doctrine, 1850–1911. *Journal of Legal Studies* 26 (1): 159–187.

Kanazawa, M. T. 2003. Origins of common-law restrictions on water transfers: Groundwater law in nineteenth century California. *Journal of Legal Studies* 32 (1): 153–180.

Kaplan, J. 1983. *The Hardest Drug: Heroin and Public Policy.* Chicago: Chicago University Press.

Kay, N. 1983. Optimal size of firm as a problem in transaction costs and property rights. *Journal of Economic Studies* 10: 29–41.

Kennedy, D. 1981. Cost-benefit analysis of entitlement problems: A critique. *Stanford Law Review* 33: 387–445.

Kessler, D., and Levitt, S.D. 1999. Using sentence enhancements to distinguish between deterrence and incapacitation. *Journal of Law and Economics* 42 (1): 343–365.

King, R.G., and Levine, R. 1993. Finance and growth: Schumpeter might be right. *Quarterly Journal of Economics* 108: 717–738.

Klein, B., Crawford, R.A., and Alchian, A. 1978. Vertical integration, appropriable rents and the competitive contracting process. *Journal of Law and Economics* 21: 297–326.

Klein, B., and Leffler, K.B. 1981. The role of market forces in assuring contractual performance. *Journal of Political Economy* 89: 615–41.

Klein, B. 1997. Why hold-ups occur: The self-enforcing range of contractual relations. *Economic Inquiry* 34: 444–463.

Klein, D.B. 1990. The voluntary provision of public goods? The turnpike companies of early America. *Economic Inquiry* 28: 788–812.

Knetsch, J.L. 1983. *Property Rights and Compensation—Compulsory Acquisition and Other Losses.* Toronto: Butterworths.

Knetsch, J.L. 1989. The endowment effect and evidence of nonreversible indifference curves. *American Economic Review* 79: 1277–1284.

Knetsch, J.L., and Sinden, J.A. 1984. Willingness to pay and compensation demanded: Experimental evidence of an unexpected disparity in measures of value. *Quarterly Journal of Economics* 99: 507–521.

Kritzer, H. 1990. *The Justice Brokers: Lawyers and Ordinary Litigation.* Oxford: Oxford University Press.

Kronman, A.T. 1978. Mistake, disclosure, information, and the law of contracts. *Journal of Legal Studies* 7: 1–34.

Kull, A. 1992. Reconsidering gratuitous promises. *Journal of Legal Studies* 21: 39–67.

Landes, W.M., and Posner, R.A. 1987. *The Economic Structure of Tort Law.* Cambridge, MA: Harvard University Press.

La Porta, R., Lopez-de-Silanes, F., Shleifer, A., and Vishny, R.W. 1998 Law and finance. *Journal of Political Economy* 106: 1113–1156.

Leamer, E.F. 1983. Let's take the con out of econometrics. *American Economic Review* 23: 31–43.

Lempert, R. 1981. Desert and deterrence: An assessment of the moral bases of the case for capital punishment. *Michigan Law Review* 79: 1177–1231.

Levmore, S. 1997. Unifying remedies: Property rules, liability rules, and startling rules. *Yale Law Journal* 106: 2149–2177.

Libecap, G. 1978. Economic variables and the development of the law: The case of Western mineral rights. *Journal of Economic History* 38: 338–362.

Libecap, G., and Smith J.L. 2002. The economic evolution of petroleum property rights in the United States. *Journal of Legal Studies* 31: 589–609.

Lindahl, E. 1919. Just taxation—A positive solution. In R.A. Musgrave and A.T. Peacock, *Classics in the Theory of Public Finance.* New York: St Martin's Press, 1967.

Lott, J.R. Jr. 2000. *More Guns, Less Crime: Understanding Crime and Gun Control Law,* 2e. University of Chicago Press.

Lott, J.R., Jr., and Mustard, D.B. 1997. Crime, deterrence and right-to-carry concealed hand-guns. *Journal of Legal Studies* 26 (1): 1–68.

Lueck, D. 1989. The economic nature of wildlife law. *Journal of Legal Studies* 18: 291–324.

Lueck, D. 1995. The rule of first possession and the design of the law. *Journal of Law and Economics* 38: 393–436.

Lueck, D. 1998. First possession. In Newman (ed.) *The New Palgrave Dictionary of Economics and the Law.*

Lueck, D., and Michael, J.A. 2003. Preemptive habitat destruction under the endangered species act. *Journal of Law and Economics* 46: 27–60.

Lynk, W. 1990. The courts and the market: An economic analysis of contingent fees in class-action litigation. *Journal of Legal Studies* 19: 247–260.

Macneil, I.R. 1974. The many futures of contracts. *Southern California Law Review* 48: 691–816.

Macneil, I.R. 1978. Contracts: Adjustment of long-term economic relations under classical, neo-classical and relational contract law. *Northwestern Law Review* 72: 854–905.

Mahoney, P.G. 2001. The common law and economic growth: Hayek might be right. *Journal of Legal Studies* 30: 503–525.

Manne, H.G. 1966. *Insider Trading and the Stock Market.* New York: Free Press.

Marceau, N., and Mongrain, S. 2003. Damage averaging and the formation of class action suits. *International Review of Law and Economics* 23: 63–74.

Markesinis, B. 1990. Litigation mania in England, Germany and the United States: Are we so very different? *Cambridge Law Journal* 49: 233–276.

Marshall, J.D., Knetsch, J.L., and Sinden, J.A. 1986. Agents' evaluation and the disparity in measures of economic loss. *Journal of Economic Behavior and Organization* 7: 115–127.

Mayer, C., and Sussman, O. 2001. The assessment: Finance law and economic growth. *Oxford Review of Economic Policy* 17: 457–466.

Meiners, R.E., and Yandle, B. 1993. *Taking the Environment Seriously.* Lanham, MD: Rowman and Littlefield.

Miceli, T.J. 2002. Over a barrel: A note on contract modification, reliance, and bankruptcy. *International Review of Law and Economics* 22: 41–51.

Miceli, T.J., and Sirmans, C.F. 1995. An economic theory of adverse possession. *International Review of Law and Economics* 15: 161–173.

Morrison, G.C. 1997. Resolving differences in willingness to pay and willingness to accept: Comment. *American Economic Review* 87: 236–240.

Mortensen, D.T. 1982. Property rights and efficiency in mating, racing, and related games. *American Economic Review* 72: 968–979.

Mumey, G.A. 1971. The Coase theorem: A reexamination. *Quarterly Journal of Economics* 85: 718–723.

Newman, P. (ed.) 1998. *The New Palgrave Dictionary of Economics and the Law.* New York: St. Martin's Press.

North, D.C. 1990. *Institutions, Institutional Change and Economic Performance.* Cambridge: Cambridge University Press.

Nutter, W. 1968. The Coase theorem on social cost: A footnote. *Journal of Law and Economics* 11: 503–507.

Oppenheimer, V.K. 1988. A theory of marriage timing. *American Journal of Sociology* 94: 563–591.

Ordover, J.A. 1991. A patent system for both diffusion and exclusion. *Journal of Economic Perspectives* 5: 43–60.

Parkman, A.M. 2002. Mutual consent divorce. In Dnes and Rowthorn (eds.) *op. cit.*

Passell, P., and Taylor, J.B. 1977. The deterrence effect of capital punishment. *American Economic Review* 67: 445–451.

Peters, E. 1986. Marriage and divorce: Information constraints and private contracting. *American Economic Review* 76: 437–454.

Pigou, A.C. 1938. *The Economics of Welfare*. London: Macmillan.

Polinsky, A.M., and Rubinfeld, D. 1998. Does the English rule discourage low-probability-of-prevailing plaintiffs? *Journal of Legal Studies* 27(2): 519–535.

Posner, E.A. 1995. Contract law in the welfare state: A defense of the unconscionability doctrine, usury laws and related limitations on freedom of contract. *Journal of Legal Studies* 24: 283–319.

Posner, R.A. 1972. A theory of negligence. *Journal of Legal Studies* 1: 29–96.

Posner, R.A. 1973. Strict liability: A comment. *Journal of Legal Studies* 2: 205–222.

Posner, R.A. 1975. The social costs of monopoly and regulation. *Journal of Political Economy* 83: 807–827.

Posner, R.A. 1977. Gratuitous promises in economics and law. *Journal of Legal Studies* 6: 411–426.

Posner, R.A. 1980. A theory of primitive society, with special reference to law. *Journal of Law and Economics* 23: 1–53.

Posner, R.A. 1981. *The Economics of Justice*. Cambridge, MA: Harvard University Press.

Posner, R.A. 1985. An economic theory of criminal law. *Columbia Law Review* 85: 1193–1231.

Posner, R.A. 2002. *Economic Analysis of Law*, 6e. Boston: Aspen.

Posner, R.A. 1997. Explaining the variance in the number of tort suits across U.S. states and between the United States and England. *Journal of Legal Studies* 26 (2): 477–491.

Posner, R.A., and Rosenfield, A.M. 1977. Impossibility and related doctrines in contract law: An economic analysis. *Journal of Legal Studies* 6: 83–118.

Priest, G.L. 1985. The invention of enterprise liability: A critical history of the intellectual history of modern tort law. *Journal of Legal Studies* 14: 461–527.

Priest, G.L. 1993. The origins of utility regulation and the "theories of regulation" debate. *Journal of Law and Economics* 36, 1(2): 289–323.

Priest, G.L. 1997. Procedural versus substantive controls of mass tort class actions. *Journal of Legal Studies* 26 (2): 491–521.

Pyle, D.J. 1983. *The Economics of Crime and Law Enforcement*. London: Macmillan.

Pyle, D.J. 1993. *An Economist Looks at Crime in Britain*. Paper given to the European Policy Forum/Social Market Fund.

Pyle, D.J. 2000. Economists, crime, and punishment. In Fielding, Clark, and Witt (eds.) *op. cit.*

Pyle, D.J., and Deadman, D.F. 1994. Crime and unemployment in Scotland: Some further results. *Scottish Journal of Political Economy* 41: 314–324.

Rasmusen, E., and Ayres, I. 1993. Mutual and unilateral mistake in contract law. *Journal of Legal Studies* 22: 309–344.

Raz, J. 2002. Two views of the nature of the theory of law. In Coleman (ed.) *op. cit.*

Regan, D. 1972. The problem of social cost revisited. *Journal of Law and Economics* 15: 427–437.

Reichman, U. 1978. Judicial supervision of servitudes. *Journal of Legal Studies* 7: 139–164.

Reichman, U. 1982. Toward a unified concept of servitudes. *Southern California Law Review* 55: 1179–1260.

Reilly, B., and Witt, R. 1992. Crime and unemployment in Scotland: An econometric analysis using regional data. *Scottish Journal of Political Economy* 39: 13–28.

Reynolds, O. 1992. Of time and feedlots: The effect of Spur Industries on nuisance law. *Washington University Journal of Urban and Contemporary Law* 75: 94–133.

Rickman, N. 1999. Contingent fees and litigation settlement. *International Review of Law and Economics* 19: 295–317.

Roth, A.E. 1988. Laboratory experimentation in economics: A methodological overview. *Economic Journal* 98: 974–1031.

Roth, A.E., and Murnighan, J. 1982. The role of information in bargaining: An experimental study. *Econometrica* 50, 1123–1142.

Rubin, P., and Bailey, M. 1994. The role of lawyers in changing the law. *Journal of Legal Studies* 23: 807–832.

Rubinfeld, D., and Scotchmer, S. 1993. Contingent fees for attorneys: An economic analysis. *RAND Journal of Economics* 24: 343–356.

Schaefer, H-B., and Ott, C. 2002. *The Economics of Law.* Northampton, MA: Edward Elgar.

Schelling, T.C. 1960. *The Strategy of Conflict.* Harvard University Press, Cambridge, MA.

Schulz, N., Parisi, F., and Depoorter, B. 2002. Fragmentation in property: Towards a general model. *Journal of Institutitonal and Theoretical Economics* 158 (4): 594–613.

Schwartz, A. 1977. A reexamination of nonsubstantive unconscionability. *Virginia Law Review* 63: 1053–1083.

Schwartz, A 1988. Proposals for products liability reform : A theoretical synthesis. *Yale Law Journal* 97: 353–419.

Schwartz, M., and Mitchell, D. 1970. An economic analysis of contingency fee and personal injury litigation. *Stanford Law Review* 22: 1125–1162.

Selten, R. 1978. The chainstore paradox. *Theory and Decision* 9: 127–159.

Shavell, S. 1980. Strict liability v. negligence. *Journal of Legal Studies* 9: 1–26.

Shavell, S. 1982. Suit, settlement, and trial: A theoretical analysis of alternative methods for allocating legal costs. *Journal of Legal Studies* 11: 55–81.

Shavell, S. 1985. Criminal law and the optimal use of nonmonetary sanctions as a deterrent. *Columbia Law Review* 85: 1232–1262.

Shavell, S. 1993. The optimal structure of law enforcement. *Journal of Law and Economics* 36: 255–287.

Shepherd, J.M. 2002. Fear of the first strike: The full deterrent effect of California's two- and three-strikes legislation. *Journal of Legal Studies* 31 (1): 159–178.

Shogren, J.F. 1993. Experimental markets and environmental policy. *Agricultural and Resource Economics Review* 22: 117–129.

Shogren, J.F., Shin, S.Y., Hayes, D.J., and Kliebenstein, J.B. 1994. Resolving differences in willingness to pay and willingness to accept. *American Economic Review* 84: 255–270.

Simon, H. 1957. *Models of Man.* New York: John Wiley.

Smith, A. 1776. *An Enquiry into the Nature and Causes of the Wealth of Nations.* Edited by R.H. Campbell, A.S. Skinner, and W.B. Todd. Oxford: Clarendon Press, 1976.

Smith, V.L. 1989. Theory, experiment, and economics. *Journal of Economic Perspectives* 3: 151–169.

Snyder, E.A., and Hughes, J.W. 1990. The English rule for allocating legal costs: Evidence confronts theory. *Journal of Law, Economics and Organization* 6: 345–380.

Stigler, G.J. 1966. *The Theory of Price,* 3e. New York: St. Martin's Press.

Stigler, G.J. 1971. The theory of economic regulation. *Bell Journal of Economics* 2: 3–21.

Stringfellow, P., and Lafferty, F. 1997. *King of Clubs.* New York: Time Warner.

Swanson, T.M., and Kantoleon, A. 2000. Nuisance. Entry 2,100 in Bouckaert and De Geest (eds.) *op. cit.*

Sykes, A.O. 1990. The doctrine of commercial impracticability in a second-best world. *Journal of Legal Studies* 19: 43–94.

Temple, J. 1999. The new growth evidence. *Journal of Economic Literature* 37: 112–156.

Thaler, R. 1980. Toward a positive theory of consumer choice. *Journal of Economic Behavior and Organization* 1: 39–60.

Thomason, T. 1991. Are attorneys paid what they are worth? Contingent fees and the settlement process. *Journal of Legal Studies* 20: 187–223.

Tideman, T.N., and Tullock, G. 1976. A new and superior process for making social choices. *Journal of Political Economy* 84: 1145–1159.

Trebilcock, M.J. 1993. *The Limits of Freedom of Contract*. Cambridge, MA: Harvard University Press.

Trebilcock, M.J., and Dewees, D.N. 1981. Judicial control of standard form contracts. In Burrows and Veljanovski (eds.) *op. cit.*

Tromans, S. 1982. Nuisance—prevention or payment. *Cambridge Law Journal* 41: 87–109.

Tullock G. 1968. The welfare costs of tariffs, monopoly, and theft. *Western Economic Journal* 5: 224–232.

Tversky, A., and Kahneman, D. 1991. Loss aversion in riskless choice: A reference-dependent model. *Quarterly Journal of Economics* 106: 1039–1061.

Ulen, T. 1984. The efficiency of specific performance: Toward a unified theory of contract remedies. *Michigan Law Review* 83: 358–403.

Umbeck, J. 1981. Might makes rights: A theory of the formation and initial distribution of property rights. *Economic Inquiry* 19: 38–51.

Van Zandt, D.E. 1993. The lessons of the lighthouse. *Journal of Legal Studies* 22: 47–72.

Veljanovski, C. 1982. The Coase theorems and the economic theory of markets and law. *Kyklos* 35: 66–81.

Walmsely, J. 1986. Personal violence. *Home Office Research Paper 89*. London: HMSO.

Weiss, R. 1989. Private prisons and the state. In R. Mathews (ed.) *Privatising Criminal Justice*. London: Sage.

Wellisz, S. 1964. On external economies and the government-assisted invisible hand. *Economica* 31: 345–362.

White, M.J. 1988. Contract breach and contract discharge due to impossibility: A unified theory. *Journal of Legal Studies* 17: 353–376.

White, M.J. 1989. An empirical test of the comparative and contributory negligence rules in accident law. *Rand Journal of Economics* 20: 308–330.

Williamson, O.E. 1985. *The Economic Institutions of Capitalism*. New York: Macmillan, The Free Press.

Williamson, O.E. 1993. The evolving science of organization. *Journal of Institutional and Theoretical Economics* 149: 36–63.

Williamson, O.E. 2000. The new institutional economics: Taking stock, looking ahead. *Journal of Economic Literature* 38: 595–614.

Willis, K. 1983. Spatial variations in crime in England and Wales. *Regional Studies* 17: 261–272.

Wilson, J., and Herrnstein, R. 1985. *Crime and Human Nature*. New York: Simon and Schuster.

Withers, G. 1984. Crime, punishment, and deterrence in Australia: An empirical investigation. *Economic Record* 60: 176–185.

Witte, A. 1980. Estimating the economic model of crime with individual data. *Quarterly Journal of Economics* 94: 57–84.

Witte, A., and Tauchen, H. 2000. *Work and Crime*. In Fielding, Clark, and Witt (eds.) *op. cit.*

Wittman, D. 1981. First come, first served: An economic analysis of coming to the nuisance. *Journal of Legal Studies* 9: 557–568.

Wittman, D. 1998. Coming to the nuisance. In Newman (ed.) *op. cit.*

Wolpin, K. 1978a. An economic analysis of crime and punishment in England and Wales 1894–1967. *Journal of Political Economy* 86: 815–840.

Wolpin, K. 1978b. Capital punishment and homicide: The English experience. *American Economic Review* 68: 422–427.

Zelder, M. 1973. Inefficient dissolutions as a consequence of public goods. *Journal of Legal Studies* 22: 503–520.

INDEX